SEEKING WESTERN WATERS

SEEKING WESTERN WATERS

WATERS

*The Lewis and Clark Trail from the
Rockies to the Pacific*

EMORY AND RUTH STRONG

EDITED BY HERBERT K. BEALS

OREGON HISTORICAL SOCIETY PRESS

Cover photo by Emory Strong. It is a canoe burial site at the outlet of Abernethy Creek, a site Lewis and Clark passed on 26 March 1806.

Seeking Western Waters could not have been produced without the generous financial support of the Wilfred W. Townes Trust of Milwaukie, Oregon, and the Jack Murdock Publication Fund.

Oregon Historical Society
1200 SW Park
Portland, OR 97205
www.ohs.org

Library of Congress Cataloging-in-Publication Data
Stong, Emory M.
    Seeking western waters: The Lewis and Clark trail from the Rockies to the Pacific / Emory and Ruth Strong; edited by Herbert K. Beals.
        p.   cm.
    Contains excerpts from the journals of Lewis and Clark.
    Includes Bibliographical references (p.   ) and index.
    ISBN 0-87595-245-3
    1. Lewis and Clark expedition (1804–1806) I. Strong, Ruth, 1904–1984. II. Beals H.K. (Herbert Kyle), 1934–   . III. Lewis, Meriwether, 1774–1809. Original journals of the Lewis and Clark expedition. Selections. IV. Title.
F592.7S77 1995
917.804'2—dc20   94-40421
Second edition   CIP

The paper used in this publication meets the minimum requirements of American National Standard for Information Sciences—Permanence of Paper for Printed Library Materials, ANSI Z39.48-1984.

Designed and produced by the Oregon Historical Society Press.

*This book
is dedicated to the memory of my wife, Helen,
partner and best friend for fifty-four years.
We knew and respected Ruth and Emory Strong,
and shared their abiding interest in Lewis and Clark.*

—Wilfred Townes

CONTENTS

LIST OF MAPS

PREFACE

When Meriwether Lewis and William Clark returned from their celebrated expedition, their first concern was to publish their reports for the use of the nation. So voluminous were the records that abridgement was considered necessary, and a promising young lawyer, Nicholas Biddle, agreed to perform the task. Other pressing matters curtailed his efforts and eventually another editor, Paul Allen, finished the work, which was not published until 1814, eight years after the expedition's return.

In 1892 Elliott Coues (pronounced "cows") edited the Biddle-Allen edition for republication. In his research he discovered the original notebooks written by Lewis and Clark in the archives of the American Philosophical Society—but not until his manuscript was already in the printer's hands. A hurried revision was necessary, and in 1893 his work, copiously annotated, was published.

At the end of the nineteenth century, the New York publishing house of Dodd, Mead and Company commissioned the historian and editor Reuben Gold Thwaites to edit the original journals found by Coues. This monumental work, published in 1905, consists of the journals transcribed verbatim; an atlas; the journals of two members of the expedition, sergeants Joseph Whitehouse and Charles Floyd (the latter of whom did not live to see western waters); and correspondence relating to the expedition. We are indebted to Dodd, Mead for permission to quote extensively from this work and to use some of the sketches and maps.

In *Seeking Western Waters*, our intent has been to let the reader see a portion of the journey at close range, through a clear glass, rather than more distantly, as on a dim screen. The details add flavor and color by illustrating landmarks, Native-American village sites, birds, animals, plants, and other remarkable things the expedition's members witnessed and recorded. The project originated with our interest in learning about the archaeological resources of the Columbia River, for which the journals of the Lewis and Clark expedition are exceedingly useful. The accurate and detailed descriptions of places we know, and the explorers' marvelous powers of observation under difficult circumstances, so impressed us that we found ourselves following the route, taking notes and pictures. We realized, from the success of our *Stone Age on the Columbia* and *Stone Age in the Great Basin*, that people are vitally interested in the places around them, where they can see and enjoy the historical and cultural heritages on every side.

We have tried to emphasize journal entries concerning the Indians, whose ancient cultures had existed on western waters for well over ten thousand years. Lewis and Clark encountered many of the native peoples before they were influenced by the white invasion, and with few exceptions they were friendly, courteous, helpful, and generous. The explorers were scrupulous observers and comparatively unbiased for their time. Their comments thus remain a reliable source of information about the indigenous inhabitants.

Little now remains of the great villages and fishing sites, the ancient trails and burial grounds, the root patches and berry fields. We ourselves were fortunate to have visited many of them before their destruction.

Using selected passages from the journals was essential to this volume, since the original texts run to some one and a half million words. However, the wording has not been altered or rearranged. Insofar as possible, we have sought to reproduce every word exactly as it was written (except for some deletions), while striving to preserve the flavor, quality, continuity, and meaning of the original. Deletions are indicated by a three-period ellipsis (. . .) when the omission occurs within a sentence, or by a four-period ellipsis (. . . .) when the omission involves a break from one sentence to another. Nothing has been added save for an infrequent punctuation mark, conjunction, or article when it seemed necessary to the reader's understanding. All such insertions are set off by brackets []. Lewis and Clark's spelling has been retained, except occasionally when a correction seemed necessary to clarify the meaning of a word or phrase, in which case it is also bracketed. Before reaching the Pacific Coast, Clark would write a preliminary or first draft, distinct from his finished or final draft, on the events of the day. We have selected excerpts from either or both. These are preceded by parenthetical notations: [Clark, first draft] or [Clark], the latter indicating the final draft.

Excerpts from the journals of Lewis, Joseph Whitehouse, John Ordway and Patrick Gass are similarly identified, with their respective names inserted in brackets at the beginning of the quoted text, or in some cases by a lead-in sentence.

EDITOR'S NOTE

The manuscript of this book came to my hands for editorial review several years after the deaths of its co-authors. Regrettable though that was, as I had known them, I entered upon the task with more confidence than might otherwise have been the case. From my first meeting with Emory in 1970 to the last opportunity I had, fifteen years later, to talk with Ruth, they were unstinting in their enthusiasm to understand and elucidate the remarkable story of Lewis and Clark's sojourn in the western wilderness. At the time of Ruth's death in September 1985, the manuscript was substantially complete, though in need of the usual editorial attention before any such work is committed to print. It also lacked a concluding section and a bibliographical list of the Strongs' sources, both of which they had clearly intended to complete. Some editorial work on the text was initiated before my involvement, most of which has been incorporated into this version of the text. Although I have found nothing to indicate explicitly what the Strongs may have intended to say in their concluding remarks, I have ventured to supply a brief epilogue. Whatever its faults may be, they are solely mine. As for sources, a list has been compiled of the publications and documents the Strongs, or I as editor, have quoted from or otherwise consulted. Brief parenthetical entries inserted in the text refer the reader to an appended list of sources. The reader will also sometimes encounter in these parenthetical inserts day-month-year entries, which refer to journal entries under the indicated date as they appear in this work.

Occasionally, footnotes are used to provide brief editorial comment or explanation. Because their labors ceased before the current effort (begun in 1983) by the University of Nebraska Press, under the editorship of Gary E. Moulton, to republish the entire Lewis and Clark journals, the Strongs relied exclusively on Reuben G. Thwaites's edition of 1905. Revising the texts they quoted from the Thwaites edition to coincide with the Moulton edition has not been attempted because the differences do not seem substantial enough to warrant it. This is no reflection on the value or accuracy of the Moulton edition, which doubtless will become the standard scholarly reference, just as the Thwaites edition has been hitherto.

Thus, all quotations attributed to Lewis, Clark, and Whitehouse are from the Thwaites edition. Those attributed to Gass are from an edition of his journal edited by Earle R. Forrest and published by Ross and Haines in 1958. Quotations from Ordway's journal are from the edition published (with excerpts from Lewis's journal) in 1916 by the State Historical Society of Wisconsin, edited by Milo M. Quaife.

As editor of this volume, I have resolutely resisted the temptation to tamper with the Strongs' selection of passages from the journals. In a few instances, however, where new information has surfaced or was otherwise unavailable to the Strongs, it has seemed to me beneficial to augment the commentary accordingly. Such additions are offered in the hope that they will increase the reader's understanding of the events described or observations made in the journal entries quoted. The most significant of these instances are: comment concerning the now largely discredited belief that some Northern Plains Indians (the Mandans in particular) may have been descendants of twelfth-century Welsh colonists in North America; revisions in the explanation of prehistoric catastrophic floods in the Columbia River Basin; expanded discussion of the madrona or arbutus tree; the European discovery of the Columbia River; the possibility of the expedition's near encounter with the American brig *Lydia* on the lower Columbia River; and comment concerning metal swords that Lewis and Clark saw among the lower Columbia River Indians.

In reviewing correspondence between the Strongs and various publishers to whom they had submitted their manuscript, it was clear to me that, in their words, "abridging [it] would not serve our purpose." In this matter, they may rest assured that their wishes have been honored.

HERBERT K. BEALS

PROLOGUE

In 1803 the United States paid France a little over two cents an acre for a vast tract of land lying between the Mississippi River and the boundary of territories to the west claimed by Spain and Great Britain. This acquisition, at the time denounced by some as a blunder and protested by Spain as a treaty violation, eventually added twelve new states to the American Union, with natural resources sufficient to generate enormous wealth for the nation.

It was an extensive domain, peopled by Indians and immense numbers of wildlife, unexplored except for its fringes. Thomas Jefferson, during whose presidency the territory was obtained, had for some time proposed sending explorers across the tract to the Pacific by way of the Missouri River and whatever pass its headwaters had sculpted through the Rocky Mountains. Even before the Louisiana Purchase was complete, Jefferson had wheedled $2,500 to equip an expedition out of a reluctant Congress

and had put the finishing touches to its organization. For the leader of the long, grueling, and dangerous journey, he appointed his twenty-nine-year-old secretary, Meriwether Lewis. It may even be that he had selected Lewis some years before and that the secretarial position was to verify his choice as well as to sharpen Lewis's bent for the natural sciences.

For his co-leader, Lewis selected the thirty-four-year-old William Clark. No better partner could have been found. Throughout all the hardships and frustrations of the almost three-year journey there was no hint of disagreement or friction. Toward the end, their association seems to have grown even closer, for the journals refer to "my good friend Capt. Clark" or "my friend Capt. Lewis." The two leaders complemented each other perfectly. Lewis was the scientist and planner, Clark the engineer and ambassador. Between them, they chose and forged a disciplined, hardy, and zealous party of explorers whose place in history will always be secure. Thirty-three persons were in the final party that made its laborious way to the Pacific Ocean and back. In selecting their crew, the leaders were strictly pragmatic, with ability alone guiding their decisions. It was a diverse group, encompassing (besides Lewis and Clark) twenty-three army privates, three sergeants, two interpreters, one African-American slave, and a Shoshone Indian woman with an infant. Other than Lewis and Clark, the party comprised sergeants Patrick Gass, John Ordway, and Nathaniel Pryor; privates William Bratton, John Collins, John Colter, Pierre Cruzatte, Joseph Field, Reuben Field, Robert Frazer, George Gibson, Silas Goodrich, Hugh Hall, Thomas Howard, François Labiche, Jean Baptiste Lepage, Hugh McNeal, John Potts, George Shannon, John Shields, John Thompson, William Werner, Joseph Whitehouse, Alexander Willard, Richard Windsor, and Peter Wiser; the interpreters, Toussaint Charbonneau and George Drouillard; York, the African American, who was Clark's personal servant on the expedition; and Sacagawea, the wife of Charbonneau, and their infant son, Baptiste. (Sergeant Charles Floyd, Jr., who had set out with the original party, had died—probably of peritonitis—on 18 August 1804, on the banks of the Missouri.) Perhaps we should add another member to the expedition, for Captain Lewis's large black Newfoundland dog, Seaman, was as devoted and sometimes as useful as anyone in the party.°

The Lewis and Clark expedition has long been viewed as an epic adventure, among the best managed, most successful explorations in history. Its leaders' fame has remained undiminished over the years, time seeming only to enhance their reputation. The reasons are clear: They kept readable and detailed journals that have become classics of discovery, and they were the first whites to see and record much that is now familiar in the continental United States. We can only be fascinated by an undertaking so utterly dependent for its success upon the determination, resourcefulness, and integrity of the two young captains and their small contingent of explorers. President Jefferson, in his lengthy instructions to Captain Lewis on the conduct of the enterprise, had written: "Other objects worthy of notice will be: The soil and face of the country; its growth and vegetable productions, especially those not of the United States; the animals of the country generally, and especially those not known in the United States" (Coues, *History of the Expedition*, 1:xxviii).

Lewis took these instructions literally. He noticed, collected, and meticulously described hundreds of plants and animals, many of them new to science. He was not, of course, their discoverer. Much had been learned over millennia by indigenous populations, who knew what was edible, medicinal, or useful as fiber. But Lewis was to bring many species to the attention of the scien-

---

°Long thought, mistakenly, to be "Scannon" because of a misreading of the original manuscript journals (*see* Jackson, "Call Him a Good Dog").

tific world for the first time. He was in a virgin field and he performed his task with diligence and acumen. The scientific accomplishments of the expedition were never really appreciated, or called to general attention, until the publication in 1969 of Paul Russell Cutright's *Lewis and Clark: Pioneering Naturalists*.

On 13 May 1804 the members of the Corps of Discovery° left their camp on the Mississippi in a fifty-five-foot keelboat and two pirogues for a long struggle with the swift current of the Missouri. Progress was painfully slow, the oars sometimes propelling the boats for miles to make a few hundred yards toward their goal, so tortuous was the wandering channel. Still, beyond the Rockies, they would often long for the stupendous dinners of prime buffalo ribs on the banks of the Missouri as they gnawed on wooden dried salmon, tasteless roots, and tainted elk. The party holed up for a bitter winter at a Mandan village near what is now Bismarck, North Dakota. There they recruited the interpreter Charbonneau and his Shoshone slave-wife, Sacagawea, with their infant son, Baptiste—an addition that would later help prevent disaster for the expedition.

As soon as the ice broke up in the spring of 1805, Lewis and Clark were on their way again, soon to enter territory completely unexplored by white men. On reaching the junction of the Missouri and Marias, they did not know which stream to take, and spent a week exploring be-

fore deciding on the southerly branch. Still unsure, Lewis went ahead to find the great falls the Indians had said were on the Missouri's main stem. When he first saw them, he was immensely impressed with their beauty and majesty (fully as impressed as some people were later with their potential for profit), but the falls were a serious obstacle to navigation. It took the party from 16 June to 15 July to portage their possessions around the cascades and build new boats to resume the journey. Lewis fretted at the delay: the Rocky Mountains were still in the distance and if they were not crossed before winter the expedition would surely fail.

As each tributary was passed the Missouri decreased in flow, and it soon became apparent that water travel must cease. Once, when Whitehouse fell, the boat passed over and nearly crushed him in the gravel, so shallow was the stream. Fortunately, this country was Sacagawea's childhood homeland. The Shoshone were the sole source of help at that point, for they had horses, and without pack animals the explorers could not transport their baggage across the mountains to western waters. By mutual consent Lewis went ahead to scout for Indians. Early in the morning of 12 August they missed a chance to make contact when a lone Shoshone let them approach within a few hundred yards before becoming alarmed and departing. Bitterly disappointed but still undaunted, Lewis resumed his trek toward the Great Divide. There, in Lewis and Clark's own words, the story of this volume begins.

°As Jefferson named the expedition.

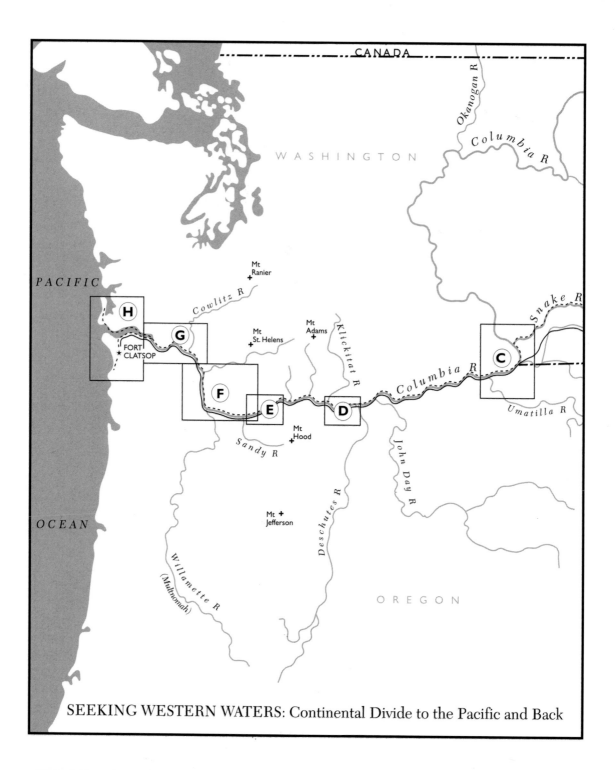

SEEKING WESTERN WATERS: Continental Divide to the Pacific and Back

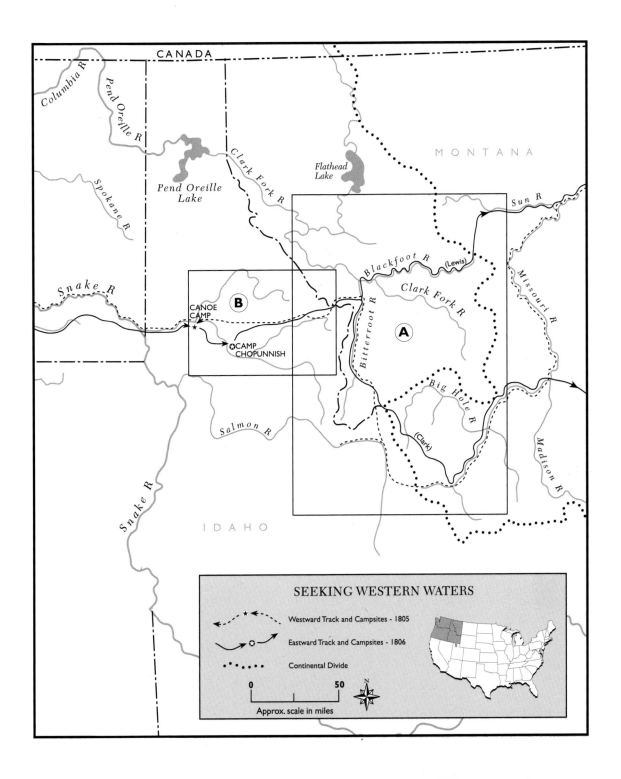

CANADA

Columbia R

Pend Oreille R

MONTANA

Spokane R

Pend Oreille Lake

Clark Fork R

Flathead Lake

Sun R

Snake R

B

CANOE CAMP

Blackfoot R (Lewis)

Clark Fork R

Missouri R

CAMP CHOPUNNISH

Bitterroot R

A

Salmon R

Big Hole R

(Clark)

Madison R

Snake R

IDAHO

SEEKING WESTERN WATERS

- ★ Westward Track and Campsites - 1805
- ⊕ Eastward Track and Campsites - 1806
- • • • • Continental Divide

0   50

Approx. scale in miles

N

"I discovered immence ranges of high mountains"
Looking westward from Lemhi Pass.

"Here I first tasted the water of the great Columbia river" (right)
Agency Creek where Lewis crossed it on the Indian trail.

I

SEEKING WESTERN WATERS

12 TO 29 AUGUST 1805

12 August 1805.
[LEWIS]

"I now determined to pursue the base of the mountains. . . . we fell in with a large and plain Indian road. . . . the road took us to the most distant fountain of the waters of the Mighty Missouri in surch of which we have spent so many toilsome days and wristless nights. thus far I had accomplished one of those great objects on which my mind has been unalterably fixed for many years, judge then of the pleasure I felt in all[a]ying my thirst with this pure and ice-cold water which issues from the base of a low moun-

tain or hill of gentle ascent . . . two miles below McNeal had exultingly stood with a foot on each side of this little rivulet [Trail Creek] and thanked his god that he had lived to bestride the mighty & heretofore deemed endless Missouri. after refreshing ourselves we proceed on to the top of the dividing range [Lemhi Pass] from which I discovered immence ranges of high mountains still to the West of us with their tops partially covered with snow. I now decended the mountain . . . to a handsome bold runing Creek [Agency] of cold Clear water. here I first tasted of the water of the great Columbia river. after a short halt of a few minutes we continued our march along the Indian road which lead us over steep hills and deep hollows to a spring, . . . here we encamped for the night having traveled about 20 Miles. . . . at the creek . . . I observed a species of deep perple currant lower in its growth [and] the stem more branched and leaf doubly as large as that of the Missouri. . . . the fruit . . . is ascid & very inferior in point of flavor."

•

Lewis was on the sunset side of the Beaverhead Mountains, where waters flow westward to the Pacific Ocean. It was a critical objective, attained after a tedious journey, but navigable tributaries of the Columbia were yet more than 250 miles away across some of the most broken and jagged land in North America. He knew neither the way nor the distance, only that he must reach those rivers and that without help the passage would be impossible, although he still must try.

Jefferson had instructed Lewis to observe the "soil and face of the country; its growth and vegetable productions; especially those not of the United States" (Coues, *History of the Expedition*, 1:xxviii). This duty Lewis performed unfailingly, describing unknown plants in great detail. The first plant he recorded new to science on western waters was the sticky currant, *Ribes viscossissimum*, which grows profusely along Agency Creek and throughout the area. But the best memorial to Meriwether Lewis on the headwaters of the Columbia at Lemhi is the vivid red Lewis's monkey flower, *Mimulus lewisii*. Wreathing the rocks of every rivulet, the bright flowers seem to commemorate the intensity of the collector whose specimens were described by Frederick Pursh at Philadelphia and first published in his *Flora Americae Septentrionalis* in 1814.

13 August 1805.

[LEWIS]

"We set out very early on the Indian road. . . . to a large creek [Pattee] . . . this we passed and on rising the hill beyond it had a view of a handsome little valley [Lemhi]. . . . I saw near the creek some bushes of the white maple . . . and a species of honeysuckle . . . [that] bear a globular berry as large as a garden pea and as white as wax. . . . we had proceeded about four miles through a wavy plain . . . when at the distance of about a mile we saw two women, a man and some dogs. . . . the women soon disappeared behind the hill, the man continued untill I arrived within a hundred yards of him and then likewise absconded. . . . we pursued the back track of these Indians . . . the road was dusty and appeared to have been much traveled lately both by men and horses. . . . we had not continued our rout more than a mile when we were so fortunate as to meet with three female savages. . . . they appeared much allarmed but saw that we were to near for them to escape by flight they therefore seated themselves on the ground, holding down their heads as if reconciled to die which the[y] expected no doubt

"*I saw . . . the white maple . . . and
a species of honeysuckle*"
Rocky Mountain maple/Snowberry.

would be their fate; I took the elderly woman by the hand and raised her up . . . and strip[ped] my shirt sleve . . . to prove to her the truth of the ascertion that I was a white man. . . . I gave these women some beads a few mockerson awls some pewter looking-glasses and a little paint. . . . after they had become composed I enformed them by signs that I wished them to conduct us to their camp. . . . they readily obeyed and we set out. . . . we had marched about 2 miles when we met a party of about 60 warriors mounted on excellent horses who came in nearly full speed . . . I advanced towards them with the flag leaving my gun. . . . the chief and two others . . . spoke to the

"small pieces such as the N. W. Company furnish the natives"
Flintlock trade gun.

women, and they informed them who we were and exultingly shewed the presents which had been given them these men then advanced and embraced me very affectionately. . . . both parties now advanced and we wer all carresed and be-smeared with their grease and paint till I was heartily tired of the national hug. I now had the pipe lit and gave them smoke; they seated them-selves in a circle around us and pulled of[f] their mockersons . . . before they would receive or smoke the pipe. . . . which is much to say that they wish they may always go bearfoot if they are not sincere; a pretty heavy penalty if they are to march through the plains of their country. . . . They were armed with b[o]ws arrow and Shields except the three whom I observed with small pieces such as the N.W. Company furnish the na-tives . . . on our arrival at their encampmen[t] on the river in a handsome level and fertile bottom. . . . we were seated on green boughs and the skins of Antelopes. . . . the chief next produced his pipe and native tobacco and began a long ceremony. . . . this pipe was made of a dense simitransparent green stone very highly polished . . . the bowl

being in the same direction with the stem. a small piece of birned clay is placed in the bottom of the bowl to seperate the tobacco from the end of the stem. . . . all the women and children of the camp were shortly collected about the lodge to indulge themselves with looking at us, we being the first white persons they had ever seen. . . . we had not taisted any food since the evening before. the Chief . . . gave us some cakes of serviceberries and Choke cherries which had been dryed in the sun; of these I made a hearty meal. . . . This eve-ning the Indians entertained us with their danc-ing nearly all night. at 12 O'Ck. I grew sleepy and retired to rest leaving the men to amuse them-selves with the Indians."

•

The "white maple" was the Rocky Mountain maple, *Acer glabrum*, unknown to science until seen by Lewis. The "species of honeysuckle" was probably the shrub now called snowberry, *Symphoricarpos albus laevigatus*, also then new to science (*see* Cutright, *Lewis and Clark*, 210; and 20 September 1805).

"this pipe was made of a dense simitransparent green stone"
Tube pipe, Columbia River.

The gun furnished by the North West Company was a musket much favored by the Indians. For more about this weapon, *see* 24 January 1806.

Use of the pipe by Native Americans has an origin lost to history. Fumes from flaming aromatic herbs and gums were used by ancient peoples throughout history to enrich ceremonies, evict diseases, and cleanse the soul, but smoking and use of the tobacco plant is distinctively American. Originally the virtue of the pungent weed was distributed by putting the fired end of a tubular vessel to the lips and blowing the soothing vapors over the afflicted or the assembled multitude; the large pipes used this way were called cloud blowers. The amount of patient work and artistic endeavor expended upon pipes indicates that smoking was an important ceremonial function; however, tobacco was also smoked for the pleasure it may have given. The typical pipe from west of the Divide was tubular and made from steatite, a soft black soapstone.

14 August 1805.
[LEWIS]

"In order to give Capt. Clark time to reach the forks of Jefferson's [Beaverhead] river I concluded to spend this day at the Shoshone Camp and obtain what information I could with rispect to the country. . . . I directed Drewyer [Drouillard] and Shields to hunt a few hours . . . the Indians furnished them with horses and most of their young men also turned out to hunt. the game which they principally hunt is the Antelope which they pursue on horseback. . . . when they discover a herd of the Antelope they seperate and scatter themselves to the distance of five or six miles in different directions arround them . . . some one or two now pursue the herd at full speed over the hills vallies gullies and the sides of precipices that are tremendious to view. thus after runing them from five to six or seven miles the fresh horses that were in waiting head them and drive them back persuing them as far or per-

"their encampmen[t] . . . in a handsome . . .bottom"
Lemhi River valley.

haps further quite to the other extrem of the hunters who now in turn pursue on their fresh horses thus worrying the poor animal down and finally killing them with their arrows. . . . I was very much entertained with a view of this indian chase; it was after a herd of about 10 Antelope and about 20 hunters. . . . my hunters returned . . . unsecuessfull. I now directed McNeal to make me a little paist with the flour and added some berries to it which I found very pallatable.

"The means I had of communicating with these people was by way of Drewyer who understood perfectly the common language of jesticulation of signs which seems to be universally understood by all the Nations we have yet seen. it is true that this language is imperfect and liabel to error but is much less so then would be expected. the strong parts of the ideas are seldom mistaken.

"I now told Cameahwait that I wished him to speak to his people and engage them to go with me tomorrow to the forks of Jeffersons river. . . . that I wish them to take with them about 30 spare horses to transport our baggage to this place where we would then remain sometime among them and trade with them for horses. . . . he . . . made a lengthey harrangue to his village. . . . and informed me that they would be ready to accompany me in the morning. . . . Drewyer who had good view of their horses estimated them at 400. most of them are fine horses. indeed many of them would make a figure on the South side of James River or the land of fine horses. . . . notwithstanding the extreem poverty of those poor people they are very merry as they danced again this evening untill midnight. each warrior keep[s] one or more horses tyed by a cord to a stake near his lodge both day and night and are always prepared for action at a moments warning. they fight on horseback altogether."

•

The power of the "language of jesticulation" and the proficiency with which Drouillard handled it is well illustrated by the abstract ideas conveyed to Cameahwait. It was no easy task to persuade a band of Shoshone, short of food and nearly defenseless, to make a two-day journey into territory of the dreaded Blackfoot.

15 August 1805.
[LEWIS]

"This morning I arrose very early and as hungary as a wolf. . . . I found on enquiry of McNeal that we had only about two pounds of flour remaining. this I directed to him to divide into two equal parts and to cook one half this morning in a kind of pudding with the burries as he had done yesterday and reserve the ballance for the evening. on this new fashoned pudding four of us breakfasted, giving a pretty good allowance also to the Chief who declared it the best thing he had taisted for a long time. he took a little of the flour . . . and examined [it] very scrutinously and asked me if we made it of roots. I explained to him the manner in which it grew. I hurried the departure of the Indians. . . . they seemed very reluctant to accompany me. . . . [the Chief] told me that some foolish persons among them had suggested the idea that we were in league with the Pahkees [Blackfoot] and had come on in order to decoy them into an ambuscade. . . . [These people] have been accustomed from their infancy to view every stranger as an enimy. . . . [Cameahwait] haranged his village a third time. . . . shortly after this harange he was joined by six or eight only and with these I smoked a pipe . . . determined to set out with them while I had them in the humour . . . several of the old women were crying and imploring the great sperit to protect their warriors as if they were going to inevitable distruction. we had not proceeded far before our party was augmented by ten or twelve more, and before we reached the Creek [Pattee] . . . it appeared to me that we had all the men of the village and a number of women with us. . . . When we arrived at the spring . . . the Chief insi[s]ted on halting to let the horses graize with which I complyed and gave the Indians smoke. they are excessively fond of the pipe; but have it not much in their power to indulge themselves with even their native tobacco as they do not cultivate it themselves. . . . about sunset we reached the upper part of the level valley of the Cove which [we] now called Shoshone Cove. the grass being birned on the North side of the river we passed over to the south encamped."

16 August 1805.

[LEWIS]

"being now informed of the place at which I expected to meat Capt. C. and the party they insisted on making a halt, which was complyed with. we now dismounted and the Chief with much cerimony put tippets about our necks such as they t[h]emselves woar I redily perceived that this was to disguise us. . . . to give them further confidence I put my cocked hat with feather on the chief and my over shirt being of the Indian form my hair deshivled and skin well browned with the sun I wanted no further addition to make me a complete Indian in appearance the men followed my example and we were so[o]n completely metamorphosed."

•

To the mortification of Lewis and dismay of the Indians, there was no sign of Clark and the boats when they arrived at the river. Determined "to restore their confidence cost what it might," Lewis gave his gun to Cameahwait and told him to shoot if he thought he had been deceived; the other men also gave up their guns to the Indians. These were desperate measures in a desperate situation, but Lewis knew that he had to hold the Indians at all costs, for if they should disperse he would never be able to approach them again. He now reverted to a "stratagem in which I thought myself justifyed by the occasion, but which I must confess set a little awkward." He convinced the Indians that a note he had left for Clark on 10

August was actually a message from the invisible party, and that they were but a short distance below.

Lewis resolved to send Drouillard in the morning to search for Clark, accompanied by one of the Indians. He slept little that night, "my mind dwelling on the state of the expedition which I have ever held in equal estimation with my own existence, and the fait of which appeared at this moment to depend in a great measure upon the caprice of a few savages who are ever as fickle as the wind."

17 August 1805.
[L E W I S]

"This morning I arrose very early and dispatched Drewyer and the Indian down the river. . . . Drewyer had been gone about 2 hours when an Indian who had straggled some little distance down the river returned and reported the white-men were coming, that he had seen them just below. they all appeared transported with joy, & the ch[i]ef repeated his fraturnal hug. I felt quite as much gratifyed at this information as the Indians appeared to be. Shortly after Capt. Clark arrived with the Interpreter Charbono, and the Indian woman, who proved to be a sister of the Chief Cameahwait. the meeting of those people was really affecting, particularly between Sah-cah-gar-we-ah and an Indian woman, who had been taken prisoner at the same time with her and who, had afterwards escaped from the Min-netares [Hidatsas] and rejoined her nation. At noon the Canoes arrived, and we had the satisfaction once more to find ourselves all together. . . . we unloaded our canoes and arranged our baggage on shore; formed a canopy of one of our large sails and planted some willow brush in the ground to form a shade for the Indians to set under while we spoke to them. . . . about 4 P.M. we called them together and through Labuish [English to French], Charbono [French to Hidatsa] and Sah-cah-gar-we-ah [Hidatsa to Shoshone] we communicated to them fully the objects which had brought us into this distant part of the country, in which we took care to make them a conspicuous object of our own good wishes and the care of our government. . . . We gave [Cameahwait] a medal of the small size with the likeness of Mr. Jefferson, the President of the U'States . . . to the other Chiefs we gave each a small medal which were struck in the Presidency of George Washing[ton] Esqr. . . . I also shot my air-gun [see 24 January 1806] which was so perfectly imcomprehensible that they immediately denominated it the great medicine."

•

That Sacagawea proved to be Cameahwait's sister was a coincidence fiction writers might hesitate to use, but it was only one of a number of remarkable occurrences that favored the progress of the expedition when most needed, some of them the result of good planning, discipline, and alertness. The foresight that Lewis and Clark used in bringing this young Indian woman, burdened with an infant, to interpret in just such a situation paid dividends proportionate to its boldness.

The slave-wife of Charbonneau was of considerable help to the expedition, which without her would probably have met with dismal failure in the Bitterroots. Many legends concern this quiet, brave Indian woman—principally that she was a guide and that there was a romantic attachment between her and Captain Clark. Between Three Forks and the Lemhi, the part of the country she knew, her services as a guide were invaluable. Clark, as well as the other members of the Corps, had immense respect for her. That Sacagawea revered Clark is unquestionable, but any *affaire de coeur* between them is in the realm of myth.

Sacagawea was born in the beautiful and fertile Lemhi Valley in about 1788. Before she reached her teens her tribe was attacked by the Hidatsa near Three Forks, Montana, while hunting buffalo. Fleeing on the Jefferson River, several of the tribe's members were killed. Sacagawea was captured with some others, and was sold to the crude and faithless Charbonneau, whose wife she later became.

Little is known about Sacagawea after her return to the Mandan villages at the end of the expedition. She may have accompanied her son, Baptiste (or Pomp, as Captain Clark called him), to St. Louis for him to receive an education. In 1811 she and Charbonneau returned to Dakota on a boat belonging to the fur trader Manuel Lisa. Henry Brackenridge wrote in his journal: "We had on board a Frenchman named Charboneau, with his wife, an Indian woman of the Snake nation, both of whom had accompanied Lewis and Clark to the Pacific, and were of great service. The woman, a good creature, of a mild and gentle disposition, greatly attached to the whites, whose manners and dress she tries to imitate, but she had become sickly and longed to revisit her native country" (Thwaites, *Brackenridge's Journal*, 32–33). Charbonneau was employed by Lisa as an interpreter at Fort Manuel and there, on 20 December 1812, the clerk of the fort, John Luttig, wrote in his journal: "this Evening the Wife of Charbonneau a Snake Squaw, died of a putrid fever she was a good and the best Woman in the fort, aged abt 25 years she left a fine infant girl" (Luttig, *Journal of a Fur Trading Expedition*, 106; *see also* Epilogue, this work).

The custom of presenting medals to prominent Indians started early in colonial times and lasted nearly one hundred years. After the Revolution it was the practice for the government to give presidential medals; of these Lewis and Clark carried at least eighty-seven, in two types. The Jefferson presidential medal was made in three sizes, although apparently only the two smaller sizes—2¼ and 3³⁄₁₆ inches in diameter— were taken on the expedition. The design was the same for all, a likeness of President Jefferson on the obverse, and clasped hands, a peace pipe, a tomahawk, and the legend "Peace and Friendship" on the reverse.

"we reached . . .
Shoshone Cove . . .
[and] encamped"
Looking east from
Lemhi Pass towards
Shoshone Cove.

Sacagawea was
born in this vicinity,
where Pattee
Creek meets the
Lemhi River.

Peace medals carried by Lewis & Clark: Jefferson medal, top, and the three types of Washington "Season" medals.

The "small" medals were ordered during Washington's administration but not delivered until later. There were three designs, all with the same reverse. The obverse came with either a man sowing grain, a man tending domestic animals, or a woman spinning. They were about 1¾ inches in diameter. All the presidential medals were struck in silver and bronze or copper, but apparently only the silver one was carried on the expedition.

No less than forty-four medals were passed out on western waters. Of these, only eight have been recovered. One, a Jefferson medal, was reported by John Kirk Townsend, who wrote on 14 October 1836: "One of Mr. Birnie's children found, a few days since, a large silver medal, which had been brought here by Lewis and Clark, and had probably been presented to some chief, who lost it" (*Narrative of a Journey*, 252).° James Swan wrote that William Tufts, supercargo of the ship *Guatimozin* of Boston, on the West Coast in 1807–08, procured a "sowing" medal that had been given to an Indian by Lewis and Clark (*Northwest Coast*, 406). Both these historical

---

°James Bernie, a native of Aberdeen, Scotland, was the Hudson's Bay Company's superintendent at Fort George (Astoria) in October 1836.

treasures are now lost. A Washington medal showing a man tending animals is in a private collection. Circumstances of the recovery of the other five are noted where appropriate in this text.

From the Indians, Lewis and Clark soon learned devastating news—the streams they would first meet across the divide were not navigable, and a long, weary trip over the mountains lay ahead before boats could be used. Since they were unwilling to accept this news without verification, they decided that Clark should choose eleven men and leave immediately to examine the Salmon River, taking tools to make canoes if the river were passable and suitable trees available. He would also take Charbonneau, Sacagawea, and all the Indians except three with him to the Shoshone camp on the Lemhi, where Sacagawea would attempt to hasten the return of the Indians with packhorses to transport the baggage.

While Clark was on his discovery mission, Lewis faced the difficult task of making packsaddles, repacking their stores, and transporting them across the Divide. Time was critical, for already there was heavy frost each morning, and an early snow would close the mountain passes. Lewis had left the Shoshone camp on the Lemhi on 15 August. It would be 30 August before he left the village again with the party intact and headed for the navigable Columbia.

18 August 1805.
[CLARK]

"Purchased of the Indians three horses for which we gave a chiefs Coat Some Handerchiefs a Shirt Legins & a fiew arrow points &c. I gave two of my coats to two of the under Chiefs who appeared not well satisfied that the first Cheif was dressed so much finer than themselves, at 10 oClock I set out . . . the fore part of the day worm. . . . We proceeded on thro' a wide leavel vallie without wood except willow & Srubs for 15 miles and Encamped."

19 August 1805.
[CLARK]

"A verry Cold morning Frost to be seen[.] we Set out at 7 oClock and proceeded on thro a wide leavel Vallie the Chief shew[ed] me the place that a number of his nation was killed about 1 years past . . . the beaver has Damed up the River in maney places we proceeded on up the main branch [Trail Creek] with a gradial assent to the head and passed over a low mountain [Lemhi Pass] and Decended a Steep Decent to a butifull Stream [Agency Creek], passed over a Second hill of a verry Steep assent & thro' a hilley Countrey for 8 miles an[d] Encamped on a Small Stream [Pattee Creek]."

[LEWIS]

"from what has been said of the Shoshones it will be readily perceived that they live in a wretched stait of poverty. yet notwithstanding . . . they are not only cheerful but even gay, fond of gaudy

"passed over a Second hill of a veery Steep assent"
Here, just west of Lemhi Pass, the trail turned north for one half mile then west over this steep hill.

dress and amusements; like most other Indians they are great egotists and frequently boast of heroic acts which they never performed. they are also fond of games of wrisk. They are frank, communicative, fair in dealing, generous with the lit-

tle they possess, extremely honest, and by no means beggarly. each individual is his own sovereign master, and acts from the dictates of his own mind; the authority of the Cheif being nothing more than mere admonition supported by

"a weapon called . . . the pog-gar-mag-gon"

the influence which the prop[r]iety of his own ex-amplary conduct may have acquired him in the minds of the individuals who compose the band. the title of cheif is not hereditary, nor can I learn that there is any cerimony of instalment, or other epo[c]h in the life of a Cheif from which his title as such can be dated. in fact every man is a chief, but all have not an equal influence on the minds of the other members of the community, and he who happens to enjoy the greatest share of con-fidence is the principal Chief. The Shoshonees may be estimated at about 100 warriors, and about three times that number of women and children. . . . their arms offensive and defensive consist in the bows and arrows shield, some, lances, and a weapon called by the Cippeways who formerly used it, the pog-gar-mag-gon. . . . from the middle of May to the first of Septem-ber these people reside on the waters of the Co-lumbia where they consider themselves in per-fect security from their enimies . . . during this season the salmon furnish the principal part of their subsistence and as this fish either perishes or returns about the 1st of September they are compelled . . . in surch of subsistence to resort to the Missouri. . . . here they move slowly down the river in order to collect and join other bands either of their own nation or the Flatheads, and having become sufficiently strong . . . venture on the Eastern side of the Rockey mountains into the plains where the buffaloe abound."

•

A "pog-gar-mag-gon" is a stone-headed club. The most familiar type consists of a wooden han-dle and a fist-sized stone encased in wet buck-skin, which, when dry, binds the whole together in one piece. It is a fearful and effective weapon at close quarters.

Clark records that he "passed over a Second hill of a verry Steep assent." Indian roads usually followed the valley or ridge crest, and when a hill had to be crossed they went straight up or down it. (For one thing, a travois was unmanageable in traversing a hillside obliquely; for another, there was less interference from fallen timber.)

20 August 1805.

[CLARK]

"Set out at half past 6 oClock and proceeded on . . . thro' a hilley Countrey to the Camp of the Indians . . . before we entered this Camp a Serimonious hault was requested by the Chief and I smoked with all that Came around, for Several pipes, we then proceeded on to the Camp & I was introduced into the only Lodge they had which was pitched in the Center for my party all other Lodges made of bushes, after a fiew Indian Seremonies I . . . requested a guide to accompany me [down the river]. . . . at 3 oClock . . . I set out accompanied by a old man as a Guide. . . . proceeded on thro a wide rich bottom on a beaten Roade 8 miles Crossed the river [Lemhi] and encamped on a Small run, this evening passed a number of old lodges, and met a number of men women children & horses. . . . Those Indians are verry attentive to Strangers &c."

•

The Indian village was near the junction of Kenney Creek and the Lemhi, having moved upstream from Sandy Creek where Lewis stayed on 13 and 14 August. There is a marker on the highway near the site.

Clark camped at or near what is now Baker, Idaho. Lewis, on the Beaverhead, wrote twenty-five hundred words on the ethnology of the Shoshone, made fifteen astronomical observations, and "made up a small assortment of medicines, together with the specimens of plants, minerals, seeds &c, which, I have collected between this place and the falls of the Missouri which I shall deposit here." On the return journey nearly a year later, Clark stopped to raise the cache and "most of the Party being Chewers of Tobacco become so impatient to be chewing it that they scercely gave themselves time to take their saddles off their horses before they were off to the deposit. I found every article safe, except a little damp."

The reason the Indians had only brush shelters is that the Blackfoot had attacked them shortly before, capturing all their possessions except some horses and the one tepee that Clark used.

21 August 1805.

[CLARK]

"Frost last night. proceeded on with the Indians . . . to there Camp, . . . I went to see the place those people take the fish, a wear across the Creek in which there is Stuk baskets Set in defferent derections So as to take the fish either decending or assending. . . . Crossed the River and went over a point of high land & Struck it again near a Bluff on the right Side. . . . They have only a few indifferent Knives, no ax, make use of Elk's horn Sharpened to Sp[l]it ther wood, no clothes except a Short Legins & robes of different animals. . . . Their ornements are Orter Skin d[e]curated with See Shells & the Skins & tales of the white weasel, See Shells of different size hung to

"Struck it again near a Bluff"
Salmon River on the right. Clark camped on the far side of this bluff 21 to 25 August.

their Ears hair and breast of their Shirts, beeds of Shells platted Grass, and Small strings of otter Skin dressed. . . . the most sacred of all the orniments of this nation is the Sea Shells of various Sizes and Shapes and colours, of the bassterd perl kind [abalone], which they inform us they get from the Indians to the South on the other Side of a large fork [Snake] of this river in passing to which they have to pass thro: Sandy & barron open plains without water to which place they can travel in 15 or 20 days. The bottoms of this day is wide & rich."

●

"The bottoms of this day wide and rich."
Salmon River valley.

The seashell trade routes ran east from the coast as far as the Navajo country. Natives sometimes crossed the desert without water or any food except a small pouch of chia (*Salvia columbariae*, a southwestern desert plant of the mint family) to permit a maximum burden of the precious shells. A thimbleful of nutritious seeds of this plant was sufficient to allay both thirst and hunger.

22 August 1805.

[CLARK]

"We Set out early passed a Small Creek [Tower] on the right side at 1 mile and the points of four mountains verry Steup high & rockey, the assent of three was So Steup that it is incredeable to describe. . . . the Indian horses pass over those Clifts hills beds & rocks as fast as a man, the three horses with me do not detain me any on account of those difficulties, passed a Small River [North Fork of the Salmon] at the mouth of which Several families of Indians were encamped and had Several Scaffolds of fish & buries drying we alarmed them verry much. . . . They offered every thing they possessed (which was very littl) to us. Some run off and hid in the bushes. The first offer of theirs were Elks tushes [tusks] from around their childrens necks, Sammon &c. my guide attempted [to] passify those people and they Set before me berri[e]s & fish to eate, I gave a fiew Small articles to those fritened people which added verry much to their pasification but not entirely as some of the women & Childn. Cried dureing my Stay of an hour at this place, I

proceeded on . . . Encamped on the lower pt. of an Island. . . . I saw to day [a] Bird of the woodpecker kind which fed on Pine burs its Bill and tale white the wings black every other part of a light brown, and about the Size of a robin."

[LEWIS]

"at 11. A.M. Charbono, the Indian Woman, Cameahwait and about 50 men with a number of women and children arrived. . . . I called the Cheifs and warriors together and addressed them . . . I had previously prepared a good meal for them all of boiled corn and beans which I gave to them as soon as the council was over and I had distributed the presents. . . . the Cheif wished that his nation could live in a country where they could provide such food. . . . I gave him a few dryed squashes . . . he had them boiled and declared them to be the best thing he had ever tasted except sugar, a small lump of which it seems his sister Sah-cah-gar Wea had given him."

•

The "fritened people" were camped where the North Fork joins the main stem of the Salmon and the reinforced stream turns westward through its magnificent wilderness canyon. "Elks tushes [tusks]," the incisors or canine teeth, were worn as necklaces or suspended from garments and were considered very valuable. Where elk were scarce, a substitute was sometimes carved from bone.

The "Bird of the woodpecker kind" was Clark's nutcracker, *Nucifraga columbiana*, de-

"I saw . . . [a] bird of the woodpecker kind"
Clark's nutcracker.

scribed and named from a specimen collected by the expedition. Its favorite food is the seed of yellow pine, and it can cling to a branch with its head down like a chickadee or hold a cone in one foot while it pries out the seed. After the nesting season, these beautiful birds gather and travel in noisy flocks (*see* Cutright, *Lewis and Clark*, 187).

23 August 1805.
[CLARK]
"We Set out early. . . . one mile to a verry bad riffle the water confined in a narrow Channel & beeting against the left Shore . . . I Deturmined to delay the party here and with my guide and three men I proceeded on. . . . Sometimes in a Small wolf parth & at other times Climing over the rocks for 12 miles to a large Creek (Indian) on the right side. . . . a road passes down this Creek which I understood passed to . . . the ground of another nation. . . . The River from the place I left my party to this Creek is almost one continued rapid, . . . with Canoes is entirely impossible. . . . those difficulties and necessary precautions would delay us an emence time in which provisions would be necessary. . . . those rapids which I had Seen [my guide] said was Small & trifleing in comparrison to the rocks & rapids below. . . . We camped about one hour after dark."
[LEWIS]
"at three p.m. the expected party of Indians arrived, about 50 men women and children. I now learnt that most of them were thus far on their way . . . towards the buffaloe country, and ob-

served . . . a good deal of anxiety on the part of some of those who had promised to assist me over the mountains to accompany this party; I felt some uneasiness . . . but as they still said they would return with me as they had promised I said nothing more to them. . . . [These people] made use of flint for knives, and with this instrument, skined the animals they killed, dressed their fish and made their arrows. . . . they renew the edge by flecking off the flint by means of the point of an Elk's or deer's horn. with [this] they also form their arrow points . . . with a quickness and neatness that is really astonishing. . . . their implements for making fire is nothing more than a blunt arrow and a peice of well seasoned soft spongey wood such as the willow or cottonwood. the point of this arrow they apply to this dry stick so near one edge of it that the particles of wood which are seperated from it by the friction of the arrow falls down by it's side in a little pile. the arrow is held between the palms of the hand . . . [and] briskly rolled . . . backwards and forwards . . . till the dust by the friction takes fire; then . . . some dry grass or dooted [rotted] wood is added. . . . in less than a minute they will produce fire."

•

The Salmon River from Salmon to Riggins is one of the great white-water streams of the world. For years it was called "The River of No Return" because downstream was the only way one could go. Native Americans were living on this wild stream centuries ago.

Flint is a mineral form of silicon dioxide that occurs only in limestone. As it is rare in the North American West, most projectile points and knives made there were from similar materials variously called—depending on the color— agate, chalcedony, jasper, or carnelian, or from the natural volcanic glass called obsidian.

24 August 1805.

[CLARK]

"Set out very early . . . on my return. . . . (I sliped & bruised my leg verry much on a rock). . . . I wrote a letter to Capt Lewis informing him of the prospects . . . and despatched one man [Colter] & horse."

[LEWIS]

"As the Indians who were on their way down the Missouri had a number of spare ho[r]ses I thought it probable that I could obtain some of them. . . . I now produced some battle axes which I had made at Fort Mandan [see 6 May 1806] with which they were pleased. knives also seemed in great demand among them. I soon purchased three horses and a mule. . . . at twelve Oclock we set out. . . . I now had the inexpressible satisfaction to find myself once more under way with all my baggage and party. . . . we . . . traveled only about six miles. . . . [The Indians] are excellent horsemen and extreemly expert in casting the cord about the neck of the horse."

•

The note Clark sent to Lewis recommended two plans, the first "of which I would be most pleased with" was to buy as many horses as possible, and with his present guide, proceed by land; the other was to divide the party, one trying the river and the other going with the guide. Another proposal, crossed out in the journal, was for one party to attempt the mountains while another returned to the Missouri, stocked up on provisions, and then tried the Medicine River. It was indeed a crucial time for the expedition.

"[These people] *make use of flint for knives*"

25 August 1805.

[CLARK]

"Set out verry early and halted one hour at the Indian Camp, they were kind [and] gave us all a little boiled Sammon & dried buries to eate, abt. half as much as I could eate. . . . a party of Squars & one man with Several boys going down to guathe[r] berries below."

[LEWIS]

"This morning loaded our horses and set out a little after sunrise. . . . proceeded within 2 Ms. of the narrow pass [Lemhi] . . . and halted for dinner. . . . sometime after we halted, Charbono mentioned to me with apparent unconcern that he expected to meet all the Indians from the camp on the Columbia tomorrow on their way to the Missouri. allarmed at this information I asked why he expected to meet them. he then informed me that the 1st Cheif had dispatched some of his young men this morning . . . requesting the Indians to meet them tomorrow and that himself and those with him would go on with them down the Missouri, and consequently leave me and my baggage on the mountain or thereabouts. I was out of patience with the folly of Charbono who had not sufficient sagacity to see the consequencies . . . and altho' he had been in possession of this information since early in the morning when it had been communicated to him by his Indian woman yet he never mentioned it untill the after noon. I could not forbear speaking to him with some degree of asperity on this occasion. I saw that there was no time to be lost in having those orders countermanded, or that we should not in all probability obtain any more horses or even get my baggage to the water of the Columbia."

•

Lewis's persuasive powers were now taxed to the utmost. He called the chiefs together, smoked, and then talked them into sending another messenger to the camp on the Lemhi to countermand the assembly orders. Cameahwait admitted he had done wrong, but "he had been induced to that measure from seeing all his people hungry." This was one of the occasions on which Sacagawea was instrumental in saving the expedition from failure. She had discovered Cameahwait's plan and realized the implications but, able to speak only Hidatsa and Shoshone, could inform no one but the dullard Charbonneau. Had the Indians met together on the Lemhi it is unlikely that Lewis could have de-

tained them longer. A hungry group with prospects of fat buffalo ahead would have been hard to control, for already they had lost over a week, with winter and starvation drawing near.

26 August 1805.
[LEWIS]

"This morning was excessively cold; there was ice . . . nearly a quarter of an inch thick. . . . Proceeded to a fine spring. . . . here I halted to dine and graize our horses. . . . I directed a pint of corn be given each Indian who was engaged in transporting our baggage. . . . one of the women . . . halted at a little run about a mile behind us. . . . I enquired of Cameahwait the cause of her detention, and was informed by him in an unconcerned manner that she had halted to bring fourth a child . . . ; in about an hour the woman arrived with her newborn babe and passed on her way to camp apparently as well as she ever was. . . . I observe the indian women collecting the root of a speceis of fennel which grows in the moist grounds and feeding their poor starved children; it is really distressing to witness the situation of those poor wretches. . . . Cameahwait requested that we would discharge our guns when we arrived in sight of the Village, accordingly . . . I drew up the party at open order in a single rank and gave them a runing fire discharging two rounds. they appeared much gratifyed with this exhibition. We then proceeded to the village . . . of brush lodges 32 in number . . . situated in a beautifull level smooth and extensive

"I observe the indian women collecting . . . a speceis of fennel"
Yampah, flower and root.

bottom . . . about 3 miles above the place I had first found them. . . . I found Colter here who had just arrived with a letter form Capt. Clark."

•

The "speceis of fennel" was Gairdner's yampah, *Perideridia gairdneri*; only an expert can differentiate between the several species. The plant has many common names, of which yampah and ipos seem the most popular; it was extremely important to the Indians, who relished it greatly (*see* Cutright, *Lewis and Clark*, 188n.). We once talked to a Paiute in Nevada who had some yampah in his pocket, dried hard as oak pegs; occasionally he would put one in his mouth, like horehound candy.

This day brings to a close the known journal of Captain Lewis on western waters until his entries resume on 1 January 1806, except for those when he and Captain Clark were separated. Specifically, that is 18–22 September and 29 November–31 December 1805. Whether Lewis kept a journal for the missing dates and it was lost or whether that important task was left to Clark is not known. Historians have argued the point endlessly, a futile debate unless the missing records are found.

27 August 1805.
[CLARK]
"Some frost this morning[.] every Man except one, out hunting. . . . Those Pore people are here depending on what fish they can catch, without anything else to depend on and appere con-

"proceeded to the village . . . in a beautiful . . . bottom"
Where the Salmon and Lemhi Rivers meet.

tented, my party hourly Complaining of their retched Situation . . . an Indian brough[t] in to the Camp 5 Sammon, two of which I purchased which afforded us a Supper."

[WHITEHOUSE]

"Capt. Lewis then began to trade with the natives for horses. . . . the Indian women are mostly employed gethering a kind of Small black Seed not So large as buck wheat, which they dry and pound or rub between 2 Stone[s] and make a Sort of meal of it[.] they also dry cherries and Servis berryes & roots &c. for food. . . . an Indian came in with a horse load of Deer meat, which our hunters killd. our hunters all returned towards evening had killed 4 Deer & 8 or 10 fine Salmon. . . . Capt. Lewis has bought 7 or 8 horses this day . . . but they Seem loth to part with anymore without asking more for them. Some of them play away whatever they git for their horses, at a game nearly like playing butten only they keep Singing all the while and do all by motions. [They] more or less play at this game & loose or win more or less they care not[.]"

•

The "Small black Seed" was from the goosefoot, or Chenopodium, family of plants. Sergeant Gass wrote: "Those of the natives, who are detached in small parties, appear to live better, and to have a larger supply of provisions, than those who live in large villages. The people of these three lodges have gathered a quantity of sunflower seed, and also of the lambs-quarter, which they pound and mix with service berries, and make of the composition a kind of bread; which appears capable of sustaining life for some time."

For a description of the gambling game, *see* 18 April 1806.

28 August 1805.
[CLARK]

"a frost this morning. . . . a Camp of about 40 Indians came from the West fork and passed up to day. . . . I dispatched one man [Gass] to the upper Camps to enquire if Cap. Lewis was comeing &c.

. . . I purchased Some fish roe of the pore but kind people with whome I am Encamped for which I gave three Small fish hooks, the use of which they readily proseved."

[WHITEHOUSE]
"a clear pleasant morning. . . . Capt. Lewis has bought 5 or 6 more [horses] to day we have now 25 in all. . . . in the evening 2 Indians arived at this village on horseback from another band which were Some distance to the South near the Spanish country. the principal men of the village all assembled to council with them. these Savages all like Salt & eat it on meat &c."

29 August 1805.
[CLARK]

"I . . . proceeded on up to join Capt. Lewis at the upper Village of Snake Indians . . . found him much engaged in Councelling and attempting to purchase a fiew more horses. . . . our wish is to get a horse for each man to carry our baggage and for some of the men to ride occasionally, The horses are handsom and much accustomed to be changed as to their Parsture. . . . I purchased a horse for which I gave my Pistol 100 Balls Powder & a Knife."

[WHITEHOUSE]
"a clear pleasant morning. . . . a number of Indians arived here from the East Side of the Mountain. they belonged to this nation but had been gone a long time and one of the warrie[r]s had been Scupled by Some war party in the plain. a number of their relation cryed aloud when they

arived in the village. . . . these natives do not incline to Sell any more horses without guns in return as they say they must have one or the other for defence, as they could jump on their horses & ride off and carry their children &c. we told them [we] could not Spare any guns if we Should git nor more horses."

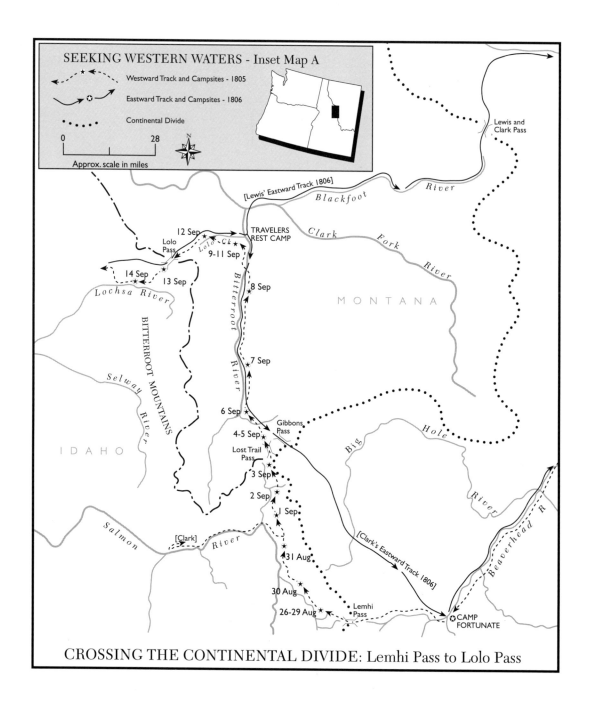

SEEKING WESTERN WATERS - Inset Map A

★···◀ Westward Track and Campsites - 1805

⟶✦⟶ Eastward Track and Campsites - 1806

··········· Continental Divide

0   28

Approx. scale in miles

N

Lewis and Clark Pass

[Lewis' Eastward Track 1806]

Blackfoot   River

Clark   Fork   River

MONTANA

12 Sep

Lolo Pass

TRAVELERS REST CAMP

Lolo Ck.

9-11 Sep

14 Sep

13 Sep

Lochsa River

Bitterroot   River

8 Sep

BITTERROOT MOUNTAINS

Selway   River

7 Sep

6 Sep

Gibbons Pass

4-5 Sep

Lost Trail Pass

IDAHO

Big   Hole   River

3 Sep

2 Sep

1 Sep

Salmon   River

[Clark]

[Clark's Eastward Track 1806]

Beaverhead R.

31 Aug

30 Aug

26-29 Aug

Lemhi Pass

CAMP FORTUNATE

CROSSING THE CONTINENTAL DIVIDE: Lemhi Pass to Lolo Pass

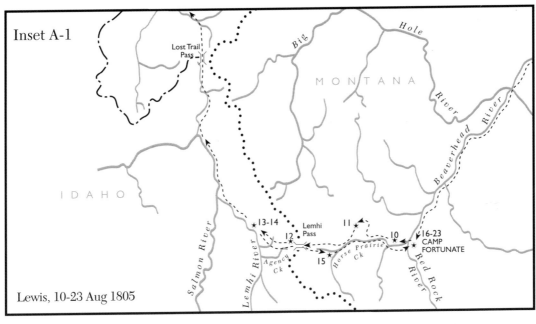

Inset A-1

Lost Trail Pass

Big

Hole

River

MONTANA

IDAHO

Beaverhead River

Salmon River

Lemhi River

13-14

Lemhi Pass

12

Agency Ck

11

15

Horse Prairie Ck

10

16-23
CAMP FORTUNATE

Red Rock River

Lewis, 10-23 Aug 1805

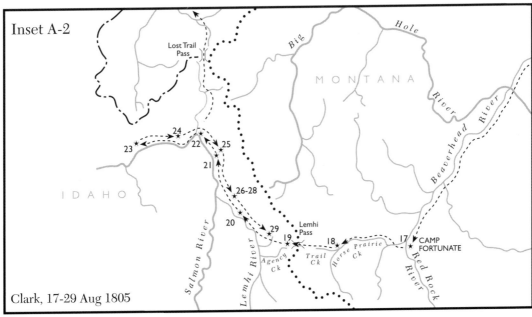

Inset A-2

Lost Trail Pass

Big

Hole

River

MONTANA

IDAHO

Beaverhead River

Salmon River

Lemhi River

24

23

22

25

21

26-28

20

29

Lemhi Pass

19

Agency Ck

Trail Ck

18

Horse Prairie Ck

17
CAMP FORTUNATE

Red Rock River

Clark, 17-29 Aug 1805

"Passed remarkable rock resembling Pirimids"

"Encamped in Some old lodges" (right)
Campsite for 31 August.

II

BY TRAIL TO NAVIGABLE RIVERS

30 AUGUST TO 6 OCTOBER 1805

30 August 1805.

[CLARK]

"finding that we Could purchase no more horse[s] . . . for our goods &c . . . I Gave my Fuzee to one of the men & Sold his musket for a horse which Completed us to 29 total horses . . . Set out on our rout down the river [Lemhi] by land guided by my old guide [and] one other who joined him . . . proceeded on 12 Miles and en-camped on the river South Side. at the time we Set out from the Indian Camps the greater Part of the Band Set out over to the waters of the Missouri."

[WHITEHOUSE]

"the guide which we engaged to go with us tells us that we could go a road which would be Smooth & leads to the Southward but we would be 2 days without water and no game on that road. but he could Show us a hilley rough roud [road] [Lolo Trail] over the mountains to the north of the River which would take us . . . in 10 days to a large fork of the River, where it would be navagable."

A fuzee (fusee or fusil) is a light musket.

The road to the southward would have been through Challis, Idaho, into the Snake River Plains, where they would have followed a route, later to become the Oregon Trail, that crossed the Blue Mountains and met the Columbia below the mouth of the Snake River.

31 August 1805.
[CLARK]

"A fine morning[.] Set out before Sun rise . . . proceeded on in the Same rout I decended the 21st Instant, halted 3 hours on Sammon [Carmen] Creek to Let our horses graze. . . . I met an Indian on horse back who fled with great Speed to Some lodges below & informed them that the Enemies were Coming down, armd. with guns &c. the inhabitents of the Lodges indisceved him, we proceeded on the road on which I had decended as far as the 1st run [Tower Creek] below & left the road & Proceeded up the Run in a tolerable road 4 miles & Encamped in Some old lodges at the place the road leaves the Creek and assends the high Countrey. . . . The Countrey is Set on fire for the purpose of Collecting the different bands . . . to go to the Missouri where they intend passing the winter near the Buffalow. . . . Passed remarkable rock resembling Pirimids on the Left Side."

•

Setting the prairie or hills afire was the traditional method of calling the tribes together or warning that enemies were approaching. Fray Silvestre de Escalante saw the Indians near Salt Lake signalling this way, as did John C. Frémont in California, and many other explorers mention the custom (*see* Bolton, *Pageant in the Wilderness*, 177; and Jackson, *Expeditions of Frémont*, 1:663). Stories of communication by the manipulation of a smoke column are romantic nonsense.

Tower Creek was until recently called Boyle Creek and is shown by that name on older maps.

1 September 1805.
[WHITEHOUSE]

"proceeded on over verry high mountains which was verry bad for our horses to climb up and down them. . . . we find a great pleanty of Servis berrys which are verry Sweet and good at this time. in the afternoon we descended a Mountain nearly as Steep as the roof of a house. . . . the wild or choke cherryes abound in this bottom. we gethered and boiled Some which eat verry well."

2 September 1805.
[WHITEHOUSE]

"we proceeded on through a bad thicket of tall Strait pitch pine bolsom fer & cotton timber. . . . the bottoms on the Creek narrow and Swampy a number of beaver dams. we Call this place dismal Swamp, and it is a lonesom rough part of the Country. we were obledged to climb Several hills with our horses, where it was So Steep and rockey that Some of the horses which was weak

"we find a great plenty of Servis berrys . . . . choke cherryes abound in this bottom"

and their feet Sore they fell back 3 or 4 fell over backwards and roled to the foot of the hills. we were then obledged to carry the loads up the hills and then load again. . . . This horrid bad going . . . was six miles and we are not out of it yet."

•

Near Gibbonsville the main Indian road the party was following turned east toward the buffalo country. Nowadays it would be a dim and rugged track up the North Fork and over the Divide by way of Lost Trail Pass. There is a historical marker on Highway 93 near the campsite for this day.

3 September 1805.
[CLARK]

"A Cloudy morning, horses verry Stiff. . . . hills high & rockey on each Side, in the after part of the day the high mountains closed the Creek on each Side and obliged us to take on the Steep Sides of those Mountains, So Steep that the horses Could Scur[ce]ly keep from Slipping down . . . with great dificuelty we made [about 8] miles & Encamped on . . . the Creek. . . . I killed 5 Pheasents & the hunter 4 with a little Corn afforded us a kind of Supper. . . . we met with a great misfortune, in haveing our last Th[er]-mometer broken, by accident."

Besides recording new flora and fauna, Lewis was charged with keeping a log on meteorology, a task he faithfully performed; the temperature, weather, and wind were set down at sunrise and 4:00 P.M. daily. The thermometer readings end on 5 September, and the notes say the thermometer was broken on 6 September. In the log were noted many interesting events, such as when berries ripened, flowers bloomed, and migratory birds arrived or departed.

4 September 1805.

[CLARK]

"a verry cold morning every thing wet and frosed, . . . we assended a mountain & took a Divideing ridge which we kept for Several Miles & fell on the head of a Creek which appeared to run the Course we wished to go, I was in front, & saw Several of the Argalia or Ibex [bighorn sheep; *see* 12 April 1806] decended the mountain by verry Steep decent to the Creek, where our hunters killed a Deer which we made use of, and prosued our Course down the creek to the forks about 5 miles [near Sula, Montana] where we met a part of the Tushepau [Flathead] nation, of 33 Lodges about 80 men 400 Total and at least 500 horses. . . . I was the first white man who ever wer on the waters of this river."

This meeting with the Flatheads was one of the most colorful events of the entire journey. The artist Charles Russell thought so, too, and painted the magnificent mural *Lewis and Clark Meeting the Flatheads* in the Capitol Building in Helena, Montana. We stood on the porch of the house where Russell had worked, and attempted to reconstruct the vivid scene in the valley below.

Whitehouse's description is graphic: "towards evening we arrived at a large Encampment of the flat head nation which is a large band of the nation of about 40 lodges. they have between 4 and 500 well looking horses now feeding in this valley or plain in our view. they received us as friends and appeared to be glad to See us. 2 of our men who were a hunting came to their lodges first the natives Spread a white robe over them and put their arms around their necks, as a great token of friendship. then Smoaked with them. when Capt. Lewis ari[ved] they Spread white robes over their Shoulders and Smoaked with them. our officers told them that they would Speak with them tomorrow and tell them our business. . . . the natives are light Complectioned decent looking people the most of them well cloathed with Mo. Sheep and other Skins. they have buffalow Robes leather lodges to live in, but have no meat at this time. but gave us abundance of their dryed fruit Such as Servis berrys cherries different kinds of roots all of which eat verry well."

"we met a part of the Tushepau [Flathead] nation"
Ross's Hole at Sula, Montana.

5 *September* 1 8 0 5 .
[W H I T E H O U S E]

"Gave 4 of their principal men meddles made them cheifs gave each of them a Shirt and a nomber of other articles also 2 flags &c. . . . these Savages has the Strangest language of any we have ever Seen. they appear to us to have an Empediment in their Speech or a brogue or bur on their tongue but they are the likelyest and honestst Savages we have ever yet Seen."

6 *September* 1 8 0 5 .
[W H I T E H O U S E]

"at 10 oClock A.M. the natives all got up their horses and Struck their lodges in order to move over on the head of the Missourie after the the buffalow. they make a large Show as they are numerous and have abundance of horses. we take these Savages to be the Welch Indians if their be any Such from the Language. So Capt. Lewis took down the names of everry thing in their Language, in order that it may be found out whether they are or whether they Sprang or origenated first from the welch or not."

•

The idea that "Welch" Indians might be found in the heart of North America stems from a supposed transatlantic voyage in the twelfth century led by a Welsh prince named Madoc og Gwynned. Proponents of this theory assert that he landed with a party of colonists on the coast of the Gulf of Mexico near Mobile, Alabama, some time in A.D. 1170, after which all of them eventually disappeared northward into the interior. The Mandan Indians, because of their relatively light complexions and linguistic dissimilarity to other Indians inhabiting the upper Missouri River basin, had been said to be descendants of Madoc's colonists. A Welshman named John Evans visited the Mandans over the winter of 1796–97, in an effort to validate such contentions—something he was unable to do. Neither Lewis nor Clark seems to have put much stock in the idea after their own winter spent among the Mandans. Whitehouse's remarks concerning the Flatheads, however, suggest that the expedition had not given up entirely on the possibility of finding "Welch" Indians, unlikely as the prospects of that must have seemed (*see* Deacon, *Madoc and the Discovery of America*).

The Flatheads were a Salishan-speaking people, buffalo hunters who roamed over much of Montana and part of Idaho. Their culture was similar to that of the Nez Perce. The two nations traded, fought, and hunted together, and intermarried. Around 1720 the acquisition of horses greatly enriched their way of life.

Although these Indians are still known as Flatheads, they did not disfigure their heads as did the Chinooks of the Lower Columbia. This custom seems to be an old tradition. The flattening process was accomplished by binding a board against an infant's head, which at that age is flexible. The skull was thus forcibly deformed, apparently without pain and certainly without any harm to the brain, for almost all the early explorers comment on the shrewdness of the Chinooks. The end result was a broad, flat face, which was considered a mark of distinction and great beauty among those whose practice it was. Actually, "Flathead" is a misnomer, since the forehead is flattened, while the head itself is brought to a point. One theory for the name "Flathead Nation" is that the heads of this group were not disfigured but naturally flat on top, instead of peaked.

The place Clark met the Flatheads is now called Ross's Hole. In the early 1800s, the Hudson's Bay Company sent trapping parties to exploit the rich western beaver streams; Alexander Ross, leading the 1824 Snake River Expedition, was snowbound there (*see* Ross, *Fur Hunters*, 206–35). Those colorful brigades—men, women, and children of up to a hundred, with triple the number of horses, ranged over a vast area for a year or more, living off the land and frequently starving.

In trapper parlance, a "hole" is a river bottom surrounded by mountains, a sheltered haven offering abundant game, forage, wood, and water.

7 September 1805.
[CLARK]

"A Cloudy & ranie Day the greater Part of the day dark & Drisley[.] we proceeded on down the river thro a Vallie passed Several Small Runs on the [right] & 3 creeks on the left The Vallie from 1 to 2 miles wide . . . Saw 2 horses left by the In-

dians those horses were as wild a[s] Elk. . . . we did not make camp untill dark, for the want of a good place."

8 September 1805.
[CLARK]

"a Cloudy morning[.] Set out early and proceeded on through an open Vallie for 23 miles passed 4 Creeks. . . . encamped [near Stevensville] on the right Side of the river. . . . I observe great quantities of a peculiar Sort of Prickly peare grow in Clusters ovel & about the Size of a Pigions egge with strong thorns which is so birded [bearded] as to draw the Pear from the Cluster after penetrating our feet. . . . we found 2 mears and a Colt, the mears were lame."

9 September 1805.
[CLARK]

"a fair morning[.] Set out early and proceeded on thro' a plain as yesterday down the valley Crossed . . . the main river at 15 miles & Encamped on a large Creek from the left which we call Travelers rest [Lolo] Creek."

[LEWIS]

"our guide could not inform us where this [Bitterroot] river discharged itself into the columbia river, he informed us that it continues it's course . . . to the N. as far as he knew it and that not very distant . . . it formed a junction with a stream nearly as large as itself [Clark's Fork] . . . which forms an excellent pass to the Missouri."

"I observe a peculiar Sort of Prickly peare"

10 September 1805.
[C L A R K]
"A fair morning[.] Concluded to Delay to day and make Some observations."
[L E W I S]
"this evening one of our hunters [Colter] re-turned accompanyed by three men of the Flat-head nation whom he had met in his exurtion up *travellers rest* [Lolo] Creek. on first meeting him the Indians were alarmed and prepared for bat-tle with their bows and arrows, but he soon re-lieved their fears by laying down his gun and ad-vancing towards them. the Indians were mounted on very fine horses . . . each man in the nation possesses from 20 to a hundred head. . . . two of them departed . . . and the third remained . . . [he said] some of his relations were at the sea last fall and saw an old whiteman who resided there by himself."

•

This "old whiteman" may have been an individ-ual known as Soto, who was then living on the lower Columbia River, and who claimed to be the offspring of a shipwrecked Spaniard and a Clatsop woman (*see* 30 March 1806).

11 September 1805.
[W H I T E H O U S E]
"a beautiful pleasant morning. we went out to hunt up our horses, but they were So Scattered that we could not find them at all untill 12 oClock, So we dined here. . . . Some of the men

who were hunting the horses detained us Untill 4 oClock at which time we Set out and proceeded on up this Creek. . . . Passed a tree on which was a nomber of Shapes drawn on it with paint by the natives. a white bear Skin hung on the Same tree. we Suppose this to be a place of worship among them. . . . Came about 7 miles this evening and Camped on a Smooth plain near the creek, where had lately been a large Encampment of Indians. Saw one house made of Earth. the pine trees pealed as far up as a man could reach. we Suppose that the natives done it to git the enside beark to mix with their dryed fruit to Eat."

12 September 1805.
[CLARK]

"a white frost. . . . proceeded on up the Creek, passed a Fork on the right on which I saw near an old Indian encampment a Swet house Covered with earth. . . . The road through this hilley countrey is verry bad passing over hills & thro' Steep hollows, over falling timber &c. &c. . . . passed Some most intolerable road on the Sides of the Steep Stoney mountains. . . . Encamped on a hill Side on the Creek after Decending a long Steep mountain, Some of our Party did not get up untill 10 oClock P.M. . . . Party and horses much fatigued."

13 September 1805.
[CLARK]

"a cloudy morning. . . . I proceeded on with the partey up the Creek at 2 miles passed Several

Springs [Lolo Hot Springs] which I observed the Deer Elk &c. had made roads to, and below one of [them] the Indians had made a whole to bathe, I tasted this water and found it hot & not bad tasted. . . . I found this water nearly boiling hot at the places it Spouted from the rocks. . . . as Several roads led from these springs . . . my guide took a wrong road and took us out of our rout 3 miles. . . . This Creek is verry much damed up with the beaver. we crossed the dividing ridge [Lolo Pass] found it only about half a mile from the head Spring of water running East to a branch running west. I proceeded on thro [a] tolerable rout for abt. 4 or 5 miles and halted to let our horses graze as well as wate for Capt. Lewis. . . . after he came up, and proceeded over a mountain . . . we fell on a Small Creek from the left which Passed through open glades . . . proceeded . . . about 2 miles . . . & Encamped."

•

Lolo Hot Springs has been a tourist attraction since 1900. The many trails were made by deer, elk, and other animals attracted to minerals deposited by the water. Similar trails may be seen at Colgate Springs on the Lochsa, where there is a visitors' center and a nature walk.

14 September 1805.
[WHITEHOUSE]

"a cloudy morning. we eat the last of our meat, and Set out as usal. . . . ascended a verry high mountain . . . went Some distance on the top

"Camped on a Smooth plain near the creek"
Lolo Creek in the vicinity of Travelers Rest,
Bitterroot Mountains beyond.

"saw . . . a Swet house Covered with earth"

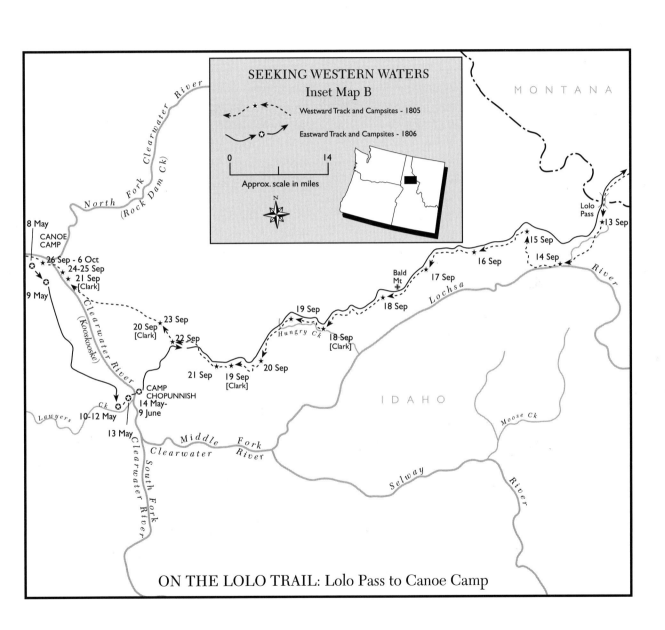

MONTANA

North Fork Clearwater River

(Rock Dam Ck)

Lolo Pass

13 Sep

8 May

CANOE CAMP

26 Sep - 6 Oct

24-25 Sep

21 Sep
[Clark]

9 May

Clearwater River
(Kooskooske)

15 Sep

14 Sep

River

16 Sep

Bald Mt

17 Sep

18 Sep

Lochsa

23 Sep

20 Sep
[Clark]

22 Sep

19 Sep

Hungry Ck

18 Sep
[Clark]

21 Sep

19 Sep
[Clark]

20 Sep

IDAHO

Moose Ck

Ck

CAMP CHOPUNNISH

10-12 May

14 May-
9 June

13 May

Lawyers

Middle Fork

Clearwater River

South Fork Clearwater River

Selway

River

ON THE LOLO TRAIL: Lolo Pass to Canoe Camp

then descended it about 6 miles. . . . came down at another fork . . . the Natives had a place made across in form of our wires [weirs] in 2 places, and worked with willows verry injeanously, for the current [was] verry rapid. passed Several late Indian Encampments. our Guide tells us that the natives catch a nomber of Sammon along here. we went down the creek abt. 4 miles and Camped [near Powell Ranger Station] for the night. Eat a little portable Soup, but the men in jeneral So hungry that we killed a fine Colt which eat verry well, at this time."

•

The trail followed the ridge between Pack and Haskell creeks to their junction. Two miles from camp the guide took a wrong fork, leading the party several miles out of the way and through some miserable going; his choice led to the fishing sites on the Lochsa. Perhaps it was the only way he knew. From the junction of the two creeks the trail passed over a mountain to the place where White Sand (named Colt-killed by the explorers) and Crooked Fork met to form the Lochsa River.

15 September 1805.
[WHITEHOUSE]

"cloudy. we loaded our horses and Set out at 7 oClock, and proceeded on down the creek a Short distance[.] crossed Several Springs and Swampy places covred with white ceeder and tall handsome Spruce pine, which would be excelent for boards or Shingles. we crossed a creek a Small pond a little below, then assended a high mountain. . . . we marched on top of this mountain untill after dark in hopes to find water . . . found plean[ty] of Snow . . . we melted what we wanted to drink and made or mixd, a little portable Soup with Snow water and lay down contented."

•

The expedition left the Lochsa four miles below today's Powell Ranger Station and ascended Wendover Ridge to the top. They were now again on the main Lolo Trail. The "Small pond below" is now called Whitehouse Pond. A Forest Service campground nearby is also named after Whitehouse.

The journals justly complain of the abominable condition of the road across the Bitterroots, for there can be no doubt that it was villainous. But one should remember that (when not closed by snow) it was in continual use by Indians going to and returning from the buffalo country—entire bands with all their baggage and hundreds of horses. In July 1877, the Nez Perce chief, Looking Glass, led his band of some two hundred men and four hundred fifty women and children, with more than two thousand horses, over this trail in nine days (see Andrist, *The Long Death*, 307; and Brown, *Bury My Heart at Wounded Knee*, 306).

16 September 1805.

[WHITEHOUSE]

"when we awoke this morning to our great Surprise we were covered with Snow. . . . Some of our men without Socks raped rags on their feet, and loaded up our horses and Set out without anything to eat."

[CLARK]

"I walked in front to keep the road and found great dificuelty in keeping it as in maney places the Snow had entirely filled up the track, . . . at 12 oClock we halted . . . to worm & dry our Selves a little as well as to let our horses rest and graze on Some long grass which I observed . . . I have been wet and as cold in every part as I ever was in my life, indeed I was at one time fearfull my feet would freeze in the thin Mockirsons which I wore, . . . I took one man and proceed on as fast as I could about 6 miles . . . halted and built fires for the party agains[t] their arrival which was at Dusk, verry cold and much fatigued. . . . Killed a Second Colt which we all Suped hartily on and thought it fine meat."

•

Ralph Space located this cold camp one-quarter mile north of the stone cairns called Indian Post Office on the present motor road.° The original trail passed below these rock piles; they are not

"passed Several Springs"
Rock formation at Lolo Hot Springs.

°Ralph Space was an acquaintance of the Strongs, and an authority on the Lewis and Clark Trail in Idaho and Montana. He was supervisor of the Clearwater National Forest (1954–63), and the author of *The Lolo Trail* (1980, privately printed) and *The Clearwater Story* (1984, USDA Forest Service).

"a Small Creek . . . Passed through open glades"

"we crossed a creek a Small pond below"
Whitehouse Pond near the Lochsa River.

The Lochsa where Lewis & Clark left it.

mentioned in the journals, but on the return trip in June the party's members did notice a cairn just west of their 17 September campsite.

Stone piles are found in great numbers throughout the American West. Many of them were built by white men for one reason or another, and it is generally impossible to tell which are aboriginal. In their constant quest for food the Indians had to know their territory as a farmer knows his fields, but ethnologists tend to discount the theory that they used trail markers. It is known that piling rocks was a task performed by youths during their puberty rites, and that some tribes habitually cast a stone at a growing pile along a trail while repeating a short prayer.

17 September 1805.
[CLARK]

"Cloudy morning[.] our horses much Scattered which detained us untill one oClock. . . . Snow on the Knobs, no Snow in the Vallies[.] Killed a fiew Pheasents which was not sufficient for our Supper. . . . A Coalt being the most useless part of our Stock he fell a Prey to our appetites. . . . we made only 10 miles to day . . . Encamped on the top of a high Knob . . . at a run passing to the left."

18 September 1805.
[LEWIS]

"Cap Clark set out this morning to go a head with six hunters. there being no game in these mountains we concluded it would be better for one of us to take the hunters and hurry on to the leavel country a head and there hunt and provide some provisions while the other remained with and brought on the party. the latter of these was my part. . . . we marched 18 miles this day and encamped on the side of a steep mountain. . . . we dined & suped on a skant proportion of portable soup, a few canesters of which, a little bears oil and about 20 lbs of candles form our stock of provisions."

[CLARK]

"we passed over a countrey Similar to the one of yesterday more fallen timber . . . from the top of a high part of the mountain at 20 [12] miles I had a view of an emence Plain and leavel Countrey to the s.w. & West. . . . Made 32 [21] miles and Encamped on a bold running Creek passing to the left which I call *Hungery* Creek as at that place we had nothing to eate."

•

Lewis and the main party camped three miles west of Bald Mountain. The stream on which Clark camped was later named Obia, but Ralph Space succeeded in having the name Hungery Creek restored—keeping the explorer's original spelling.

19 September 1805.
[LEWIS]

"Set out this morning a little after sun rise and continued our rout about the same course of yesterday or s.20.w. for 6 miles when the ridge terminated and we to our inexpressable joy discov-

"Indian Post Office" on the Lolo Trail.

ered a large tract of Prairie country lying to the s.w. . . . this plain appeared to be about 60 Miles distant, but our guide assured us that we should reach it's borders tomorrow. . . . the road was excessively dangerous along [this] creek being a narrow rockey path. . . . Fraziers horse fell from this road in the evening and roled with his load near a hundred yards into the Creek. we all expected that the horse was killed but to our astonishment when the load was taken off he arose to his feet & appeared to be but little injured. . . . we took a small quantity of portable soup, and retired to rest much fatiegued."

Original Lolo Trail.

[CLARK]

"proceeded on up the Creek [Hungery] passing through a Small glade at 6 miles at which place we found a horse. I derected him killed and hung up for the party after takeing a brackfast off for our Selves which we thought fine . . . passed over a mountain, and the heads of a branch of hungary Creek, two high mountains, ridges and through much falling timber . . . Struck a large Creek passing to our left which I Kept down for 4 miles and left it to our left & passed over a mountain to a Small Creek . . . and Encamped."

•

The prairie they were so delighted to see was not the one their guide was heading for, but the present Camas Prairie, a rich farmland fifty miles away across the Clearwater.

20 September 1805.

[CLARK]

"I set out early . . . decended the mountain to a leavel pine Countrey proceeded on through a butifull Countrey . . . to a Small Plain which I found maney Indian lodges . . . I met 3 boys, when they saw me [they] ran and hid themselves, searched[,] found [two] gave them Small pieces of ribin & Sent them forward to the village[.] a man Came out to meet me & Conducted me to a large Spacious Lodge which he told me (by Signs) was the Lodge of his great Chief who had Set out 3 days previous with all the Warriers of the nation to war . . . & would return in 15 or 18

days. . . . those people gave us a Small piece of Buffalow meat, Some dried Salmon beries & roots in different States, Some round and much like an onion which they call Pas she co Sweet, of this they make bread & Supe . . . I gave them a fiew Small articles as preasents, and proceeded on with a Chief to his Village 2 miles in the Same Plain. . . . They call themselves *Cho Pun-nish* or *Pierced Noses*. . . . Emence quantity of *Pas-shi-co* root [camas] gathered & in piles about the plain, those roots grow much like an onion in marshey places. . . . I find myself verry unwell all the evening from eateing the fish & roots too freely."

[LEWIS]

"I have also observed two birds of a blue colour . . . the one of a blue shining colour with a very high tuft of feathers on the head a long tale . . . its note is cha-ah cha-ah. it is about the size of a pigeon. saw . . . a kind of honeysuckle which bears a white bury . . . not common but to the western side of the rockey mountains."

•

Clark met the Indians on Weippe Prairie near the town of Weippe (pronounced Wé-ipe). Here the main party camped on 22 September 1805, as they did on 10–14 and 21–23 June 1806, on the return trip.

The camas, *Cammasia quamash*, was as important to the Nez Perce Indians as the bison was to the warriors of the Great Plains or the salmon to the wanderers of the Columbia Plateau. It was their staple food, since it grew in great abun-

Here Clark met the Indians on Weippe Prairie.

dance and could be easily preserved. Without the camas, few could have subsisted in the vast area between the Rockies and the Columbia River fisheries.

The bird with the peculiar note, new to science, was the black-headed jay, *Cyanocitta stelleri annectens*, a subspecies of Steller's jay (*see*

Cutright, *Lewis and Clark*, 210). The honeysuckle was the snowberry, *Symphoricarpos albus*, one of the most interesting of the plants collected by Lewis. President Jefferson wrote to Mme. la Comtesse de Tresse, an aunt of Mme. de Lafayette, in 1813: "Lewis' journey across our continent to the Pacific has added a number of new plants. I have growing, which I destine for you, a very handsome little shrub of the size of a currant bush. Its beauty consists in a great production of berries the size of currants, and literally as white as snow" (Thwaites, *Journals*, 7:393).

The snowberry is abundant in the Columbia River watershed. The flowers are small pink cups; the fruit hangs from the branchlets like popcorn balls, ornamental and useful, too, as winter forage for birds.

21 September 1805.
[CLARK]

"A fine Morning[.] sent out all the hunters . . . I my self delayed with the Chief to prevent Suspission and to Collect by Signs as much information as possible about the river and the Countrey in advance. The Chief drew me a kind of chart of the river, and informed me that a greater Chief than himself was fishing at the river half a days march from his Village called the twisted [hare], and that the river forked . . . and passed thro' the mountains at which place was a great fall [Celilo], at those falls white people lived from whome they precured the white beeds & Brass &c. which the womin wore. . . . Set out to the river, met a man at dark . . . whome I hired . . . to polit [pilot] me to the Camp of the twisted hare . . . found at the Camp five Squars & 3 Children. my guide called to the Chief who was Encamped with 2 others on a Small Island [one mile above Orofino] in the river, he soon joind. me, I found him a Chearfull man with apparant siencerity, I gave him a Medal

"roots . . . much like an onion"
Camas bulbs.

&c. and Smoked untill 1 oClock a.m. and went to Sleep. . . . The weather verry worm after decending into the low Countery."

[LEWIS]

"We were detained this morning untill 11 OCk. in consequence of not being able to collect our horses. we then set out . . . passed a broken country heavily timbered great quantities of which had fallen and so obstructed our road that it was almost impracticable to proceed in many places. . . . encamped in a small open bottom where there was tolerable food for our horses. I directed the horses be hubbled to prevent delay in the morning being determined to make a forced march tomorrow in order to reach if possible the open country. we killed a few Pheasants, and I killed a prarie woolf which together with the ballance of our horse beef and some crawfish which we obtained in the creek enabled us to make one more hearty meal, not knowing where the next was to be found. the Arborvita [red cedar] increases in quantity and size. I saw several sticks today large enough to form eligant perogues of at least 45 feet in length."

22 September 1805.

[CLARK]

"a fine morning[.] I proceed on down the little river [Clearwater] to about 1½ a mile & found the chi[e]f in a canoe comeing to meet me[.] I got into his canoe & crossed over to his camp. . . . Set out with the Chief & his Son . . . for the Village at which place I expected to meet Capt

Lewis[,] this young horse in his fright threw himself and me 3 times and hurt my hip much . . . arrived at his Village [at Weippe] at Sunset where I found Capt. Lewis & the party Encamped, much fatigued, hungery, much rejoiced to find something to eate . . . I cautioned them of the Consequences of eateing too much &c. The planes appeared covered with Spectators viewing the white men and the articles which we had . . . the supply I Sent by R. Fields proved timely and gave great encouragement to the party. . . . I got the Twisted hare to draw the river from his Camp down which he did with great Cherfullnes on a white Elk skin. . . . I precured maps of the Country & river with the Situation of Indians, Towns from Several men of note Seperately which varied verry little."

23 September 1805.

[WHITEHOUSE]

"a clear pleasant morning. we purchased considerable quantity of Sammon and root or potatoe bread from the natives. . . . the women are engaged laying up food for the winter as they tell us that they intend going over to the Missourie in the Spring after buffaloe &c. Some of the natives have copper kittles, and beeds a fiew knives &c. . . . they are verry fond of our marchandize. the large blue beeds they are the fondest of but are glad to git anything we have. . . . these natives live well and are verry kind and well dressed in mountain Sheep & deer & Elk Skins well dressed. they have buffalo robes but are verry

choise of them. . . . these Savages at this village
. . . are numerous and talk loud & confused. they
live [with] much comfort in their villages. Several lodges all join. the most of them have leather
lodges, and are makeing flag [or mat] lodges &c."

•

Concerning flag or mat lodges, *see* 17 October
1805.

24 September 1805.
[CLARK]

"a fine morning . . . proceeded on by the Same
rout I had previously traveled, and at Sunset we
arrived at the Island on which I found the
Twisted hare, and formed a Camp on a large Island a little below, Capt. Lewis scercely able to
ride on a jentle horse which was furnished by the
Chief, Several men So unwell that they were
Compelled to lie on the Side of the road for
Some time others obligded to be put on horses. I
gave rushes Pills to the Sick this evening. Several
Indians follow us."

25 September 1805.
[CLARK]

"a verry hot day. . . . I Set out early with the Chief
and 2 young men to hunt Some trees Calculated
to build Canoes, as we had previously deturmined to proceed on by water . . . proceeded on
down the river Crossed a Creek at 1 mile . . .
verry rockey which I call rock dam Creek [North
Fork of the Clearwater] & Passed down on the N

"encamped in a small open bottom"

*"the Arborvita increases
in . . . size"*
Western red cedar.

side of the river to a fork . . . which is about the Same size . . . with the other fork. . . . one of the young men took his guig [fish spear] and killed 6 fine Salmon two of them were roasted and we eate, two Canoes Came up loaded with the furniter & provisions of 2 families, those Canoes are long Stedy and without much rake, I crossed the South fork and proceeded up on the South side . . . thro' a narrow Pine bottom in which I Saw fine timber for Canoes[.] one of the Indian Canoes with 2 men with Poles Set out from the forks at the Same time I did and arrived at our Camp . . . within 15 minits of the Same I did, not withstanding 3 rapids which they had to draw the Canoe thro' in the distance, when I arrived at Camp found Capt. Lewis verry Sick, Several men also verry Sick, I gave Some Salts & Tarter *emetic*."

26 September 1805.
[CLARK]

"Set out early and proceeded on down the river to a bottom opposit the forks of the river on the South Side and formed a Camp. . . . I had the axes distributed and handled . . . ready to commence building canoes on tomorrow, our axes are Small & badly calculated to build Canoes of the large Pine, Capt. Lewis Still verry unwell, Several men taken Sick on the way down, I administered Salts Pils Galip [jalap] Tarter emetic &c. I feel unwell this evening. . . . we purchase fresh Salmon of the Indians."

•

In July 1826 the Scottish botanist David Douglas wrote: "On Friday reached the mountains at nine o'clock and took my breakfast among some very large trees of *Thuya occidentalis*, the spot pointed out to me by the Indians where Lewis and Clarke built their canoes, on their way to the ocean, twenty-one years ago" (*Journal*, 200–01).

Donald Culrose Peattie, in his *Natural History of Western Trees* (218), writes: "Near the present town of Orofino, Idaho, he [Clark] located his boat timber, and here the party felled the trees whose stumps were still pointed out as late as 1900. And on the morning of October 7, they set out borne on the great boles of the Giant Canoe Cedar (*Thuja plicata*) which lumbermen today call the Western Red Cedar."

There are still some magnificent groves of red cedar on the Clearwater, but most Lewis and Clark students believe the canoes were made from ponderosa pine, which is also plentiful along the Clearwater (*see* Cutright, *Lewis and Clark*, 217).

27 September 1805.
[CLARK]

"All the men able to work commen[c]ed building 5 Canoes, Several taken Sick at work, our hunters returned Sick without meet. . . . the day verry hot. . . . Several Indians come up the river from a Camp Some distance below."

"a narrow Pine bottom in which I saw fine timber for Canoes"
Canoe Camp, right center; North Fork Clearwater River, left center. Photo ca. 1890.

28 September 1805.
[C L A R K]
"Our men nearly all Complaining of their bowels, a heaviness at the Stomach & Lax, Some of those taken first getting better, a number of Indians about us gazeing &c. &c. . . . one old man informed us that he had been to the white people fort at the falls & got white beeds &c."

29 September 1805.
[C L A R K]
"a cool morning. . . . men Sick as usial, all the men [that are] able to [at] work, at the Canoes[.]"

30 September 1805.
[C L A R K]
"a fine fa[i]r morning[,] the men recruiting a little, all at work which are able. Great number

of Small Ducks pass down the river this morning. maney Indians passing up and down the river."

•

The western Indians had no axes, and used an adze for woodworking. Trees were felled and canoes shaped with the assistance of fire, controlled and guided by wet moss or mud. After burning for the desired time, the fire was removed and the charcoal scraped out with the adze. For more on canoe making, *see* 1 February 1806.

1 October 1805.
[C L A R K]

"A cool Morning . . . had Examined and dried all our Clothes and other articles, and laid out a Small assortment of such articles as those Indians were fond of to trade with them for Some provisions. . . . nothing to eate except a little dried fish which the men complain of as working of them as a dost of the Salts. . . . Several Indians visit us from the different tribes below."

[G A S S]

"All the men are now able to work; but the greater number are weak. To save them from hard labour, we have adopted the Indian method of burning out the canoes."

2 October 1805.
[C L A R K]

"despatched 2 men Frasure & S. Guterich back to the village with 1 Indian & 6 horses to pur-

chase dried fish, roots &c. . . . To the Indians who visited us yesterday I . . . divided my Handerchief between 5 of them, with a Small piece of tobacco & 1 pece of riebin & to the 2 principal men each a ring & brooch. I walked out with my gun on the hills which is verry steep & high could kill nothing. . . . Hunters killed nothing excep a Small Prarie wolf. Provisions all out, which compells us to kill on[e] of our horses to eate."

3 October 1805.
[C L A R K]

"a fine morning . . . all our men getting better in helth, and at work at the Canoes &c. The Indians who visited us from below Set out on their return early. Several others Come from different directions."

4 October 1805.
[C L A R K]

"I displeased an Indian by refuseing him a pice of Tobacco which he tooke the liberty to take out of our Sack. . . . The two men Frasure and Guterich return late from the Village with Fish roots &c."

[W H I T E H O U S E]

"we continue at the canoes[.] Some of them ready to dress and finish off."

5 October 1805.
[C L A R K]

"had all our horses 38 in number Collected and branded [*see* 23 November 1805] Cut off their

Monolithic stone adze, Columbia River.

fore top and delivered them to the 2 brothers and one son of one of the Chiefs who intends to accompany us down the river to each of those men I gave a Knife & Some Small articles &c. they promised to be attentive to our horses untill we Should return. . . . Capt. Lewis and myself eate a Supper of roots boiled, which Swelled us in Such a manner that we were Scercely able to breath for Several hours. finished and lanced [launched] two of our canoes this evening which proved to be verry good. . . . Several Squars Came with fish and roots which we purchased of them for Beeds, which they were fond of."

6 October 1805.

[CLARK]

"had all our Saddles Collected a whole dug and in the night buried them, also a Canister of powder and a bag of Balls at the place the Canoe which Shields made was cut from the body of a tree. The Saddles were buried on the Side of a bend about 1/2 a mile below. all the Canoes finished this evening ready to be put into the water. I am taken verry unwell with a pain in the bowels & Stomach, which is certainly the effects of my diet which last all night. . . . The river below this forks is *Called Kos kos-kee*[. Now called the Clearwater River.] it is Clear rapid with Shoals or Swift places."

*"Some of them ready to . . .
finish off"*
Ruth Stong examines a dugout
canoe like the ones made by Lewis
and Clark, on display at the Fort
Clatsop National Historic Site.

"Had a whole dug"
Marker on the cache site at
Canoe Camp.

"rockey rapids at the foot of an Island"
Outlet of Colter Creek, now Potlatch River. The canoe accident was at the end of this island.

III

DOWN THE KOOSKOOSKEE AND THE SNAKE

7 TO 15 OCTOBER 1805

7 October 1805.
[CLARK]
"I continued verry unwell but obliged to attend to every thing all the Canoes put into the water and loaded . . . and Set out. . . . proceded on passed 10 rapids which wer dangerous[.] the Canoe in which I was Struck a rock and Sprung a leak . . . we proceeded on 20 miles and Encamped on a Star'd. point opposit a run. . . . passed Several Camps of Indians to day."

8 October 1805.
[WHITEHOUSE]
"a fair day. we dilayed loading &c. burryed a canister of powder [on] the Northe Side of a broken toped tree. . . . Set out and proceeded on down the River. . . . took Some water in the canoes by the waves dashing over the Sides. the current rapid the most part of the way some places deep. passed clifts of rocks and bare hills on each Side.

about 12 oClock we Came to Some Indians Camps . . . only 4 or 5 lodges of well looking Indians and Squaws. they had Several Small canoes and catch considerable quantitys of Sammon. we purchased Some from them by giving them a fiew green or blue or red beeds, and tin &c. . . . Some of the men bought 2 dogs from them. they have a great many horses feeding along the Shores. . . . as we were descending a rockey rapids at the foot of an Island on which was Some Indian Camps, one of the canoes Struck a rock and whe[e]led round then Struck again and cracked the canoe and was near Spliting hir in too. throwed the Stearsman [Gass] over board, who with difficulty go to the canoe again, but She soon filled with water, and hang on the rocks in a doleful Situation. Some of the men on board could not Swim, and them that could had no chance for the waves and rocks. an Indian went in a Small canoe to their assistance. our little canoe went also and took out Some of the loading. . . . got all to Shore below the rapid, and Camped at dark. . . . we have come about 18 miles this day before the Sad axident hapended to us."

•

The cache was made near their camp at Lenore, Idaho, opposite Jacks Creek. The powder, in sealed lead containers, was found by Indians and returned (*see* 7 May 1806). These lead canisters were an ingenious invention. Besides the fact that the powder was well protected and kept perfectly dry, each empty canister could also be melted down and used for making bullets. The canisters' only fault was that they were heavy; an upset canoe meant a serious loss unless the lading was well lashed down.

The unhappy accident occurred just below the outlet of the present-day Potlatch River, a stream Lewis and Clark named for John Colter; for more on this stream *see* 5 May 1806. The rapids on the Clearwater (or Kooskooskee as the explorers knew it) and Snake were not necessarily those of today. Most are caused by gravel bars that change constantly but slowly, sometimes creeping downstream and sometimes eroding away or growing larger. Those caused by rock ledges or debris spilled from tributaries are, of course, stationary. Not all the rapids of the Clearwater, Snake, and Columbia rivers were as bad as the journals might lead one to believe. The explorers were surveying rivers for future naviga-

tion; even small rapids would be an obstacle, especially for upstream traffic, and many of them were so dangerous and difficult as to require great skill and judgment in the handling of the expedition's clumsy, overladen dugouts.

9 *October 1805.*
[CLARK]

"In examoning our Canoe found that by putting Knees & Strong peces pined to her sides and bottom &c. She could be made fit for Service in by the time the goods dried, Set 4 men to work at her . . . at 1 oClock she was finished stronger than ever[.] The wet articles not sufficiently dried to pack up obliged us to delay another night . . . at Dark we were informed that our old guide & his son had left us and had been Seen running up the river Several miles above, we would not account for the cause of his leaveing us at this time, without receiving his pay. . . . we requested the Chief to Send a horseman after our old guide to come back and receive his pay &c. which he advised us not to do as his nation would take his things from him before he passed their camps. The Indians and our party were verry merry this after noon[.] a woman fain'd madness &c. &c. Singular acts of this woman in giveing in small po[r]tions all she had & if they were not received She would Scarrify her self in a horid manner &c."

•

Ordway writes that after this woman fainted she "came too by thier puting water on hir and

Seemed to take great care of hir &C." (Quaife, *Journals*, 296).

The Shoshone guides, Old Toby and his son, were enemies of the Nez Perce and in dangerous territory. They had performed an essential and vital service with patience and diligence, as Lewis and Clark recognized. The guides did help themselves to a horse apiece from the expedition's herd, a well-deserved reward.

10 October 1805.
[CLARK]

"a fine Morning[.] loaded and Set out. . . . at 3 miles lower passed a Creek [Lapwai] on the Lard.° with wide cotton willow bottoms. . . . at 8½ miles lower we arrived at the heade of a verry bad *riffle*, at which place we landed near 8 Lodges of Indians on the Lard side to view the riffle . . . two canoes were taken over verry well; the third stuck on a rock which took us an hour to get her off. . . . at five miles lower and Sixty miles below the forks arrived at a large southerly fork [Snake] which is the one we were on with the *Snake* or *So-so-Nee* nation. . . . our diet extemely bad haveing nothing but roots and dried fish to eate, all the Party have greatly the advantage of me, in as much as they all relish the flesh of the dogs, Several of which we purchased. . . . The *Cho-pun-nish* or Pierced nose Indians are Stout likeley men, handsom women, and verry dressey in their way. . . . The women dress in a Shirt of Ibex or Goat Skins . . . ornemented with quilled Brass, Small peces of Brass Cut into different forms, Beeds, Shells & curious bones &c. . . . Their amusements appear but fiew as their Situation requires the utmost exertion to pr[o]cure food they are generally employed in that pursute, all the Summer & fall fishing for the Salmon, the winter hunting the deer on Snow Shoes in the plains and takeing care of their emence numbers of horses, & in the Spring cross the mountains to the Missouri to get Buffalow robes and meet &c. at which time they frequent[ly] meet with their enemies & lose their horses & maney of their people."

●

In the fall of 1836, the Rev. Henry H. Spalding and an artisan, William H. Gray, built a mission on Lapwai Creek near the Clearwater. At the same time, Dr. Marcus Whitman established one at Waiilatpu on the Walla Walla River. Neither mission was successful. The white men attempted to recast an ancient culture into their own pattern, while the Indians had little tolerance for autocracy. Both Waiilatpu and Lapwai are now National Historic Sites.

The word "quilled" apparently refers to porcupine quills, small barbed needles that are white with black tips. They were flattened, trimmed, dyed, and sewn to garments in a decorative pattern. After the white invasion colored beads were favored for the same purpose.

°Larboard. Nautical term referring to the left side of the boat. Later changed to "port" to reduce confusion with starboard, the right side of the boat.

"arived at a large southerly fork"
Clearwater River, left, debouching into the Snake at Lewiston. Photo ca. 1890.

"We set out early"
The Snake River at the 10 October campsite.

"Came to and encamped at 2 Indian Lodges"
Almota Creek, right center near trees.

From this day until May on the return trip, dog flesh was an important part of the daily fare, but Clark could never bring himself to eat it, sometimes to his great inconvenience.

The party camped on the right bank of the Snake River opposite Clarkston, Washington, just downstream from Lewiston, Idaho. Both towns are named in honor of Lewis and Clark.

11 October 1805.

[CLARK]

"a cloudy morning. . . . We set out early . . . passed a rapid at two miles, at 6 miles we came too at Some Indian lodges and took brackfast, we purchased all the fish we could and Seven dogs of those people for Stores of Provisions down the river[.] at this place I saw a curious Swet house underground, with a Small whole at top to pass in the hot Stones, which those in[side] threw on as much water as to create the temporature of heat they wished[.] at 9 mile passed a rapd at 15 miles halted at an Indian Lodge . . . we procured some *Pash-he-quar* roots five dogs and a few fish dried . . . we proceeded on. Came to encamped at 2 Indian Lodges at a great place of fishing [Almota Creek]. . . . we Passed today nine rapids all of them great fishing places, at different places on the river saw Indian houses . . . near each of those houses we observe grave yards picketed."

12 October 1805.

[CLARK]

"a fair Cool morning . . . after purchaesing every Sp[e]cies of the provisions those Indians could spare we set out . . . at three miles passed 4 Islands, Swift water and bad rapid oppisit those Islands on the Lard. side at 14½ miles passed a large Creek [Deadman] . . . here the Countrey assends with a gentle assent to the high plains. We passed today rapids several of them very bad and came to at the head of one (at 30 miles) . . . to view it before we attemptd. to d[e]send through it. The Indians had told us [it] was very bad we found [it] long and dangerous about 2 miles in length, and maney turns necessary to Stear Clare of the rocks, which appeared to be in every direction[.] The Indians went through & our small canoe followed them, as it was late we deturmined to camp above untill the morning. . . . fire wood is verry Scerece. The hills or assents from the water is faced with a dark ruged Stone."

•

The party camped at the head of Texas Rapids near Riparia, now deep beneath the backwater of Lower Monumental Dam.

13 October 1805.

[CLARK, FIRST DRAFT]

"The wife of Shabono our interpreter we find reconsiles all the Indians, as to our friendly intentions a woman with a party of men is a token of peace."

[CLARK]

"A windey dark raney morning . . . we took all our Canoes through this rapid without any injurey[.]

"here the Countrey assends with gentle assent"
Snake River near Central Ferry.

a little below passed through another bad rapid. . . . passed the Mo: of a large Creek [Tucannon River]. . . . At 10 Ms. [a] little river [Palouse] in a Stard. bend, imediately below a long bad rapid in which the water is confined in a Chanel of about 20 yards between rugid rocks for the distance of a mile and a half. . . . This must be a very bad place in high water, here is great fishing place, the timber of Several houses piled up, and a number of wholes of fish, and the bottom appears to have been made use of as a place of deposit for their fish for ages past. . . . we passed a rapid about 9 mile lower. at dusk came to on the Std. Side & Encamped."

"The Indians told us [it] was very bad"
Texas Rapids of the Snake River.

14 October 1805.
[CLARK]

"a verry Cold morning wind from the West. . . . at 12 miles we came too at the head of a rapid which the Indians told me was verry bad. . . . in decending three Stern Canoes stuck fast for some time on the head of the rapid and one struck a rock in the worst part, fortunately all landed Safe below the rapid which was nearly 3 miles in length. here we dined, and for the first time for three weeks past I had a good dinner of Blue wing Teel, after dinner we Set out and had not proceded on two miles before our Stern Canoe in passing thro a Short rapid [Pine Tree] opposit the head of an Island, run on a Smothe rock and turned broad Side, the men got out on the [rock] all except one of our Indians Chiefs who swam on Shore, The canoe filed and sunk a number of articles floated out . . . the greater part of which were cought by 2 of the Canoes, whilst a 3rd. was unloading & Steming the Swift current to the relief of the men on the rock, who could with much dificuelty hold the Canoe [.] however in about an hour we got the men an[d] canoe to shore with the Loss of Some bedding Tomahaw[k]s shot pouches skins Clothes &c. &c. all wet[.] we had every article exposed to the Sun to dry on the Island. . . . In this Island we found some Spilt [Split] timber the parts of a house which the Indians had verry securely covered with Stone, we also observed a place where the Indians had buried their fish, we have made it a point at all times not to take any thing belonging to the Indians even their wood. but at this time we are Compelled to violate that rule and take apart of the split timber we find here bur[i]ed for fire wood, as no other is to be found in any direction."

"The hills or assents . . . is faced with dark ruged Stone"

"the water is confined in a Chanel"
Looking up the Snake River from the mouth of the Palouse.

Palouse River at its
junction with the Snake.
A Jefferson peace medal given
to Ke-powh-kan by Lewis and
Clark was found in a cemetery
near the left of the photo.

15 October 1805.

[CLARK]

"a fair morning. . . . The plaines on each side is
wavering. . . . at two oClock we loaded & Set out.
. . . passed Eleven Island[s] . . . of different sizes
and all of round Stone and Sand, no timber of
any kind in Sight of the river, a fiew small willows
excepted. . . . passed thro: narrows for 3 miles
where the clifts of rocks juted to the river on each
side compressing the water of the river through a
narrow chanel; below which it widens into a kind
of bason. . . . at the lower part of this bason is a
bad dificuelt and dangerous rapid [Fish Hook]
. . . which we found more dificuelt to pass than
we expected from the Indians information—a
suckcession of sholes, appears to reach from
bank to bank for 3 miles which was also inter-
septed with large rocks Sticking up in every direction, and the chanel through which we must
pass crooked and narrow. We only made 20 miles
today, owing to the detention in passing rapids
&c."

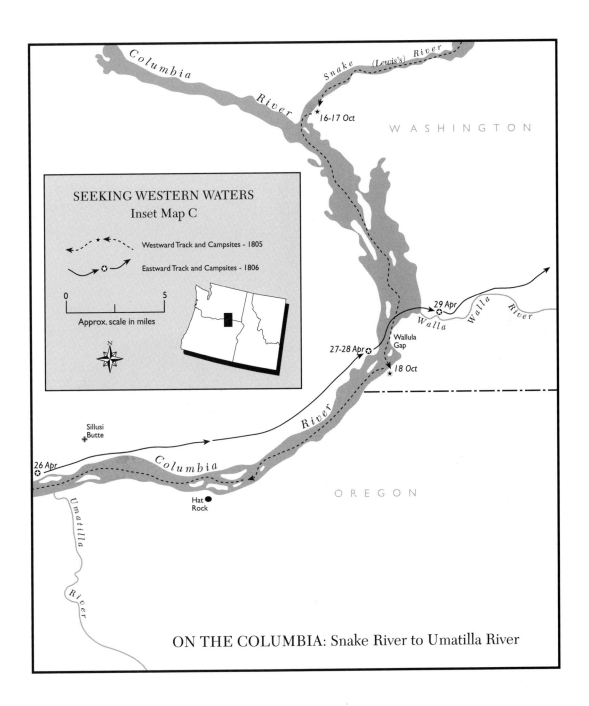

Columbia *River*

Snake (Lewis's) *River*

★ 16-17 Oct

WASHINGTON

SEEKING WESTERN WATERS
Inset Map C

★----- Westward Track and Campsites - 1805

✪----- Eastward Track and Campsites - 1806

0   5

Approx. scale in miles

N

29 Apr ✪

Walla   *Walla*   *River*

27-28 Apr ✪

Wallula
Gap

★ 18 Oct

Sillusi
✚ Butte

River

26 Apr
✪

Columbia

OREGON

Hat ● Rock

Umatilla

River

ON THE COLUMBIA: Snake River to Umatilla River

Jefferson medal found on the Palouse (obverse).

Jefferson medal found on the Palouse (reverse)

DOWN THE COLUMBIA

SNAKE RIVER TO THE LONG NARROWS

16 TO 24 OCTOBER

16 October 1805.

[CLARK]

"A cool morning, deturmined to run the rapids. . . . the canoes all passed over Safe except the rear Canoe which ran fast on a rock . . . with the early assistance of the other Canoes & the Indians, who was extremely ellert . . . the Canoe . . . got off. at 14 miles passed a bad rapid [Five Mile] at which place we unloaded and made a portage. . . . after getting Safely over the rapid and haveing taken Diner Set out and proceeded on Seven miles to the junction of this river and the Columbia which joins from the N.W. . . . In every direction from the junction . . . the countrey is one continued plain low and rises from the water gradually, except a range of high Countrey [Horse Heaven Hills] . . . on the opposit Side about 2 miles distant from the Collumbia. . . . We halted above the point on the river Kimooenim to smoke with the Indians who had collected

therein great numbers to view us. . . . after Smokeing with the Indians who had collected to view us we formed a camp at the point near which place I saw a fiew pices of Drift wood[.] after we had our camp fixed and fires made, a Chief came from this camp which was about 1/4 of a mile up the Columbia river at the head of about 200 men singing and beeting on their drums Stick and keeping time to the musik, they formed a half circle around us and Sung for Some time, we gave them all Smoke, and Spoke to their Chief as well as we could by signs informing them of our friendly disposition to all nations, and our joy in Seeing those of our Children around us, Gave the principal chief a large Medal, Shirt and Handkf. a 2nd Chief a Meadel of Small size and to the Cheif who came down from the upper villages a Small *Medal* & Handkerchief. The Chiefs then returned with the men to their camp; Soon after we purchased for our

*"Great quantities
of . . . prickley pares"*

Provisions *Seven* Dogs, Some fiew of these people made us presents of fish and Several returned and delayed with us untill bedtime. . . . one man made me a present of a [sic] about 20 lb. of verry fat Dried horse meat. great quantities of a kind of prickley pares, much worst than any I have before seen of a tapering form and attach themselves by bunches."

•

A Lewis and Clark Interpretive Center now occupies the campsite at the junction of the Snake and Columbia rivers. There is also a fine display of local Indian artifacts.

The large medal given to the principal chief was almost certainly the one found at the mouth of the Palouse in an Indian burial ground while it was being moved to accommodate Lower Monumental Dam. In 1854 George Gibbs visited Pichias, the main village there, and an Indian proudly showed him a Jefferson medal given to his father, Ke-powh-kan, by Lewis and Clark (*see* Gibbs, *Indian Tribes*, 9). Another Palouse village was Kosith, at the junction of the Columbia and Snake, where the medal may have been presented to the chief.

The "prickley pare" was *Opuntia fragilis*, the most common cactus growing on the Columbia.

"Prarie Cock a large fowl"
Sage hen or grouse.

It is indeed one of the most wicked, having a pro-fusion of long, sharp spines that readily break off in the wound. It is plentiful in the sagebrush areas and hot canyons of eastern Oregon and Washington; its bright blossoms adorn the desert in the spring.

17 October 1805.
[CLARK]
"send out Hunters to shute the Prarie Cock a large fowl which I have only Seen on this river . . . they are the size of a Small turkey, of the pheasant kind. . . . they feed on grasshoppers and the Seed of the wild plant which is also peculiar to this river and the upper parts of the Missoury

"with a wedge of the Elk's horn and a malet of Stone curioesly carved"

somewhat resembling the whins [prickly, thorny shrubs]. . . . I took *two* men in a Small canoe and assended the Columbia river 10 miles to an Island [Borgen] near the Stard. Shore on which two large Mat Lodges of Indians were drying Salmon. . . . The number of dead Salmon on the Shores & floating in the river is incredible to say. . . . passed three large lodges . . . near which great number of Salmon was drying on scaffolds[.] one of those Mat lodges I entered found it crouded with men women and children and near the enterance of those houses I saw maney squars engaged [in] splitting and drying Salmon. I was furnished with a mat to set on, and one man set about prepareing me something to eate, first he brought in a piece of a Drift log of pine and with a Wedge of the elks horn, and a malet of stone curioesly carved he Split the log into Small pieces and lay'd it open on the fire on which he put round Stones, a woman handed him a basket of water with the fish which was soon sufficiently boiled for use[.] it was then taken out put on a platter of rushes neetly made, and set before me. . . . the natives Showed me the mouth of the Tapteel [Yakima] River about 8 miles above on the West Side. . . . Those people appears to live in a State of comparitive happiness: they take a great[er] share [in the] labor of the woman, than is common among Savage tribes. . . . Those people respect the aged with Veneration. I observed an old woman in one of the Lodges I entered. She was entirely blind and as I was informed by signs, had lived more than 100 winters, She oc-

*"The Houses or Lodges
. . . is of large Mats of
rushes"* (above)

*"Supported by poles
on forks in the iner
side"* (below)

"they use flint Spikes"

cupied the best position in the house, and when She Spoke great attention was paid to what she Said. . . . I have observed amongst those, as well in all other tribes which I have passed on these water who live on fish maney of different sectes who have lost their teeth about middle age, Some have their teeth worn to the gums. . . . The Houses or Lodges of the tribes of the main Columbia river is of large Mats made of rushes, those houses are from 15 to 60 feet in length generally of an Oblong squar form, Supported by poles on forks in the in[n]er side, Six feet high, the top is covered also with mats leaveing a Seperation in the whole length of about 12 of 15 inches wide, left for the purpose of admitting light and for the Smok of the fire to pass which is made in the middle of the house. The roughfs are nearly flat, which proves to me that rains are not common in this open Countrey. Those people appear of a mild disposition and friendly disposed. They have in their huts independant of their nets gigs and fishing tackling each bows & large quivers of arrows on which they use flint Spikes."

[WHITEHOUSE]
"we bought in all 26 dogs from the natives this day. . . . a nomber of them have not any thing to cover their nakedness, but the greater part of them have dressed deer & Elk Some rabit Skins &c. to cover themselves. . . . we have lately Seen a number of their grave yards pickeded in &c."

•

The "Prarie Cock" was the sage hen or grouse, *Centrocercus urophasianus*, the largest and most impressive member of the grouse family. Its range is limited to the sagebrush plains of the upper Sonoran Zone and it survives principally upon the buds and leaves of the sage, which is one of the most nutritious of all plants.

Clark noted here, as elsewhere on western waters, that the Indians had sore eyes and that many were partially or totally blind. This affliction was probably often caused by trachoma, an inflammation of the eye's mucous membranes, and possibly sometimes by venereal diseases. The teeth were not lost, but worn away by fine sand borne by high thermal winds, which settled on drying salmon and acted as an efficient abrasive when the fish was eaten. The Canadian artist Paul Kane wrote in 1848: "The drifting of the sand is a frightful feature of this barren waste. . . . The salmon, while in the process of drying, also become filled with sand to such an extent as to wear away the teeth of the Indians, and an Indian is seldom met with over forty years of age whose teeth are not worn quite to the gums" (*Wanderings of an Artist*, 190). Anyone who has not experienced a sandstorm on the Columbia River would have difficulty visualizing its ferocity.

The veneration of the elderly and the sharing of labor between the sexes observed by Clark were typical of aboriginal peoples whose living was easy and whose enemies were few. In the plains and deserts where existence is a constant struggle, those who cannot keep the pace must be abandoned, a practice necessary for group survival. Similarly, where enemies abound the male must always be alert; thus an Indian woman would be laden with baggage so that her mate would remain unencumbered in case of attack.

The graves Whitehouse noted were one method of interment on the Columbia River. The body was wrapped in mats and placed in a pit beneath cedar planks; the pit was lined with cedar pickets extending above ground before it was filled.

18 October 1805.

[CLARK]

"The Great Chief and one of the *Chim-na-pum* [Yakima] nation drew me a sketch of the Columbia above and the tribes of his nation, living on the bank[s], and its waters, and the *Tape-tett* [Yakima] river which falls in about 18 [10] miles above on the westerly side. . . . we thought it necessary to lay in a Store of Provisions for our voyage, and the fish being out of Season, we purchased forty dogs for which we gave articles of little value, such as bells, thimbles, knitting pins, brass wire and a few beeds [with] all of which they appeared well Satisfied and pleased. . . . Took our leave of the Chiefs and all those about us and proceeded on down the great Columbia river[.] passed a large Island at 8 miles . . . [and] a Island on the Stard. Side . . . which . . . reaches 3½ miles below the 1st Island and opposit to this near the middle of the river nine Lodges are Situated on the upper point at a rapid; great num-

"gave articles of little value"

ber of Indians appeared to be on this Island, and emence quantities of fish scaffold[s] . . . at 16 [12] miles from the point the river passes into the range of high Countrey, at which place the rocks project into the river from the high clifts."

•

Brass thimbles were a favorite trade item, but they were never used for sewing. Instead, a hole was punched in the top of them, and they were then attached with a thong to garments or baby cradles.

The explorers were entering Wallula Gap, with its picturesque landmark subsequently called by some The Two Captains, in honor of Lewis and Clark. On either side of the gap the barren hills rise steeply from the water's edge to an elevation of over fifteen hundred feet, forming a narrow pass for a the river through the Horse Heaven Hills.

During Ice Age pluvials,° the greatly enlarged Columbia was a roaring torrent through the chasm. At the end of the Ice Age, some twelve to fifteen thousand years ago, about forty catastrophic floods, triggered by the collapse of ice dams in the mountains of western Montana, each unleashed as much as five hundred cubic miles of water to sweep across Idaho and eastern Washington. These were calamities of appalling magnitude, and when the raging waters reached Wallula Gap they filled it to the brim and spilled over

---

°Prolonged climatic wet spells.

"the rocks project into the river from high clifts"
Wallula Gap, looking downstream from the mouth of the Walla Walla River. Lewis and Clark crossed the Columbia here, 29 April 1806, homeward bound.

the hills on either side, gushing out to extinguish all life in the valley as far as the sea, 325 miles distant (*see* Allen, *Cataclysms on the Columbia*).

Ordway wrote: "passed Several Smooth Islands on which was large fishing Camps. large quantity of Sammon on their Scaffels. we Saw a great many dead Sammon floating in the River, and Saw the living jumping verry thick" (Quaife, *Journals*, 300).

Lewis and Clark marvelled at the prodigious

"The Two Captains" rock formation near 18 October 1805 camp.

number of dead salmon floating in the Columbia or washed ashore, a feast for ravens, condors, and vultures. The anadromous Pacific salmon do not return to the sea after spawning, as do their Atlantic relatives. We have occasionally seen them in Columbia tributaries, blinded, bruised, and covered with grisly fungus, feebly resisting being touched as their life drained away. The decaying bodies enrich the waters with proteins that promote the growth of organisms on which the returning fingerling salmon sustain themselves during their journey to the sea.

Camp was made this day on the Oregon shore near Spring Gulch, about three miles below the Walla Walla River.

19 October 1805.

[CLARK]

"The great chief *Yel-lep-pit* two other chiefs, and a chief of [a] Band below presented themselves to us verry early this morning. . . . we gave a Medal, a Handkercheif & a String of Wompom to *Yelleppit* and a String of wompom to each of the others. *Yelleppit* is a bold handsom Indian, with a dignified countenance about 35 years of age, about 5 feet 8 inches high and well perpotioned."

•

At nine o'clock they set out, passing Skinner, Techumtas, Sheep, Mottinger, and Memaloose islands, all heavily populated with native fishing communities and all now deep beneath the waters of Lake Wallula behind McNary Dam. Opposite Mottinger Island, Clark noted "a rock in a Lar'd bend resembling a hat," the present Hat Rock in the state park with the same name. He ascended the cliffs and "descovered a high mountain of emece hight covered with Snow" which he thought was Mount St. Helens but was more likely Mount Adams.

Below Hat Rock commenced the fierce Umatilla Rapids. Walking along the Oregon shore, Clark named them Muscle Shell, for the great heaps of freshwater mussel shells (*Margaritifera* *sp.*) along the banks. Shell heaps are found in all middens on the Columbia.

[CLARK]

"while Setting on a rock wateing for Capt. Lewis I shot a crain which was flying over of the common kind [sandhill crane, *Grus canadensis tabida*]. I observed a great number of Lodges on the opposit Side at some distance below, and Several Indians on the opposit bank passing up to where Capt. Lewis was with the Canoes, others I saw on a knob [Sillusi Butte] nearly oppoist to me at which place they delayed but a Short time, before they returned to their Lodges as fast as they could run, I was fearfull that those people might not be informed of us, I deturmined to take the little canoe which was with me and proceed with the three men in it to the Lodges, on my aproach not one person was to be seen except three men off in the plains, and they sheared off as I aproached near the Shore, I landed in front of the five Lodges which was at no great distance from each other, Saw no person[.] the enterance or Dores of the Lodges wer Shut with the Same materials of which they were built a Mat, I approached one with a pipe in my hand entered a lodge which was the nearest to me found 32 persons men, women and a few children Setting permiscuisly in the Lodge, in the greatest agutation, Some crying and ringing their hands, others hanging their heads. I gave my hand to them all and made signs of my friendly dispo[si]tion. . . . made signs to the men to come and Smoke with me[.] Not one come out untill the canoes arrived

"a rock in a Lar'd bend resembling a hat"
Hat Rock.

with the 2 cheifs. . . . They said we came from the clouds &c. &c. and were not men &c. &c. . . . as Soon as they Saw the Squar wife of our interperter they pointed to her and . . . imediately all came out and appeared to assume new life, the sight of This Indian woman . . . confirmed . . . our friendly intentions, as no woman ever accompanies a war party."

•

The sound of a gun, which they may never have heard before, and the sight of the crane falling from the sky, coupled with Clark's use of a burning glass to light his pipe, had convinced the Indians that he had descended from the heavens with a crash of thunder.

The magnificent sandhill crane, *Grus canadensis tabida*, a four-foot-tall wading bird, inhabits the open prairie and marshlands east of the Cascades. The birds are gregarious and migrate in large flocks, disturbing the morning calm with harsh croaks as they fly over or alight in western valleys. No wild call is more haunting than theirs. During breeding season the males have a crown of brilliant red.

[CLARK]

"proceeded on passed a Small rapid [Devils Bend] and 15 Lodges . . . and Encamped below on Island . . . nearly opposit to 24 Lodges on an Island near the middle of the river. . . . Soon after we landed which was at a fiew willow trees about 100 Indians came from the different Lodges, and

"others I saw on a knob opposit"
Sillusi Butte and McNary Dam. The "fritened village" was on the far shore, extreme left.

a number of them brought wood which they gave us, we smoked with all of them . . . and two of our Party Peter Crusat & Gibson played on the violin which delighted them greatly."

•

Wood was about the most welcome present the explorers could receive, for there are few trees along the middle Columbia and the driftwood cast ashore by annual spring floods quickly vanished in the campfires of thousands of fish-hungry Indians. Clark records that, at this village, the

Indians were "drying fish & Prickley pares to Burn in winter."

Cruzatte's violin was another example of Lewis and Clark's insight. They permitted it to be taken despite the difficulty of transporting it, where every ounce, every bulky package, had to be carefully considered. The music proved of immense value in establishing friendly relations with the natives. It never failed to delight them greatly.

[WHITEHOUSE]

"the natives came to See us in their canoes. brought us Some fish which had been roasted and pounded up fine and made up in balls, which eat verry well. . . . we passed. over Several [rapids] today but no exident hapened. . . . When any of these natives die they deposite all their property with them. . . . we Saw one of their grave yards to day, even a canoe was Split in peaces and Set up around the yard Several other art. [articles] also."

20 October 1805.

[CLARK]

"after brackfast we gave all the Indian men Smoke and we Set out leaveing about 200 of the nativs at our Encampment. . . . passed a rapid at seven miles one at a Short distance below we passed a verry bad rapid, a chane of rocks makeing from the Stard. Side and nearly chokeing the river up entirely with hugh black rocks, and Island below . . . on which was four Lodges of Indians drying fish. . . . at one oClock we landed on the lower point of an Island at Some Indian Lodges, a large Island on the Stard. Side nearly opposit and a Small one a little below. . . . on those three Island[s] I counted seventeen Indian lodges. . . . on the upper part of this Island [Blalock] we discovered an Indian Vault, our curiosity induced to examine the method those nativs practiced in depos[it]eing the dead, the vau[l]t was made of broad poads [boards] and pieces of Canoes leaning on a ridge pole which was Suported by 2 forks Set in the ground six feet in hight . . . and about 60 feet in length, and 12 feet wide, in it I observed great numbers of humane bones of every description perticularly in the pile near the center of the vault, on the East End 21 Scul bomes [bones] forming a circle on Mats; in the westerly part of the Vault appeared to be appropriated for those of more resent death, as many of the bodies of the deceased raped in leather robes lay on board[s] covered with mats, &c. we observed, independant of the canoes which served as a covering, fishing nets of various kinds, Baskets of different Sizes, wooden boles, robes Skins, trenchers, and various kinds of trinkets, in and suspended on the ends of the pieces forming the vault; we also Saw the Skeletons of Several Horses at the vault a great number of bones about it."

•

The "verry bad rapid" was in the north channel at the head of Cooks Island, not in the main stream, and the party did not have to pass through it.

"great numbers of humane bones"

There were two vault burial sites. The one nearest the river has been covered with sand for years and is now flooded. When we first visited the other there were still many split cedar boards and horse bones about. The entire island was a favorite hunting ground for searchers of Indian relics, and for those who wanted to linger for a bit in an atmosphere of the past.

21 October 1805.

[CLARK]

"A verry cool morning wind . . . we set out verry early. . . . last night we could not collect more dry willows the only fuel, than was barely Suffi[ci]ent to cook Supper, and not a sufficiency to cook brackfast this morning, passd. a Small Island . . . [then] a large one . . . in the middle of the river, some rapid water [Owyhee Rapids] at the head and Eight Lodges of nativs opposit its Lower point on the Stard. Side. we came too at those lodges, bought some wood and brackfast, Those people recived us with great kindness, and examined us with much attention. . . . we got from those people a fiew pounded roos [roots] fish and Acorns of white oake, those *Acorns* they make use of as food raw & roasted and inform us they precure them of the natives who live near the falls below which place they all describe by the term *Timm*[.] at 2 miles lower passed a rapid [Blalock] large rocks stringing into the river of large Size . . . opposit to this rapid on the Stard. Shore is Situated *two* Lodges of the Nativs drying fish[.] here we halted a fiew minits to examine the rapid before we entered which was our Constant Custom, and at [as] all that was verry dangerous put out all who Could not Swim to walk around, after passing this rapid we proceeded on passed another rapid [Rock Creek] at 5 miles lower down, above this rapid on the Stard. Side five Lodges of Indians fishing &c. . . . [at] one mile passed an Island . . . below which is two Lodges of nativs, a little below is a bad rapid [Squally Hook] which is bad crouded with hugh rocks scattered in every Direction. . . . 5 Lodges a little below . . . and one lodge on an Island . . . opposit to which is a verry bad rapid [Indian], thro which we found much dificuelty in passing . . . a Small river [John Day] on the Larboard Side 40 yards wide descharges but little water at this time. . . . imediately above and below this little river comences a rapid [John Day] which is crouded with large rocks in every direction, the passage both crooked and dificuelt, we halted at a Lodge to examine those noumerous Islands of rock . . . great nums. of Indians came in canoes to View us at this place. . . . proceeded on about two miles lower . . . and encamped near *five* Lodges of nativs . . . we purchased a little wood to cook our Dog meat and fish. . . . All [the natives] have *pierced noses* and the men when Dressed ware a long taper'd piece of Shell [dentalium] or beed put through the nose. . . . the hills are high and rugid a fiew scattering trees to be Seen on them either Small pine or Scrubey white oke. . . . One of our party J. Collins presented us with Some varry good *beer* made of the *Pa-shi-co-quar-mash* bread . . . which by being frequently wet molded & sowered &c."

•

The village where the Corps stopped for breakfast was at the outlet of Old Lady Canyon; another large village site was at Sundale, two miles below. One of the finest panels of petroglyphs on the river was at the foot of Blalock Rapids. Just below was Fountain Bar (*see* 23 April 1806), perhaps the most heavily occupied area on the river except for The Dalles. An early attempt at homesteading broke the sod and permitted the wind to blow a large part of the bar away, exposing relics to be picked up by the curious. In some places the spalls of colorful agate—flakes discarded during the chipping of arrow points and knives—lay a foot deep in the deflated gullies.

"a verry bad rapid thro which we found much difficuelty in passing"
Indian Rapids.

Opposite the end of Fountain Bar on the Oregon shore was another area densely populated with native fishers. Rows of boulders on the beach showed where later Chinese miners panned for gold, early in the twentieth century. There is gold all along the middle Columbia, but it is so fine that its extraction presents unsurmountable difficulties, yet attempts to exploit the sands on Blalock Island were being made as late as 1960.

Lewis and Clark named the "Small river" Lepage, after a member of the expedition, Jean Baptiste Lepage, but the name was later changed to John Day, for a member of the overland Astor party, led by Wilson Price Hunt in 1811–12. John Day and Ramsay Crooks, after a winter of incredible hardships in Idaho, were attempting to reach Astoria by land when they were stripped of all their possessions near this river by Indians. Managing to work their way back to friendly tribes near the Umatilla River, they were rescued weeks later by a passing brigade from Astoria. Crooks eventually became one of the most influential fur traders in North America.

Near the "Small river" trees began to appear, the first the party had seen for over a hundred miles. With the scattered hackberry, *Celtis douglasii*, the hills bore an occasional ponderosa pine or a few white oaks, *Quercus garryana*.

22 October 1805.
[CLARK]

"We set out at 9 oClock passed a verry bad rapid [Biggs] at the head of an Island close under the Stard. side above this rapid . . . is six Lodges of nativs Drying fish [at Maryhill], at 9 mls. passed a bad rapid at the head of a large Island [Miller] of high and uneaven [rocks], jutting over the water, a Small Island in a Stard. Bend opposit the upper point, on which I counted 20 parcels of dryed and pounded fish; on the main Stard. Shore opposit to this Island *five* Lodges of Indians are Situated, Several Indians in canoes killing fish with gigs [fish spears] &c. opposit the center of this Island of rocks which is about 4 miles long we discovered the enterence of a large river [Deschutes] on the Lard. Side. . . . we proceeded on pass[ed] the mouth of this river. . . . at *two* miles below this River passed Eight Lodges on the Lower point of the Rock Island aforesaid. . . . below this Island on the main Stard. Shore is 16 Lodges of nativs, here we landed a fiew minits to Smoke, the lower point of one Island opposit . . . 6 miles below the upper mouth of *Towornehiooks* [Deschutes] River the commencement of the pitch of the great falls. . . . we landed and walked down accompanied by an old man to view the falls [Celilo], and the best rout for to make a portage. . . . the waters is divided into Several narrow chanels which pass through a hard black rock forming Islands of rocks at this Stage of the water, on those Islands of rocks as well as at and about their Lodges I observe great numbers of Stacks of pounded Salmon neetly preserved in the following manner, i.e. after [being] suffi[c]iently Dried it is pounded between two Stones fine, and put into a speces of basket neetly made of grass and rushes better than two feet long and one foot Diamiter, which basket is lined with the Skin of Salmon Stretched and dried for the purpose, in this it is pressed down as hard as is possible, when full they Secure the open part with the fish Skins which they fasten th[r]o. the loops of the basket that part very securely, and then on a Dry Situation they Set those baskets the corded part up, their common custom is to Set 7 as close as they can Stand and 5 on top of them, and secure them with mats which is raped around them and made fast with cords and covered also with mats, those 12 baskets of from 90 to 100 lbs. each forms a Stack. thus preserved those fish may be kept Sound and sweet Several yars."

23 October 1805.
[CLARK]

"we were obliged to let the Canoes down by strong ropes of Elk Skins which we had for the purpose, one Canoe in passing this place got loose by the cords breaking, and was cought by the Indians below. I accomplished this necessary business and landed Safe with all the canoes at our Camp below the falls by 3 oClock P.M. nearly covered with flees which were so thick amongst the Straw and fish Skins at the upper part of the portage at which place the nativs had been Camped not long since; that every man of the party was obliged to Strip Naked dureing the time of takeing over the canoes, that they might have an oppertunity of brushing the flees of[f]

their legs and bodies. Great numbers of Sea Otters in the river below the falls, I shot one in the narrow chanel to day which I could not get."

•

The "sea otters" were seals that followed the salmon up the Columbia in great numbers (*see* 23 February 1806). The portage was on the Oregon shore, close below the present boat landing at Celilo Park. The canoes were dragged nearly five hundred yards over the rocks and launched in the channel below. Camp was made on a sandbar just downstream from the present railroad bridge, on the Washington side.

On the beach along the edge of Celilo Park are a number of large rectangular boulders, which once covered the graves of fishermen in a burial ground above the falls. Fine sculpted stone pieces have been found there, and the shore is littered with agate spalls and broken camp rock.

24 October 1805.
[CLARK]

"from Some obstruction below, the cause of which we have not yet learned, the water in high fluds (which are in the Spring) rise below these falls to a leavel with the water above the falls; the marks of which can be plainly tracd. around the falls. . . . At 9 o'Clock a.m. I Set out with the party. . . . at 2½ miles the river widened into a large bason to the Stard. Side on which there is five Lodges of Indians. here a tremendious black rock [Browns Island] Presented itself high and

"a large island of high uneaven [rocks]"
Miller Island.

Steep appearing to choke up the river . . . the current was drawn with great velocity to the Lard. Side of this rock at which place I heard a great roreing. I landed at the Lodges and the natives went with me to the top of this rock. . . . at this place the water of this great river is compressed into a chanel . . . not exceeding *forty five* yards wide. . . . I deturmined to pass through this place notwithstanding the horrid appearance of this agitated gut swelling, boiling & whorling in every direction . . . we passed Safe to the astonishment of all the Inds. of the last Lodges who viewed us

*"we . . . walked down
. . . to view the falls"*
B. A. Gifford,
Celilo Falls ca. 1905.

from the top of the rock. i passed one Lodge below this rock, and halted on the Stard. Side to view a very bad place, the current divided by 2 Islands of rocks . . . this place being verry bad I sent by land all the men who could not Swim and such articles as were most valuable to us . . . and proceeded down with the canoes two at a time to a village of 20 wood houses in a Deep bend to the Star'd Side below which [was] a rugid black rock [*see* 20 April 1806] about 20 feet hiter than the Common high fluds of the river. . . . The nativs of this village re[ce]ived me verry kindly, one of whome invited me into his house, which I found to be large and comodious, and the first wooden houses in which Indians have lived Since we left those in the vicinity of Illinois, they are scatterd permiscuisly on a elivated Situation near a mound of about 30 feet above the Common leavel, which mound has . . . every appearance of being artificial. those houses are about the same Shape Sise and form 20 feet Square . . . [they were] sunk into the earth six feet, the roofs of them was Supported by three Strong pieces of Split timber. . . . Light is admited thro' an opening at top which also Serves for the Smoke to pass through, one half of those houses is apropriated for the storeing away Dried & pounded fish which is the principal food, and the other part next the dore is the part occupied by the nativs who have beds raised on either side, with a fire

Celilo Falls and vicinity before The Dalles Dam.

1. Miller Island
2. Deschutes River
3. canoe portage
4. baggage portage
5. Maryhill Museum
6. Celilo Canal

place in the center of this Space. I . . . with two men walked down three miles to examine the river Over a bed of rocks . . . on those rocks I saw Several large scaffols on which the Indians dry fish . . . I counted 107 stacks of dried pounded fish in different places on those rocks . . . the chanel is narrow and compressed for about 2 miles. . . . I returned to the village. . . . here we formed a camp. . . . Peter Crusat played on the *violin* and the men danced which delighted the nativs, who Shew every civility toward us."

[WHITEHOUSE]

"their has been white people tradeing among these Savages Saw one half white child among them."

•

Ten Mile Rapid, or the Short Narrows, was between Brown Island and the Oregon shore, two and one-half miles below Celilo Falls; Clark's estimate of the width should be doubled. The writers have passed through this "agitated gut" three times in a small boat, and it would indeed be a trial for cumbersome dugout canoes. The larger of the "Islands of rocks" became known as Upper Memaloose Island, and was used by the Indians as a vault burial site until shortly before The Dalles Dam was constructed, when the remains of venerable warriors were removed by helicopter and reburied one mile north of The Dalles Bridge. The tip of the island is still visible two miles below Browns Island. It is now a gull rookery.

The "rugid black rock" was the obstruction causing the falls above to be flooded in high water (*see* 25 October 1805 and 17 April 1806). The explorers here entered the Grand Dalles or Long Narrows of the Columbia, one of the most furious of all river rapids and the site of the ancient Indian village of Wishram, the great aboriginal trade mart of the West. From east of the Cascades came the Cayuse, the Nez Perce, and many other nomadic dwellers of the semi-arid plains; from the west came the sedentary coastal and riverine tribes led by the Chinook—all to meet on the barren rocks beside the violent waters to fish, trade, visit, and gamble.

From the rocks overhanging the Long Narrows, fishermen dipped or speared innumerable salmon from the hordes passing close to the walls of the chasm to evade the swift currents in midstream. Governor George Simpson of the Hudson's Bay Company wrote in 1824: "The population on the banks of the Columbia River is much greater than in any part of North America that I have visited" (*Fur Trade and Empire*, 94). The salmon was as important to the western Indians as was the bison to the dwellers of the Great Plains.

Clark was correct in perceiving the mound as artificial, since it was the accumulated trash of many centuries on a living site, called by the Indians Wakemap. From it were taken many archaeological treasures before it was flooded by The Dalles Dam. Both sides of the river for two miles along the narrows were one extended living

"a mound of about 30 feet above the Common leavel" Wakemap Mound.

area. On the Oregon shore, opposite Wakemap Mound, from 1953 to 1958 researchers from the University of Oregon dug through thirty feet of camp refuse; the top layer revealed modern trade goods, while the bottom held material from between ten thousand and eleven thousand years ago. The site is one of the oldest continuously occupied villages in the world (*see* Cressman, *Cultural Sequences*).

A few pictographs still remain on the cliffs, and faint trails may be traced over the rocks, worn smooth by generations of moccasined feet. In the talus slopes surrounding the Long Narrows are hundreds of rock-slide burials, although many have been looted of the few death offerings the grieving relatives placed within them. Park facilities have been built over the ancient burial sites. The high rocky point upstream is Avery Butte, around which once flowed the antecedent Columbia River, thundering over the cliffs in a grand waterfall into the plunge basin once called Colewash Bottom, now known as Horsethief Lake. On and around Avery Butte are paintings, pit-house remains, and burials. From the top there is a splendid view, although it is a poor substitute for the scenes lost beneath the water.

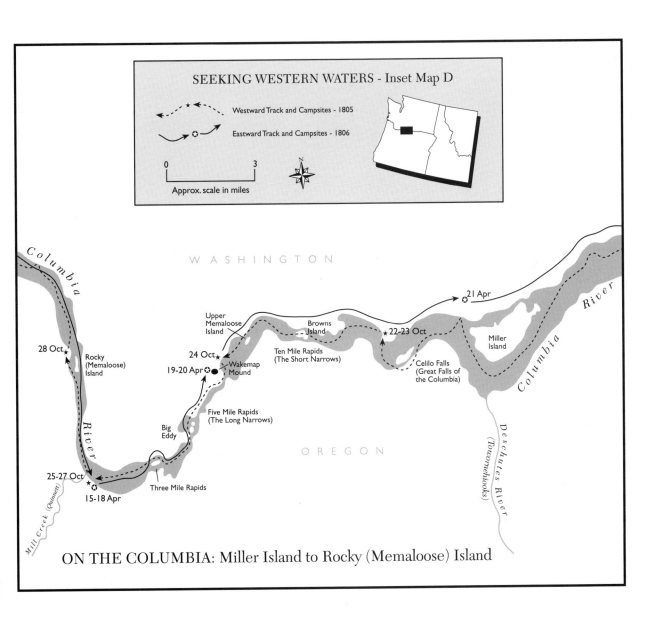

SEEKING WESTERN WATERS - Inset Map D

★----- Westward Track and Campsites - 1805

✿------ Eastward Track and Campsites - 1806

0   3
Approx. scale in miles

N

WASHINGTON

Columbia

21 Apr

Upper
Memaloose
Island

Browns
Island

22-23 Oct

Miller
Island

Columbia River

28 Oct

Rocky
(Memaloose)
Island

24 Oct

19-20 Apr   Wakemap
            Mound

Ten Mile Rapids
(The Short Narrows)

Celilo Falls
(Great Falls of
the Columbia)

River

Five Mile Rapids
(The Long Narrows)

Big
Eddy

OREGON

Deschutes River
(Tocanohooks)

25-27 Oct

15-18 Apr

Three Mile Rapids

Mill Creek (Quinnett)

ON THE COLUMBIA: Miller Island to Rocky (Memaloose) Island

"bad whorl & Suck"

On the Long Narrows. Note the Indian fishing platform, right center. The white line above it is the high water mark.

DOWN THE COLUMBIA
LONG NARROWS TO THE SEA
25 OCTOBER TO 9 NOVEMBER 1805

25 October 1805.

[CLARK]

"Capt. Lewis and my Self walked down to See the place the Indians pointed out as the worst place in passing the gut, which we found difficuelt of passing without great danger, but as the portage was impracti[c]able with our large canoes, we concluded to Make a portage of our most valuable articles and run the canoes thro. accordingly on our return divided the party Some to take over the Canoes, and others to take our Stores across a portage of a mile to a place below this bad whorl & Suck, with Some others I had fixed on the Chanel with roapes to throw out to any who Should unfortunately meet with difficuelty in passing through; great number of Indians viewing us from the high rocks under which we had to pass the 3 fir[s]t canoes passed thro very well, the 4th. nearly filled with water, the last passed through by takeing in a little water, thus Safely below what I conceved to be the worst part of this chanel felt my self extreamly gratified and pleased. We loaded the Canoes & set out. . . . this Chanel is through a hard rough black rock, from 50 to 100 yeards wide, swelling and boiling in a most tremendious manner Several places on which the Indians inform me they take the Salmon as fast as they wish; we passed through a deep bason [Big Eddy] on the Stard. Side of 1 mile below which the River narrows and [is] divided by a rock . . . here we met our two old chiefs who had been to a village below to smoke a friendly pipe and at this place they met the Chief & party from the village above . . . this chief we found to be a bold pleasing looking man of about 50 years of age dressd. in a war jacket a cap Legins & mockesons. . . . we gave this Chief a Medal, &c. [had] a parting Smoke with our two faithful friends the chiefs who accompanied us from the head of the river . . . we proceeded on

"this Chanel is through a hard rough black rock"
The Long Narrows.

down. . . . came too, under a high point of rocks on the Lard. Side below a creek [Mill] of 20 yards wide and much water, as it was necessary to make Some Selestial observations we formed our camp on the top of a high point of rocks, which forms a kind of fortification. . . . our Situation will [well] calculated to defend our selves from any designs of the natives, Should they be enclined to attack us."

•

The start of the Long Narrows, where the river contracts from half a mile wide to about 240 feet, forms a savage whirlpool in which we once saw an entire house, floating down on a flood, disappear to be ejected half a mile below as a few splintered boards. The current in the chasm, which was nearly three miles long, was so violent that it gouged holes in the riverbed that are 175 feet below the level of the sea, two hundred miles distant. This current had sufficient force to pluck rocks from the bottom and hurl them over the rim of the chute (*see Journal of Geology*, 32:139). In flood the water in the center of the race would be six feet or more higher than on the edges, heaped up by the drag of the current along the rocky sides. In low water we have been through this channel, but in flood no craft could survive an instant. The Long Narrows is the grave of dozens of early trappers and voyagers and innumerable Indians. Clark had good reason to be much gratified to pass this place safely.

The war jacket the chief wore, according to Whitehouse, "was made of Some kind of worked Splits which would defend off the arrows" (Thwaites, *Journals*, 7:180). This was one kind of armor worn by the Columbia River Indians; the other was a jacket made from elk skin. Ross Cox writes: "Their armour consists of a shirt of elk-skin remarkably thick, doubled, and thrown over the shoulders, with holes for the arms. It descends to the ankles; and from the thickness of the leather is perfectly arrow-proof. . . . In addition to the above they have another kind of armour, which they occasionally wear in place of the leathern shirt. It is a species of corset, formed of thin slips of hard wood ingeniously laced together by bear grass, and is much lighter and more pliable than the former; but it does not cover so much of the body" (*Columbia River*, 1:294–95).

The wood slips were the size of a lead pencil, laid parallel and close to each other. Remains of these "worked splits" sometimes appear in cremations, roasted to charcoal.

26 October 1805.

[CLARK]

"In the evening two Chiefs and 15 men came over in a Small Canoe. . . . one of those Chiefs made Capt. Lewis and my self each a Small present of Deer meat, and small cakes of white bread made of roots, we gave to each cheif a Meadel of the Small Size a red Silk handkerchief, arm band Knife & a piece of Paint, and acknowledged them as chiefs; as we thought it necessary at this time to treat those people verry friendly & ingratiate our Selves with them, to insure us a kind & friendly reception on our return, we gave Small presents to Several, and half a Deer to them to eate. we had also a fire made for those people to sit around in the middle of our camp, and Peter Crusat Played on the violin, which pleased those nativs exceedingly. . . . one of the guards at the river guiged [speared] a Salmon Trout, which we had fried in a little Bears oil. . . . this I thought one of the most delicious fish I have ever tasted[.] Great numbers of white crain flying in different Directions verry high. . . . The *Flees* which the party got on them at the upper & great falls, are very troublesom and dificuelt to get rid of, perticulary as the me[n] have not a Change of Clothes to put on, they strip off their Clothes and kill the flees, dureing which time they remain nakid."

•

The "white crain" was identified by Elliott Coues as the whooping crane, *Grus americana*, a magnificent bird now nearly extinct (*History of the Expedition*, 2:671). Most authorities, however, contend that the Oregon Country was outside the range of the whooping crane. What Lewis and Clark saw may have been snow geese or swans. The "Salmon Trout" was the steelhead, *Salmo gairdnerii*, a trout that has gone to sea and returned to spawn.

27 October 1805.
[CLARK]
"Wind hard from the west all the last night and this morning. Some words with Shabono our interpreter about his duty. . . . The two Chiefs & party was joined by seven other from below in two canoes, we gave them to eate & Smoke several of those . . . returned down the river in a bad humer, haveing got into this pet by being prevented doeing as they wished with our articles which was then exposed to dry. . . . Those [Indians] at the *great falls* call themselves *E-nee-shur* and are understood on the river above; Those at the Great Narrows call themselves *E-che-lute* and is understood below. . . . all the Bands flatten the heads of the female children, and maney of the male children also."

•

The explorers here first met the famous thermal winds of the Columbia River Gorge. In summer, during the day the treeless plains of eastern Oregon and Washington warm rapidly in the sun, and ascending currents of heated air cause a partial vacuum. Cooler air from the west of the Cascades jets through the gorge with terrific force, engendering waves on the river that have been known to founder a steamboat. Trees exposed to the wind have their limbs all on one side; those branches not sheltered by the trunk cannot withstand the blasts. In winter the wind is reversed, blowing from the east and bringing cold air from the plains. The explorers became well acquainted with the winds of the gorge before they left its waters.

The Long Narrows was the upper limit of the Chinook Nation. Those above were of the Sahaptin family of many different tribes.

28 October 1805.
[CLARK]

"A cool windey morning[.] we loaded our canoes and Set out at 9 o'Clock a.m. . . . river inclosed on each Side by high clifts of about 90 feet of loose dark Coloured rocks[.] at four miles we landed at a Village of 8 houses on the Stard. Side under some rugid rocks, Those people call themselves *Chil-luckit-te-quaw*, live in houses similar to those described. . . . I entered one of the houses in which I saw a British musket a cutlash and Several brass Tea kittles of which they appeared verry fond. Saw them boiling fish in baskets with Stones, I also Saw figures of animals & men cut & painted on boards in one Side of the house which they appeared to prize, but for what purpose I will not venter to say, here we purchased five Small Dogs, Some dried buries, & white bread made of roots, the wind rose and we were obliged to lie by all day at mile below on the Lard. Side. we had not been long on Shore before a Canoe came up with a man woman & 2 children who had a fiew roots to Sell, Soon after maney others joined them from above, The winds which is the cause of our delay, does not retard the motions of those people at all, as their canoes are calculated to ride the highest waves,

they are built of white cedar or Pine verry light wide in the middle and tapers at each end, with aperns, and heads of animals carved on the bow, which is generally raised. . . . we encamped on the Sand, wet and disagreeable."

•

The village was on the Washington side a couple of miles below The Dalles, near Rocky Island, formerly Memaloose Island in the Columbia River. Camp was made in a nook on the Oregon shore just below this island; we have been windbound in the same recess and welcomed its shelter.

Cooking by dropping hot stones into a vessel containing food and water was widespread among Native American peoples. Northwestern Indians, having no pottery, used waterproof baskets.

29 October 1805.
[CLARK]

"A cloudy morning wind from the west but not hard, we Set out at day light, and proceeded on about five miles came too on the Stard. Side at a village of 7 houses built in the Same form and materials of those above, here we found the Chief we had Seen at the long narrows . . . we entered his lodge and he gave us to eate Pounded fish, bread made of roots, Filbert nuts, & the berries of Sackecomme. we gave to each woman of the lodge a brace of Ribon of which they were much pleased. . . . we call this the friendly village. I observed in the lodge of the chief sundery articles which must have been precured from the white people, Such [as] a Scarlet & blue cloth Sword Jacket & hat. I also observed two wide Split boards w[i]th images on them cut and painted in emitation of a man; I pointed to this image and asked a man to what use he put them to Said Something the only word I understood was 'good,' and then Steped to the image and took out his Bow & quiver to Show me, and Some other of his war emplemints, from behind it. The Chief then directed his wife to hand him his medison bag which he opened and Showed up 14 fingers which he said was the fingers of his enemies which he had taken in wear. . . . The chief painted those fingers with Several other articles which was in the bag red and securely put them back, haveing first mad[e] a short harrang which I suppose was bragging of what he had done in war. we purchased 12 Dogs and 4 Sacks of fish, & some fiew ascid berries, after brackfast we proceeded on . . . at 4 miles lower we observed a small river falling in with great rapidity on the Stard. Side below which is a village of 11 houses, here we landed to Smoke a pipe with the nativs and examine the mouth of the river, which I found to be 60 yards wide rapid and deep. . . . we purchased 4 dogs and set out. . . . the countrey on each side begin[s] to be thicker timbered with Pine and low white oake; verry rockey and broken. passed three large rocks in the river the middle rock is large long and has Several Squar vaults on it, we call this rockey Island the Sepulchar [Lower Memaloose Island]. The last river we passed we Shall Call the Cataract River [Klicki-

tat] from the number of falls which the Indians say is on it, passed 2 Lodges of Indians a short distance below the Sepulchar Island on the Stard. Side. river wide, at 4 mile passed 2 houses on the Stard. Side, Six miles lower passed 4 houses above the mouth of a Small river [Hood] 40 yards wide on the Lard. Side a thick timbered bottom above & back of those houses. . . . about 4 miles lower and below the Sand bar is a butifull cascade falling over a rock of about 100 feet [Wahgwingwin Falls, 200 feet], a Short distance lower passed 4 Indian houses on the Lard. Side in a timbered bottom [Ruthton Point], a fiew miles further we came too at 3 houses on Stard. Side, back of which is a pond [Drano Lake] in which I Saw great numbers of Small Swan, Capt. Lewis and [I] went into the houses of those people who appeared Somewhat surprised at first. . . . I also Saw a mountain Sheap [goat] skin the wool of which is long, thick, & corse with long corse hare on the top of the neck and back something resembling bristles of a goat . . . those animals these people inform me by signs live in the mountains among the rocks, their horns are Small and streight. . . . Those people gave us *High bush cramberries* [huckleberries], bread made of roots, and roots; we purchased three dogs for the party to eate; we Smoked with the men, all much pleased with the violin."

•

Lower Memaloose Island, one of the prominent landmarks on the Columbia, is three miles down-

"their horns are Small and streight"
Mountain goat.

stream from Lyle, Washington; parks overlook it on both sides of the river. A stone obelisk marks the grave of Victor Trevitt, a pioneer of The Dalles, who expressed a wish to be buried on the island "with my friends the Indians." Lower Memaloose Island was used as a vault burial site until about 1880 by the Indians of The Dalles.

The second small river they passed they named Labiche after a member of the party; later it was Dog River and is now Hood River. One of our most fascinating experiences on the Columbia was visiting an Indian woman who was born in the very village seen by Lewis and Clark on this stream. Her head was flattened in the aboriginal fashion. She spoke enough English to converse with difficulty, and told us that the flattened head was a mark of nobility and that her sister's head had been flattened also. She talked about digging roots and how good they were, "especially with a little sugar."

30 October 1805.
[CLARK]

"a remarkable circumstance in this part of the river is, the Stumps of pine trees are in maney places, are at Some distance in the river, and gives every appearance of the river being damed up below. . . . we landed above the mouth of a Small river [Wind] on the Stard. Side and Dined. . . . this day we Saw Some fiew of the large buz-

"Saw Some fiew of the large buzzard"
California condor.

zard[.] Capt. Lewis Shot at one, those Buzzards are much larger than any other of ther Spece or the largest Eagle white under part of their wings &c. The bottoms above the mouth of this little river is m[u]ch covered with grass & firm & is about 3/4 of a mile wide rich and rises gradually, below the river and Countery rises with steep assent. we call this little river from a Speces of Ash that wood grows on its banks. . . . passed maney large rocks in the river and large creek [Rock Creek] . . . and landed on an Island close under the Stard. side at the head of the great Shute [Cascades], and a little below a village of 8 large houses. . . . I took two men and walked down three miles to examine the Shute and the river below[.] proceeded along an old Indian path, passd. an old village at 1 mile on an ellevated Situation of, this village contained verry large

houses built in a different form from any I had seen, and laterly abandoned, and the most of the boa[r]ds put into a pond of water near the village, as I conceived to drown the flees, which was emensely noumerous about the houses, I found by examonation that we must make a portage of the greater perportion of our stores 2½ miles and the canoes we could haul over the rocks."

•

The small river was christened New Timbered, then changed to Cruzatte's; now it is Wind River. The "Speces of Ash" was the Oregon or broad-leaf maple, *Acer macrophyllum* (*see* 10 February 1806). The "Buzzard" was the California condor, *Gymnogyps californianus*, the largest of all American birds, with a wingspread of nine feet—four more than the bald eagle's. It belongs to the

"the great Shute" or Cascades of the Columbia.

same family as the vulture and the South American condor (*see* 28 March 1806). The botanist David Douglas, after whom the Douglas fir is named, wrote in October 1820: "The Large Buzzard, so common on the shores of the Columbia, is also plentiful here [the southern Willamette Valley]; saw nine in one flock" (*Journal*, 216).

The "village of 8 houses" was called Yehuh. The "Great Shute," the Cascades of the Columbia, was one of the three great obstructions to navigation on the lower and middle Columbia River; the other two were Celilo Falls and the Long Narrows. A portage road was built around the Cascades in 1850, on the Washington side, with wooden rails and a car pulled by a mule. The road, improved several times and with steam locomotives added, enjoyed a lucrative business until the opening of the Cascade Locks in 1896. Upon completion of Bonneville Dam in 1938, the free-running river, with its treacherous rapids and its wealth of historical heritage, was submerged forever.

31 October 1805.

[CLARK]

"I proceeded down the river to view with more attention [the rapids] we had to pass on the river below. . . . the Great Shute which commenced at the Island on which we encamped continued with great rapidity and force thro a narrow chanel much compressd. and interspersed with large rock for 1/2 a mile, at a mile lower is a verry considerable rapid at which place the waves are remarkably high, and proceeded on in a old Indian parth . . . thro a thick wood & hill Side, to the river where the Indians make a portage, from this place I Dispatched Peter Crusat (our principal waterman) back to follow the river and examine the practibility of the canoes passing, as the rapids appeared to continue down below as far as I could See, I with Joe Fields proceeded on, at 1/2 a mile below the end of the portage passed a house where there had been an old town for ages past . . . about 1/2 a mile below this house in a verry thick part of the woods is 8 Vaults, which appeared closely covered and high deckerated with orniments. Those vaults are all

nearly the Same size and form 8 feet square, 6 feet high, sloped a little so as to convey off the rain, made of Pine or cedar boards . . . with a Dore left in the East side which is partially stoped with wide boards curiously engraved. In Several of those vaults the dead bodies w[e]re raped [wrapped] up verry securely in Skins tied around with cords of grass and bark, laid on a mat, all east & west and some of those vaults had as maney as 4 Bodies laying on the Side of each other. . . . on the tops and on poles attached to those vaults hung Brass kittles & frying pans pearced through their bottoms, baskets, bowls of wood, sea Shels, skins, bits of Cloth, hair, bags of Trinkets & Small pieces of bone &c. and independant of the curious engraveing and Paintings on the boards which formed the Vaults I observed Several wooden Images, cut in the figure[s] of men and Set up on the Sides of the vaults all round . . . I also observed the remains of Vaults rotted entirely into the ground and covered with moss. This must bee the burying place for maney ages for the inhabitants of those rapids. . . . at 2 miles lower and 5 below our Camp I passed a village of 4 large houses . . . I looked into those houses and obsirved as much property as is usial in the houses of those people which induced me to conclude that they w[e]re at no great distance, either hunting or Colecting roots, to add to their winter subsistance. . . . a Short distance below this village is a bad Stoney rapid and appears to be the last in view[.] I observed at this rapid the remains of a large and

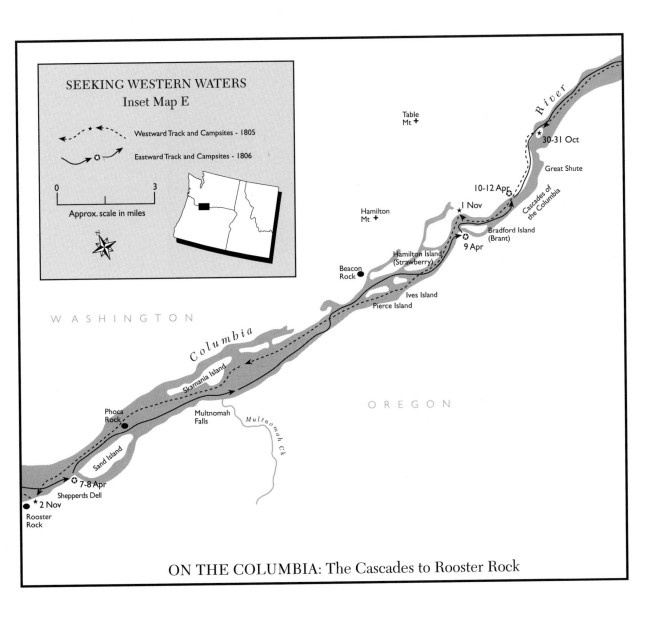

SEEKING WESTERN WATERS
Inset Map E

- - ★ - - Westward Track and Campsites - 1805
——✿—— Eastward Track and Campsites - 1806

0   3
Approx. scale in miles

N

River

Table
Mt +

★ 30-31 Oct

Great Shute

10-12 Apr ✿

Cascades of
the Columbia

Hamilton
Mt +

★ 1 Nov

Bradford Island
(Brant)

✿ 9 Apr

Beacon
Rock ●

Hamilton Island
(Strawberry)

Ives Island

Pierce Island

WASHINGTON

Columbia

Skamania Island

OREGON

Phoca
Rock ●

Multnomah
Falls

Multnomah Ck

Sand Island

✿ 7-8 Apr

Shepperds Dell

● ★ 2 Nov

Rooster
Rock

ON THE COLUMBIA: The Cascades to Rooster Rock

"the dead bodies w[e]re raped [wrapped] up verry securely"

antient Village which I could plainly trace by the Sinks in which they had formed their houses. . . . immediately below this rapid the high water passed through a narrow chanel . . . forming an Island . . . which I found to be verry rich land, and had every appearance of haveing been at some distant period cultivated[.] at this time it is covered with grass intersperced with strawberry vines, I observed Several places on this Island where the nativs had dug for roots and from its lower point I observed 5 Indians in a Canoe below the upper point of an Island . . . which induced me to believe that a village was at no great distance below . . . a remarkable high detached

rock Stands in a bottom on the Stard. Side . . . about 800 feet high and 400 paces around we called the *Beaten* [Beacon] *Rock*. . . . This Great Shute or falls is about 1/2 a mile, with the water of this great river compressed within the space of 150 paces in which there is great numbers of both large and Small rocks, water passing with great velocity [foaming] & boiling in a most horriable manner, with a fall of about 20 feet. . . . Several rocks above in the river & 4 large rocks in the head of the Shute; those obstructions together with the high Stones which are continually braking loose from the mountain on the Stard. Side and roleing down into the Shute aded to those which brake loose from these Island above and lodge in the Shute, must be the cause of the rivers daming up to such a distance above, where it shows such evidant marks of the common current [level] of the river being much lower than at the present day."

•

The vaults were on the river bank opposite the upstream end of the railroad tunnel above the Bonneville power house; traces of them may still be seen. All early explorers vividly describe these burial sheds. The "high detached rock" is Beacon Rock, a spectacular geological formation, the vent plug of an ancient volcano. There is a trail up its precipitous sides, and from the top is a grand view of all the historical area about the Cascades.

Clark came close to uncovering the real origin of the Cascades in an enormous landslide precipitated into the river from the north. The mountains here consist of soft volcanic material called the Eagle Creek formation, overlain with more resistant Columbia River basalt. As the mountains were being uplifted, the Columbia River cut through the basalts into the softer Eagle Creek materials, which rapidly eroded and thus undercut the harder lava. Some time about A.D. 1250 parts of two mountains, Table Mountain and Greenleaf Peak, could no longer support their own weight and collapsed, producing an enormous landslide. It dammed the river, flooding forests along the shore above and

"grass intersperced with strawberry vines"

"a remarkable high detached rock Stands in a bottom"
Beacon Rock.

drowning Indian villages upstream at least as far as the Snake River. Stumps of the old submerged forest standing in the river (*see* 14 April 1806) puzzled early explorers and hampered navigation. Hamilton, Pierce, and Ives islands near Beacon Rock consist of debris from the slide washed down as the river cut through the dam.

Misinterpreted Indian legends, aided and abetted by a delightful novel by Frederick Balch, have perpetuated the fable that the Cascades resulted from the collapse of a natural stone arch spanning the river. Although geological studies have shown conclusively that there was no such bridge, the myth persists.

The Cascade Range of mountains, reaching from the Canadian border to Mount Lassen in California, may have been named after the rapids but are more likely named after the many waterfalls cascading over the vertical walls of the gorge. The name seems to have appeared first in an entry dated 13 October 1826 in David Douglas's *Journal* (221; *see also* McArthur, *Oregon Geographic Names*, 132).

1 November 1805.
[CLARK]

"The Indians who arrived last evening took their Canoes on ther Sholders and carried them below the Great Shute. . . . We got all our baggage over the Portage of 940 yards, after which we got the 4 large canoes over by slipping them over the rocks on poles placed across from one rock to another. . . . I visited the Indian Viallage found that the construction of the houses [was] Similar to those abov[e] described, with this difference only, that they are larger say 35 to 50 feet by 30 feet. . . . Their beads [beds] are raised about 4½ feet, under which they Store away their dried fish, between the part on which they lie and the back wall, they Store away their roots burries nuts and valuable articles on mats, which are Spread also around the fireplace which is Sunk about one foot lower than the bottom flore of the house, this fireplace is about 8 feet long and Six feet wide secured with a fraim, those houses are calculated for 4, 5 & 6 families, each familey haveing a nice painted ladder to assend up to their beads. . . . I cannot lern certainly as to the traffick those Inds. carry on below, if white people or the indians who trade with the whites who are either settled or visit the mouth of this river. . . . the articles which they appear to trade i.e. Pounded fish, Beargrass, and roots; cannot be an object of commerce with furin merchants. However, they git in return for those articles Blue and white *beeds* copper Kettles, brass arm bands, some scarlet and blue robes and a fiew articles of old clothes, they prefer beeds to anything . . . those beeds the[y] trafick with Indians Still higher up this river for roabs, Skins, cha-pel-el bread, beargrass &c. who in their turn trafick with those under the rockey mountains for Beargrass, *quarmash* roots & robes &c. . . . The noses are all pierced and when they are dressed they have a long tapered piece of white shell [dentalium] or wampum put through the nose, those Shells are about 2 inches in lenth."

•

The bear grass, also known as elk grass, is *Xerophyllum tenax*, a showy decoration on mountain ridges when its snowy plume bursts forth in early summer. The plant is a hummock of tough leaves, each one-quarter inch wide and a foot or more long. Immense quantities of this basket-making material were gathered, and temporary

Bear grass: a showy decoration on mountain ridges.

camps were made in the mountains for the harvest. Leaves for trade were trimmed, dried, and tied in bundles of a standard size.

2 November 1805.
[CLARK]

"Examined the rapid below us ... the danger appearing too great to Hazzard our Canoes loaded, dispatched all the men who could not Swim with loads to the end of the portage below ... everry articles was brought over and the canoes arrived Safe. ... 7 Squars came over loaded with Dried fish, and bear grass neetly buldled up, Soon after 4 Indian men came down over the rapid in a large canoe. ... passed three islands covered with tall timber opposit the Beaten [Beacon] rock ... imediately below on the Stard. Side passed a village [Wahclellah, see 9 April 1806] ... which is

Situated between 2 Small creeks. . . . At 17 miles passed a rock near the middle of the river, about 100 feet high and 80 feet Diameeter [Phoca Rock] . . . saw great numbers of waterfowl of Different kinds, such as Swan, Geese, white & grey brants, ducks of various kinds, Guls, & Pleaver. . . . we encamped under a high projecting rock [Rooster Rock] on the Lard. Side."

3 *November 1805.*
[CLARK, FIRST DRAFT]

"The fog so thick this morning we did not think it prudent to set out until 10 oClock. . . . The Countrey has a handsome appearance in advance[,] no mountains[,] extensive bottoms. . . . we coasted [followed the shore] and halted at the mouth of a large river on the Lard. Side, this river [Sandy] throws out emence quantitys of sand and is verry shallow, much resembling the river Plat . . . dischargeing it[s] waters by 2 mouths, and crowding its corse sand so as to throw the Columbian waters on its Northern bands."

[CLARK]

"A mountain which we Suppose to be Mt. Hood, is about 47 miles distant from the mouth of quick Sand river. This Mtn. is covered with Snow. . . . proceeded on to the center of a large Island [Government] in the middle of the river which we call Dimond Island from it appearance, here we met 15 Indn. men in 2 canoes from below . . . we landed on the North side of this Dimond Island and encamped. . . . emense numbers of fowls flying in every direction."

•

The Sandy River arises on Mount Hood and collects several other glacial streams on its way to join the Columbia; the sand is detritus from the mountain, fast eroding away. Soft volcanic pebbles from the banks of the Sandy were favored by the Indians for stone boiling because they were less inclined to shatter when dropped hot into the water. The river was once famous for its smelt runs (*see* 24 February 1806). We have seen these succulent fish in a solid stream, a living rope the thickness of a wine cask, passing for hours and days without a break.

4 *November 1805.*
[CLARK]

"A cloudy cool morning wind from the West[.] we Set out at 1/2 past 8 oClock. . . . near the lower part of this dimond Island is the head of a large Island [Lemon] . . . on the Main Lard. Shore a Short distance below the last Island we landed at a village of 25 *houses*; 24 of those houses we[re] thatched with Straw, and covered with bark, the other House is built of boards in the form of those above, except that it is above ground and about 50 feet in length[.] This village contains about 200 men. . . . I counted 52 canoes on the bank in front of his village maney of them verry large and raised in bow. we recognized the man who over took us last night, he invited us to a lodge in which he had Some part and gave us a roundish roots about the Size of a Small Irish

(top) *passed a rock near the middle of the river* Phoca Rock.

encamped under a high projecting rock Rooster Rock.

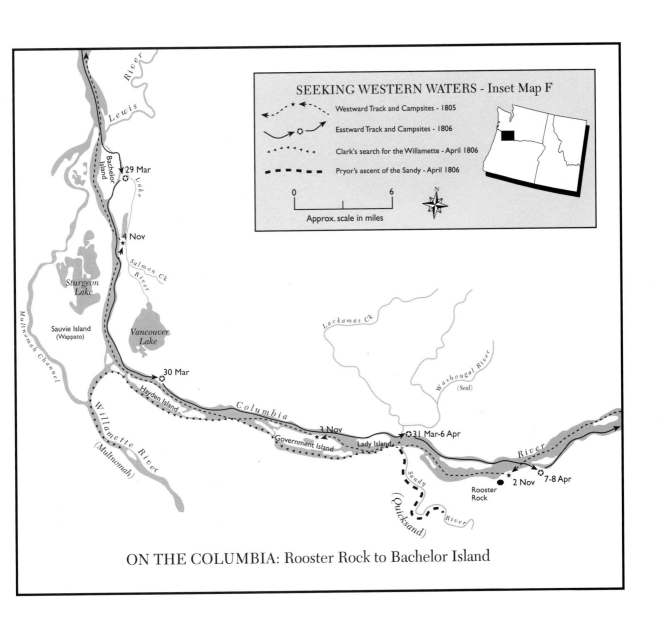

Lewis River

Bachelor Island

29 Mar

4 Nov

Lake

Salmon Ck River

Sturgeon Lake

Multnomah Channel

Sauvie Island (Wappato)

Vancouver Lake

Willamette River (Multnomah)

30 Mar

Hayden Island

Columbia

3 Nov

Government Island

Lady Island

Lackamas Ck

Washougal River (Seal)

31 Mar-6 Apr

Sandy (Quicksand) River

River

2 Nov

7-8 Apr

Rooster Rock

ON THE COLUMBIA: Rooster Rock to Bachelor Island

"This root they call Wap-pa-to"

potato which they roasted in the embers until they become Soft, This root they call *Wap-pa-to*. . . . at 7 miles below this village passed the upper point of a large Island [Hayden] nearest the Lard. Side. a Small prarie in which there is a pond opposit . . . here I landed and walked on Shore, about 3 miles . . . and joined Capt. Lewis at a place he had landed with the party for Diner. Soon after Several canoes of Indians from the village above came down dressed for the purpose as I supposed of Paying us a friendly visit. . . . Those fellows we found assumeing and disagreeable, however we Smoked with them and treated them with every attention & friendship. dureing the time we were at dinner those fellows Stold my pipe Tomahawk [*see* 9 April 1806] which they were Smoking with, I imediately serched every man and the canoes, but could find nothing. . . . while Serching for the Tomahawk one of those

Scoundals Stole a cappoe [coat] of one of our interperters, which we found Stufed under the root of a tree, near the place they Sat, we became much displeased with those fellows, which they discovered and moved off. . . . we proceeded on met a large canoe and a Small canoe . . . the large canoes was orniminted with Images carved in wood the figures of a Bear in front & a man in Stern, Painted & fixed verry netely on the canoes, rising to near the hight of a man . . . passed the lower point of the Island which is nine miles in length. . . . the Indians make Signs that a village is Situated back of the Islands. . . . at 3 miles lower . . . passed a village of four large houses [Multnomah] on the Lard. Side. . . . about a mile lower passed A Single house on the Lard. Side, and one on the Stard. Side . . . we proceeded on untill one hour after dark with a view to get clear of the nativs who was constantly about us, and trouble-

"passed a village of four large houses"
Reeder Beach, site of the Multnomah village.

som, finding that we could not get Shut of those people for one night, we landed and encamped on the Stard. Side."

•

The village of twenty-five houses was on the riverbank near what is now the Portland International Airport; it was used by residents of the Cascades while gathering wappato. The "straw" was matting made from tules or cattails. The mat lodge was not used on the Columbia below the Long Narrows; what Clark saw were temporary huts (*see* 20 April 1806). Here the explorers were introduced to the Indian potato, the wappato or common arrowhead, *Sagittaria latifolia*, a plant that was crucial to the local Indians. Without it their culture could not have flowered; wappato traffic with tribes to the east and west made them rich, for it grew in abundance only in the flooded lowlands about the mouth of the Willamette River and along the nearby Columbia. On the banks of every stream, lake, and slough are broken cooking stones and ancient fire lines, evidence of many generations of wappato gath-

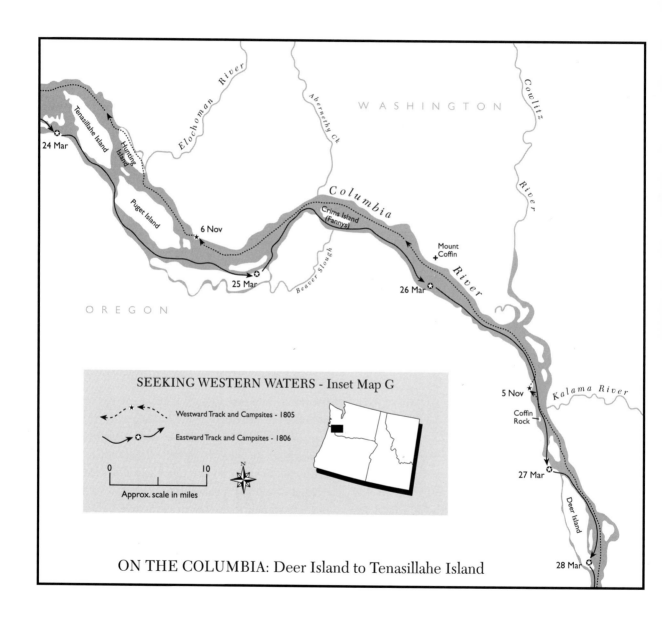

WASHINGTON

Coweliss River

Elochoman River

Abernethy Ck

Tenasillahe Island

Hunting Island

Puget Island

24 Mar

6 Nov

25 Mar

OREGON

Beaver Slough

Columbia

Crims Island
(Fannys)

Mount
Coffin

River

26 Mar

Kalama River

5 Nov

Coffin
Rock

27 Mar

Deer Island

28 Mar

SEEKING WESTERN WATERS - Inset Map G

Westward Track and Campsites - 1805

Eastward Track and Campsites - 1806

0   10

Approx. scale in miles

N

ON THE COLUMBIA: Deer Island to Tenasillahe Island

erers. The word "wappato" is from the Cree "wa-patow" or Chippewa "wapato."

Women were the harvesters. Sometimes they would wade in mud and water, towing a small canoe, and root out the tubers with their toes, throwing them in the canoe as they floated to the surface. The women's role in accumulating wealth was responsible for their position of equality and influence within the tribe.

The country about the mouth of the Willamette River, passed this day, was one of the most heavily populated areas in aboriginal America. We have counted more than sixty village sites between the Cascades and the Lewis River; however, not all were occupied at the same time. The area was a benign one for the Indians, with its mild climate, abundant food, water transportation, and the always useful cedar for canoes and house planks.

Because the Willamette's outlet was hidden behind Hayden Island and three other smaller islands that have long since been washed or dredged away, the explorers did not see this important river until their return (*see* 2 April 1806). Camp for this day was on the Washington shore near what is now Post Office Lake.

5 November 1805.
[CLARK]

"I [s]lept but verry little last night for the noise Kept [up] dureing the whole of the night by the Swans, Geese, white & Grey Brant Ducks &c. on a Small Sand Island . . . they were emensely noumerous, and their noise horid. we Set out early. . . . passed an Isld. covered with tall trees & green briers Seperated from the Stard. Shore by a narrow chanel [Bachelors Island and Slough]. . . . a short distance above its lower point is Situated a large village, the front of which occupied nearly 1/4 of a mile fronting the Chanel, and closely connected, I counted 14 houses. . . . Seven canoes of Indians came out from this large village to view and trade with us, they appeared orderly and well disposed. . . . about 1½ miles below this village on the Lard. Side behind a rockey Sharp point [Warrior Rock], we passed a chanel 1/4 of a mile wide [Multnomah Channel], which I take to be the one the Indian canoe entered yesterday from the lower point of *Immaged Canoe* Island so named. . . . an extensive Island [Deer], seperated from the Lard. side by a narrow chanel, on this Island we Stoped to Dine. . . . I walked out [and] found . . . the remains of an old village on the lower part of this Island. . . . The valley which is from above the mouth of Quick Sand [Sandy] river to this place may be computed at 60 miles on a Derect line, & extends to a great Distance to the right & left. . . . This is certainly a fertill and a handsom valley, at this time crouded with Indians."

•

The large village was Quathlahpootle (*see* 29 March 1806). Camp was made this day about two miles below Coffin Rock (*see* 27 March 1806).

Ruth Strong on a village site near the 4 November camp. The gravel on the beach consists of stones broken when dropped hot into baskets of water for boiling.

"passed an Isld. . . . Separated from the Stard. Shore by a narrow chanel" Bachelor Island and Slough.

6 November 1805.

[CLARK]

"A cool wet raney morning[.] we Set out early at 4 miles pass 2 Lodges of Indians in a Small bottom on the Lard. Side. . . . at 14 miles (*from our camp*) . . . the hills leave the river on the Lard. Side, butifull open and extensive bottom in which is an old Village [opposite Oak Point, *see* 26 March 1806], one also on the Stard. Side a little above both of which are abandened by all their inhabitents except Two Small dogs nearly starved, and an unreasonable portion of flees. The Hills and Mountains are covered with Sever[al] kinds of Pine, *Arber Vitea* or white cedar, *red Loril*, alder and Several Species of under groth, the bottoms have common rushes, nettles, & grass[.] the Slashey parts have Bull rushes & flags [cattails]. . . . the Stard. Hills are verry [high] from the river bank and continues high and rugid on that Side [North] all day. . . . No place for Several Miles suff[i]cently large and leavil for our camp. we at length Landed at a place which by moveing the stones we made a place Suffently large for the party to lie leavil on the Smaller Stones clear of the Tide. Cloudy with rain all day we are all wet and disagreeable, had large fires made on the Stone and dried our bedding and kill the flees. . . . I have like to have forgotten a verry remarkable Knob [Mount Coffin] riseing from the edge of the water to about 80 feet high, about 200 paces around at its Base and Situated on the long narrow Island above and near opposit to the 2 Lodges we passed to day."

The "red loril" was the madrona, *Arbutus menziesii,* a tree not abundant on the Columbia. The bark exfoliates, presenting a fresh, smooth, rust-colored trunk to decorate the dark forest and brushy hillsides. This tree species first came to European attention when it was noted by Fray Juan Crespi, a Franciscan missionary who accompanied the Portolá expedition to California in 1769. He called it *madroño* because it resembled a tree native to Spain, commonly known by that name. Today the Spanish species is scientifically designated *Arbutus unedo,* while the name that Crespi gave its American relative has been anglicized to madrona or madrone. It was also reported by the Scots botanist Archibald Menzies, who, as a member of the Vancouver expedition, saw it in 1792 growing on the shores of Vancouver Island in what is now British Columbia—a fact memorialized in the tree's scientific name, *Arbutus menziesii* (*see* Peattie, *Natural History,* 666; and McKelvey, *Botanical Exploration,* 31).

Clark found the woods "thick with under groth," and the contrast from barren desert to impenetrable forest must have astonished the Corps. The modern traveler can pass from rain forest to semi-arid plateau in less than an hour through the Columbia River Gorge. East of the Cascades the annual rainfall averages about ten inches, while to the west it can exceed one hundred and twenty.

Mount Coffin was the "verry remarkable

"red Loril"
Madrona.

Knob," one of many promontories used by the Indians for canoe burials. Lieutenant William Broughton named this feature on 27 October 1792. Captain Vancouver's log reads: "They [Broughton's party] now again approached high land, and on the northern shore was a remarkable mount, about which were placed several canoes, containing dead bodies; to this was given the name of Mount Coffin" (*Voyage of Discovery*, 2:754). On the following day, 28 October, Vancouver's log continues: "Broughton . . . passed a small rocky islet, about twenty feet above the surface of the water. Several canoes covered the top of this islet, in which dead bodies were deposited" (*Voyage of Discovery*, 2:754–55). This "rocky islet," known today as Coffin Rock, on the south side of the Columbia River, has been confused with Mount Coffin, the site of which is downstream on the north side. This confusion seems to have begun with Alexander Ross, who wrote in 1811: "Crossing to the [Columbia's] north side . . . we passed a small, rocky height, called Coffin Rock or Mount Coffin, a receptacle for the dead. All over this rock—top, sides, and bottom—were placed canoes of all sorts and sizes, containing relics of the dead, the congregated dust of many ages" (*Adventures of the First Settlers*, 113–14). Alexander Henry, a North West Company employee, noted in 1814: "We breakfasted at Mount Coffin. One of the canoes, that contained a corpse, measured five feet broad and four feet high at the stern, made out of one log; there was also a large, handsome sea

"I have liked to have forgotten a verry remarkable Knob"
Mount Coffin on the Columbia.

canoe, well studded, outside and inside, with sea shells of various kinds, the same as those Captain Cook mistook for human teeth" (*Journals*, 2:828).

Lewis and Clark camped on one of the small sandy beaches below Cape Horn, near where the Columbia divides to encompass Puget Island. Here the impressive headlands rise steeply from the water's edge. This point is one of three on the river christened "Cape Horn" by sturdy paddlers of early canoe brigades because they were so difficult to double in a head wind. One of them is opposite Rooster Rock, and one on the Oregon shore two miles above Lower Memaloose Island. People fishing for salmon and steelhead now pass pleasant summer days on the beach where the expedition cleared away stones to make a disagreeable camp.

This day of the expedition marks the end of the published portion of the remarkable journal of that stalwart Kentuckian Joseph Whitehouse, faithfully kept day by day except for two weeks at Fort Mandan during the first winter. A transcription of his journal from this day until 2 April has recently been discovered, but at this writing it has not been edited and published. It is difficult to appreciate how odious is the task of writing up a journal after the hardships and privations of a day from dawn to dark, often with making camp and preparing a meager meal yet to be done. Whitehouse's journal contains sixty-seven thousand words, many homely details, and much human interest. Like those of Ordway and Gass, it is rich in supplemental details confirming or amplifying the entries of Lewis and Clark.

Little is known of Whitehouse before or after the expedition. He was in Kaskaskia, some fifty miles south of St. Louis, when he joined the Corps. Later he sold his land grant to George Drouillard (all the expedition's members except York, Sacagawea, and Baptiste were awarded land grants after the journey). In 1807 he was arrested for debt and thereafter vanished without a trace.

7 November 1805.
[CLARK]

"we Set out early proceeded under . . . a high rugid hills with Steep assent the Shore boalt and rockey . . . two cano[e]s of Indians met and returned with us to their village which is Situated . . . behind a cluster of Marshey Islands, in a narrow chan . . . through which we passed to the *village* of 4 Houses, they gave us to eate Some fish, and Sold us, fish, *Wap pa to* roots three *dogs* and 2 otter skins for which we gave fish hooks principally of which they were verry fond. . . . about 14 miles below . . . we landed at a village of the same form of those above, here we purchased a Dog some fish, *wap ap to*, roots and I purchased 2 beaver Skins for the purpose of makeing me a *roab*, as the robe I have is rotten and good for nothing. . . . We proceeded on about 12 miles . . . and Encamped under a high hill . . . opposit to a rock Situated half a mile from the shore, about 50 feet high and 20 feet in Deamieter. . . . Great joy in camp we are in *view* of the *Ocian*, this great Pacific Octean which we have been so long anxious to See."

•

After passing what is now Cathlamet they entered Elochoman Slough behind Hunting Islands; the village was at the mouth of the Elochoman River. Camp was made directly opposite Pillar Rock, which still bears the name given to it by the explorers. From this place the ocean cannot be seen, but the river widens to four or five miles, an expanse easily mistaken for open ocean.

8 November 1805.

[CLARK]

"A cloudy morning Some rain. . . . passed 2 old villages . . . and at 3 miles entered a nitch of about 6 miles wide and 5 miles deep . . . we came too at the remains of an old village . . . and dined. . . . here we found a great number of flees which we treated with the greatest caution and distance; after Diner the Indians left us and we took the advantage of a returning tide and proceeded on to the Second point on the Std. here we found the Swells or Waves so high that we thought it imprudent to proceed; we landed unloaded and drew up our Canoes. . . . The Seas roled and tossed the Canoes in such a manner this evening that Several of our party were Sea sick."

•

"opposit to a rock Situated half a mile from the shore" Pillar Rock.

The two old villages were near Elliot Point and Altoona. To avoid the open water, far from shore in their unstable craft, the party coasted Grays Bay. The village "remains" were at the mouth of Deep River, while the second point was Grays Point, in the lee of which the expedition's members camped.

From Elochoman Slough to the Columbia River bar there are scattered "marshey islands," often mentioned in the journals and rich in wildlife. Some were wooded, some were bare and so low that they might be covered at high tide, and it was these that became so valuable as bases for seining, one method of harvesting the prodigious salmon runs. Long nets were laid out to surround the fish; then horses, frequently wading withers deep, dragged the nets ashore with the catch. Some of the horses never saw dry land during the fishing season; they were quartered in barns elevated on pilings above high tide. Remains of canneries may still be seen at Brookfield, Altoona,

Pillar Rock, and many other places. There were some thirty canneries between Astoria and the Cascades before the runs were destroyed.

9 November 1805.

[CLARK, FIRST DRAFT]

"the [tide] which rose untill 2 oClock PM to day brought with it such emence swells or waves, aded to a hard wind from the south which loosened the drift trees which is verry thick on the shores, and tossed them about in such a manner, as to endanger our canoes very much . . . the strictest attention by the party was scercely sufficient to defend our canoes from being crushed to pieces between those emecly large trees maney of them 200 feet long and 4 feet through. . . . not withstanding the disagreeable time of the party for several days past they are all chearfull and full of anxiety to see further into the Ocian, the water is too salt to drink, we use rain water."

"drift trees which is verry thick on the shores"

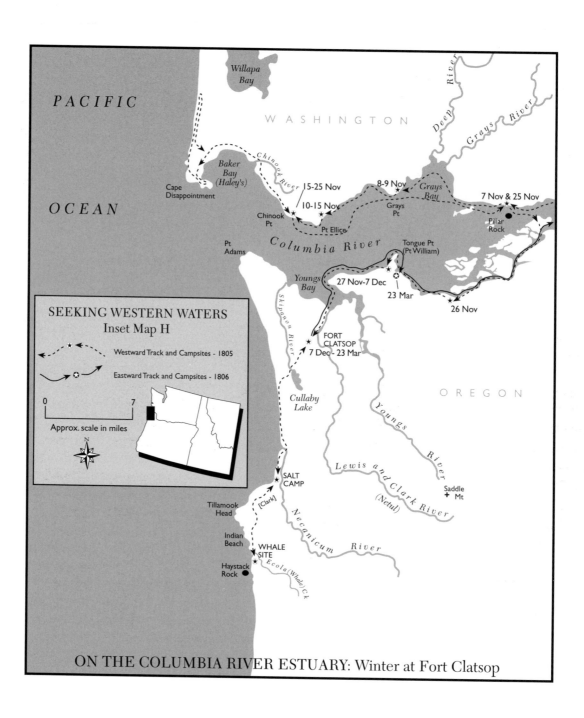

PACIFIC

OCEAN

Willapa Bay

WASHINGTON

Deep River

Grays River

Chinook River

Cape Disappointment

Baker Bay (Haley's)

15-25 Nov

10-15 Nov

8-9 Nov

Grays Bay

7 Nov & 25 Nov

Chinook Pt

Pt Ellice

Grays Pt

Pillar Rock

Pt Adams

Columbia River

Tongue Pt (Pt William)

Youngs Bay

27 Nov-7 Dec

23 Mar

26 Nov

Skipanon River

FORT CLATSOP
7 Dec - 23 Mar

OREGON

Cullaby Lake

Youngs River

Lewis and Clark River (Netul)

Saddle Mt

SALT CAMP

[Clark]

Necanicum River

Tillamook Head

Indian Beach

WHALE SITE

Haystack Rock

Ecola (Whale) Ck

SEEKING WESTERN WATERS
Inset Map H

★ - - - ★ Westward Track and Campsites - 1805

✦ Eastward Track and Campsites - 1806

0   7

Approx. scale in miles

N

ON THE COLUMBIA RIVER ESTUARY: Winter at Fort Clatsop

ORDEAL ON A STORMY COAST

10 NOVEMBER TO 7 DECEMBER 1805

10 November 1805.

[CLARK]

"Rained verry hard. . . . we loaded our canoes and . . . proceeded on about 10 miles [.] saw great numbers of Sea Guls . . . and the waves became So high that we were compelled to return about 2 miles to . . . a Small nitch at the mouth of a Small run on a pile of drift logs. . . . when the river appeared calm we loaded and set out; but was obliged to return finding the waves too high for our canoes to ride, we again unloaded the canoes . . . and formed a camp on the Drift Logs. . . . we were all wet the rain haveing continued all day. . . . nothing to eate but dryed fish pounded."

•

Failing to round Point Ellice, they were driven back to Hungry Harbor west of Cliff Point. After again starting and failing, they returned and established camp between Point Ellice and Megler.

11 November 1805.

[CLARK]

"rain falling in torrents, we are all wet as usial— and our Situation is truly a disagreeable one; the great quantities of rain which has loosened the Stones on the hill Sides; and the Small stones fall down upon us, our canoes at one place at the mercy of the waves, our baggage in another; and our selves and party Scattered on floating logs and Such dry Spots as can be found on the hill sides, and crivicies of the rocks. we purchased of the Indians 13 red charr [sockeye salmon] which we found to be an excellent fish. we have seen those Indians above and are of a nation who reside above and on the opposit Side call themselves *Calt-har-mar* [Cathlamet]. . . . those people left us and crossed the river (which is about 5 miles wide at this place) and through the highest waves I ever Saw a Small vestles ride. Those Indians are certainly the best Canoe navigaters I ever Saw."

•

The "red charr" was the sockeye or blueback salmon, *Oncorhynchus nerka* (*see* Cutright, *Lewis and Clark*, 270, and 14 January, 1806.)

12 November 1805.
[CLARK, FIRST DRAFT]

"A tremendious thunder storm abt. 3 oClock this morning . . . untill about 6 oClock at intervales[.] It then became light for a short time when the heavens became darkened by a black cloud from the s.w. & a hard rain suckceeded which lasted untill 12 oClock with a hard wind which raised the seas tremendiously. . . . as our situation became seriously dangerous, we took the advantage of a low tide & moved our camp around a point a short distance to a small wet bottom at the mouth of a small creek. . . . Three men Gibson Bratten & Willard attempted to decend in a canoe built in the Indian fashion and abt. the size of the one the Indians visited us in yesterday, they could not proceed, as the waves tossed them about at will. . . . Cought 3 salmon tds. [towards] evining in a small branch above about 1 mile[.]"

•

Erosion and construction have carved the riverbanks about Point Ellice since Lewis and Clark sought shelter there. The nights of 10 and 11 November were spent just west of Megler. On 12 November they moved upstream to Hungry Harbor west of Cliff Point, a "dismal nitich"

where they camped 12, 13, and 14 November.

13 November 1805.
[CLARK]

"I walked up the Brook & assended the first Spur of the mountain with much fatigue . . . through an intolerable thickets of Small pine, a groth much resembling the arrow wood on the Stem of which there is thorns, this groth about 12 or 15 feet high interlockd. into each other and scattered over the high fern & fallen timber. . . . I Saw in my ramble to day a red berry resembling Solomons Seal berry which the nativs call Sol-me and use it to eate. . . . we dispatched 3 men Colter, Willard & Shannon in the Indian canoe to get around the point [Ellice] if possible and examine the river, and the Bay below for a go[o]d harbor for our canoes to lie in safty &c."

•

The "groth much resembling the arrow wood" was the salmonberry *Rubus spectabilis*, its shoots growing long and straight like arrows. A beautiful plant, it bears colorful purple flowers and a raspberry-like, salmon-pink fruit. It was an important berry to the Indians, and the young tender shoots were valued as food, especially in the spring when the diet of fish began to pall.

The "red berry resembling Solomons Seal berry" was probably bunchberry, *Cornus canadensis*, although its identity has been the subject of some controversy. The plant has also been identified as being "a species of Smilacina com-

mon in the Northwest, apparently *S. sessilifolia*"
(Coues, *History of the Expedition*, 3:826, n. 12).
In referring to it by the native name "Sol-me,"
Clark introduced another possibility, namely
wild cranberry, *Vaccinium oxycoccus* (*see* Ray,
Lower Chinook Ethnographic Notes, 122, n.16;
Cutright, *Lewis and Clark*, 266; and Moulton,
Journals, 6:45, n.3). For more on the "red berry,"
see 27 January 1806.

"groth much resembling the arrow wood"
Salmonberry.

14 November 1805.
[CLARK]

"5 Indians came up in a canoe, thro' the waves,
which is verry high and role with great fury. They
made Signs to us that they saw the 3 men we Sent
down yesterday. only 3 of those Indians landed.
. . . at this time . . . Colter returnd. by land and informed us that those Indians had taken his Gigg
[fish spear] & basket, I called to the Squar to land
and to give back the gigg, which they would not
doe untill a man run with a gun, as if he intended
to Shute them when they landed, and Colter got
his gig and basket. . . . Capt. Lewis concluded to
proceed on by land & find if possible the white
people the Indians say is below and examine if a
Bay [Baker] is situated near the mouth of this
river as laid down by Vancouver."

•

There is no further mention of the "white people the Indians say is below," and their identity
remains a mystery. They might have been from
the American brig *Lydia* (Samuel Hill, captain),

which some evidence suggests may have been at the Columbia's mouth some time in mid- to late November 1805.*

15 *November 1805.*
[CLARK, FIRST DRAFT]

"from the 5th. in the morng. until the 16th. is *eleven* days rain, and the most disagreeable time I have experenced confined on a tempiest coast wet, where I can neither git out to hunt, return to a better situation, or proceed on."

[CLARK]

"about 3 oClock the wind luled, and the river became calm, I had the canoes loaded in great haste and Set Out, from this dismal nitich where we have been confined for 6 days passed."

[CLARK, FIRST DRAFT]

"passed the blustering Point [Ellice] below which is a sand beech, with a small marshey bottom . . . on which is a large village of 36 houses deserted by the Inds & in full possession of the flees. . . . Shannon & 5 Indians met me here, Shannon informed me he met Capt. Lewis some distance

below & he took Willard with him. . . . the Inds. with him wer rogues, they had the night before stold both his and Willards guns from under their heads, Capt. Lewis and party arrived at the camp of those Indians at so timely a period that the Inds. were allarmed & delivered up the guns &c."

[CLARK]

"I landed and formed a camp on the highest Spot I could find. . . . this I could plainly See would be the extent of our journey by water."

•

The village of thirty-six houses was about half a mile downstream from today's Astoria-Megler bridge; another half-mile below is the historical marker at McGowan where Lewis and Clark camped. This village was the home of Chief Concomly, a one-eyed despot with whom the explorers would soon be well acquainted. Alexander Henry visited the chief in 1813 and wrote of his residence: "I measured an inhabited house and found it to be 70 feet long by 25 feet wide; the entrance in the gable end, as usual, cut through a plank 5½ feet wide, and nearly oval. A board suspended on the outside answered for a door; on the other side of the broad plank was rudely carved a large painted figure of a man, between whose legs was the passage" (*Journals*, 2:754).

This town, too, was the "Village Chenoak" opposite which Robert Gray anchored his ship, the *Columbia Rediviva*, in May 1792, having bestowed its name on the river. John Boit, one of the ship's company, wrote in his log: "we directed

---

*Moulton, however, is not convinced the *Lydia* visited the Columbia in November 1805, believing instead that there were two visits, one in April 1805 and another in April or July 1806, neither of which coincides with Lewis and Clark's presence on the lower Columbia. He offers no explanation as to the identity of the "white people" Clark mentions on 14 November 1805 (*see* Moulton, *Journals*, 6:29 n.15 and 86 n.6; and 18 March 1806).

"this dismal nitich where we have been confined for 6 days past"
Behind Point Ellice.

our course up this noble river in search of a Village. The beach was lin'd with Natives, who ran along the shore following the Ship. . . . at length we arriv'd opposite to a large village, situate on the North side of the river about 5 leagues from the entrance" (Howay, *Voyages of the Columbia*, 397).

Captain Gray "discovered" the Columbia River only in the sense that he and his crew are the first persons of European descent known to have entered and explored its lower estuary. Aside from its prior discovery in 1775 by the Spanish explorer Bruno de Hezeta, who was prevented by circumstances from entering the river's mouth, it had been known and populated by indigenous peoples for many centuries. It is a pity Gray did not name it Oregon, a name that was popularized by Jonathan Carver in his book

"this I could plainly See would be the extent of our journey by water"
At McGowan, Washington.

Travels Through the Interior Parts of North America, published in 1778. The river was then still unseen by whites and known to them only from Indian accounts, with the exception of Hezeta and his men or possibly the victims of some unrecorded shipwreck. One might even prefer the euphonious sound of *Río de San Roque*, as it was called on Spanish charts after

Hezeta's discovery in 1775. While off the river's mouth on 17 August, Hezeta realized from the currents and the appearance of the water that it probably was, in his words, "the mouth of some great river or some passage to another sea" (Hezeta, *For Honor and Country*, 86). Exhaustion and sickness among his crew, however, prevented him from attempting to cross the river's treacherous bar. He named the river's estuary *Bahía de la Asuncion* (Assumption Bay), and gave the name *Cabo de San Roque* to its northern headland, a name that also came to be applied to the river believed by the Spaniards to exist nearby. In 1788 the British fur trader John Meares attempted to sail into Baker Bay, in the lee of Hezeta's *Cabo de San Roque*, but, remaining unconvinced that a great river was to be found, he wrote: "we can now with safety assert that there is no such river as that of San Roc" (*Voyages*, 168). He thus named the point of land he had just rounded Cape Disappointment, a name it still bears today, and the nearby waters of the Columbia's estuary Deception Bay.

The episode of the stolen gun was another of those remarkable coincidences that contributed so much to the success of the journey. When Shannon and Willard missed their guns they bluffed the Indians by threatening to bring a large party from above. Almost immediately Lewis and his men arrived and "alarmed the Indians so they instantly produced the Guns."

16 November 1805.
[CLARK]

"my man York killed 2 geese and 8 brant, 3 of them white with a part of their wings black [snow geese]."

●

York, the African-American slave, was one of the most dependable members of the party. He par-

took in all the strenuous and dangerous missions of the journey, and his good humor made him a favorite with the men. His great size, agility, feats of strength, and novelty of color fascinated the Indians, and made him an admirable ambassador of goodwill. John Bakeless says that York was eventually freed and set up in the drayage business by Captain Clark. The venture failed, however, and on the way to rejoin Clark in St. Louis he died of cholera in Tennessee (*see* Bakeless, *Lewis and Clark*, 442–43; *see also* Epilogue, this work).

17 November 1805.
[CLARK]

"Capt. Lewis returned haveing traversed Haley Bay to Cape Disappointment and the *Sea* Coast to the North for Some distance. Several *Chinnook* Indians . . . made us a present of a rute boiled and much resembling the common liqorice in taste and Size: [*They call cul-wha-mo*]. . . . This *Chinnook* Nation is about 400 Souls inhabid the countrey on the Small rivers which run into the bay below us and on the Ponds to the N.W. of us, live principally on fish and roots, they ar well armed with fusees and Sometimes kill Elk Deer and fowl. I directed all the men who wished to see more of the Ocean to get ready to set out with me tomorrow day light."

●

Haley Bay, named after a trader who occasionally anchored there, is now Baker Bay. The Chi-

"a rute . . . resembling the common liqorice in taste"
Seashore lupine.

nookan Indians proper lived along the north side of the Columbia's mouth and on Willapa Bay to the north. The Chinookan language family, however, included the Clatsops, who lived south of the Columbia at its mouth, extended up several tributaries such as the Willamette and Cowlitz rivers, and reached inland as far as the Long Narrows.

The "cul-wha-mo" was the wild blue seashore lupine, *Lupinus littoralis*. This lupine grows in great abundance in the sand along the Pacific Coast. After being roasted, the root was pounded to loosen the coarse spines from the edible fibers. Douglas, near Cape Disappointment in 1825, wrote: "We remained here several days faring scantily on roots of *Sagittaria sagittifolia* [wappato] and *Lupinus littoralis*, called in the Chenook tongue Somuchtan" (*Journal*, 61).

18 November 1805.
[CLARK]

"I set out with 10 men and my man York to the Ocian by land. . . . proceeded on a Sandy beach . . . 1 Mile to a point of rocks about 40 feet high [Chinook Point], . . . then . . . 7 Mile[s] to the enterance of a creek [Chinook River] at a lodge or cabin of Chinnooks. . . . here we were set across all in one canoe by 2 squars. to each I gave a small hook. . . . 5 Miles to the mouth of *Chin nook* [Wallacut] river. . . . This river is 40 yards wide at low tide. here we made a fire and dined on 4 brant and 48 plever. . . . Rubin Fields Killed a Buzzard of the large Kind [condor]. . . . measured

"1 Mile to a point of rocks about 40 feet high"
Chinook Point.

from the tips of the wings 9½ feet. . . . after dineing we crossed the river in an old canoe which I found on the sand near Some old houses. . . . 4 Miles to a Small rock island in a deep nitch[,] passed a nitch at 2 miles. . . . the land low opposite this nitch a bluff of yellow clay and soft Stone. . . . 2 miles to the iner extremity of *Cape Disappointment* passing a nitch in which there is a small rock island. . . . I crossed the neck of Land low and 1/2 mile wide to the main Ocian, at the foot a high open hill [North Head] projecting into the ocian. . . . I assended this hill. . . . decended to the N. of it and camped. . . . the waves appear to brake with tremendious force in every direction quite across[.] a large Sand bar lies within the mouth. . . . men appear much Satis-fied with their trip beholding with estonishment the high waves dashing against the rocks & this emence Ocian[.]"

19 November 1805.
[CLARK]

"after takeing a Sumptious brackfast of Venison which was rosted on stiks exposed to the fire, I proceeded on through ruged Country of high hills and Steep hollers 5 miles . . . to the commencement of a Sandy coast. . . . I proceeded on . . . 4 miles, and marked my name on a Small pine . . . and returned to the foot of the hill, from which place I intended to Strike across to the Bay. . . . The Deer of this Coast differ materially from our Common deer in as much as they are

"7 Mile[s] to the enterance of a creek at a lodge . . . of Chinooks"
The crossing of the Chinook River was about opposite the trees, right center. Cape Disappointment, distant left center.

"passing a nitch in which there is a small rock island"
Looking north from Cape Disappointment, across Baker Bay, toward Ilwaco, Washington.

much darker, deeper bodied, Shorter ledged [legged] horns equally branched from the beem[.] the top of the tail black from the rute to the end. Eyes larger and do not lope but jump."

•

This is the original description of the Columbian black-tailed deer, *Odocoileus hemionus columbianus*. Smaller than the mule deer, they inhabit the forests and woodlands from the western slopes of the Cascades to the sea. The course this day was over the hills of Cape Disappointment past North Head to about the vicinity of today's Long Beach, then back to the Wallacut River, where the expedition camped.

20 November 1805.
[CLARK, FIRST DRAFT]
"The Morning cleared up fare we proceeded on by the same route we went out, at the [Chinook] River we found no Indians, made a raft & Ruben Fields crossed and brought back a small canoe which lay at the Indian cabin. . . . I proceeded on to camp & on my way was over taken by 3 Indians one gave us sturgeon & *Wapto roots* to eate. I met several parties on [the] way all of them appeared to know me & was distant."
[CLARK]
"found maney of the *Chin nooks* with Capt. Lewis of whome there was 2 Chiefs *Com com mo ly* & *Chil lar la wil* to whome we gave Medals and to one a flag. one of the Indians had on a roab made of 2 Sea Otter Skins both Capt. Lewis and

"The deer of this Coast differ materially from our Common deer"

myself endeavored to purchase the *roab* with different articles[.] at length we precured it for the belt of blue beeds which the Squar-wife of our interpreter Shabono wore around her waste."

21 November 1805.
[CLARK, FIRST DRAFT]

"The nation on the opposit side is small & called *Clap-sott* [Clatsop], Their great chief name *Stil-la-sha*. The nation liveing to the North called *Chieltz* [Chehalis]. The chief is name[d] *Ma-laugh* not [a] large nation. . . . I made a chief & gave a medel. . . . this man is name[d] *Tow-wále* and appears to have some influence with the nation and tells me he lives at the great shute [Cascades]. we gave the squar a coate of Blue Cloth for the belt of Blue Beeds we gave for the Sea otter skins purchased of an Indian."

[CLARK]

"great numbers ofthe dark brant passing to the south."

•

Clark noted that the Indian women tattooed their legs, wore their hair loose, and used ear but not nose ornaments, and that both men and women had flattened heads. The women wore a short skirt made of twisted strands of cedar bark attached to a belt and sometimes a short robe. Writing in his first draft, Clark observed that "maney of the women are handsom." He also recorded that the men wore robes of animal or bird skins but usually went naked, and that no one in the group wore any foot gear.

The "dark brant" could be either the black brant, *Branta nigricans*, or the brown, *B. bernicla hrota*, but was probably the former because the Pacific is its natural habitat, whereas the Atlantic is that of the latter. Both species breed in the Arctic tundra of Sibera and Alaska, and each prefers its own coast for wintering. Their natural food is eel grass, and one may see large rafts of them feeding in the patches. The brant is a small but distinctive water bird. The head is entirely black, the neck almost encircled with a broad white collar, the upper parts sooty brown, the breast black, and the stern a conspicuous white when upended. (Hunters sometimes apply the term "brant" to all geese.)

22 November 1805.
[CLARK, FIRST DRAFT]

"before day the wind increased to a storm . . . and blew with violence throwing the water of the river with emence waves out of its banks almost over whelming us in water, O! how horriable is the day. . . . one canoe split by the Tossing of those waves[.] we find the Indians easy ruled and kept in order by a stricter indifference towards them."

23 November 1805.
[CLARK, FIRST DRAFT]

"I marked my name the Day of the Month & year on a Beech [alder] tree & . . . Capt. Lewis

Branded his and the men all marked their nams on trees about the camp. . . . In the Evening 7 Indians of the *Clatt-sopp* nation, opposit came over, they brought with them 2 Sea orter skins, for which the[y] asked such high prices we were uneabled to purchase. . . ."

[CLARK]

"mearly to try the Indian who had one of those Skins, I offered him my Watch, handkerchief, a bunch of red beads and a dollar of the American coin, all of which he refused and demanded 'ti-á-co-mo-shack' which is *Chief beads* and the most common blue beads, but fiew of which we have at this time."

•

Among the Oregon Historical Society's treasures is the very iron with which Lewis "branded" his name on the tree, while all the others merely "marked" theirs. It was found some time during 1892, 1893, or 1894, on one of the Memaloose Islands, above the Long Narrows (*see* 20 April 1806). The iron was used to identify property.

"Chief beads" we believe to be the dark, translucent, cobalt blue, faceted or cut-glass beads. They are most plentiful near the coast where sea peddlers could have brought them. Along the mid-Columbia, faceted blue glass and rolled copper beads are sometimes the only kind found in the oldest sites. Sheet copper was a favorite trade item. Captain Gray's ship, the *Columbia Rediviva*, had almost thirty-five hundred pounds of it aboard when it left Boston in 1790

Captain Lewis's branding iron.

[*see* Howay, *Voyages of the "Columbia,"* 460]. From the sheets the Indians fashioned their own ornaments and rolled beads. Copper beads of "moderate " size were called seed beads, and measured about 1/16 to 1/5 inch in diameter. They were usually used for decorating clothing, in place of dyed porcupine quills.

24 November 1805, the time had now arrived to select a place for winter quarters. As with the crucial decision at the junction of the Missouri and Marias rivers, when following the wrong branch would have meant the expedition's failure, its members were again to vote their pref-erence. The votes of York and Sacagawea were recorded with the rest. All except Sacagawea and Joseph Shields voted to examine the southern or Oregon shore and winter there if game were plentiful; if it were not, they would then return to the vicinity of the Sandy River or Celilo Falls. Shields wanted to return immediately to the Sandy, and Sacagawea was in favor of going any-place "where there is plenty Potas." She was un-commonly fond of wappato.

Lewis and Clark were determined to stay at the mouth of the Columbia if they could find game, hoping that one of the trading ships then plying the coast would come into the river, be-

cause their letters of credit would enable them
to procure a fresh supply of trinkets to barter on
the return journey. Then, too, they could send
copies of their journals, their specimens, and
perhaps even some members of the party back
to the United States by sea, thus increasing the
chances that the knowledge they had gained and
recorded would not be lost. Their supply of salt
was exhausted and could be replenished on the
coast. And there the weather also promised to be
warmer than the interior—"it will most Certainly
be," as Clark noted, "the best Situation of our
Naked party dressed as they are altogether in
leather." Despite the captains' democratic in-
stincts, it is probable that the vote would have
been overruled had it gone otherwise.

"he . . . demanded . . . the most common blue beads"

25 November 1805.
[CLARK]

"The Wind being high rendered it impossible for
us to cross the river from our Camp, we deturmined to proceed on up where it was narrow, we
Set out early accompanied by 7 Clátsops for a
fiew miles, they left us and crossed the river
through emence high waves; we . . . encamp[ed]
a little after night near our Encampment of the
7th instant [of November, at Pillar Rock]."

26 November 1805.
[CLARK, FIRST DRAFT]

"proceeded on up on the North Side of this great
river to a rock in the river from thence we
crossed to the lower point of an Island . . . and

proceeded down the South Side, passed 2 Inlets & halted below the 2nd. at a Indian village of 9 large houses those Indians live on an emenence behind a Island or [on?] a Channel of the river [at Knappa] not more than 300 yds wide. . . . they call them selves *Cat-tar-bets* [Cathlamets]. . . . "

[CLARK]

"a short distance below on the Island which is Opposit [probably Mimaker] I observed Several Canoes Scaffold[ed] in which [were] contained their dead."

•

The party proceeded upriver to about Jim Crow Point, crossed the river, and passed between Woody and Horseshoe islands, then southwest through Prairie Channel, Knappa and Callender sloughs, and South Channel. They camped two miles below Settler Point.

27 November 1805.

[CLARK]

"at day light 3 Canoes and 11 Indians Came from the Village with roots mats, Skin &c. to sell, they asked such high prices that we were unable to purchase any thing of them, as we wer about to Set out missed one of our axes which was found under an Indians roab. I smamed [shamed] this fellow verry much. . . . we proceded on between maney Small Islands passing a Small river . . . which the Indians Call Kekemarke [John Day] and around a verry remarkable point [Tongue Point] which projects into the river, we call this

Point William[.] below this point the waves became So high we were compelled to land. . . . here we formed a camp on the neck of Land which joins Point William to the main at an old indian hut."

•

Two John Day rivers flow into the Columbia River from Oregon; the one Clark mentions here, the other is above The Dalles (*see* 21 October 1805). Camp was made on the site of the present Coast Guard Station on Tongue Point, and here the members of the main party were stormbound until 7 December. The point where they camped is only about 350 yards wide, completely exposed to the prevailing winds.

28 November 1805.

[CLARK, FIRST DRAFT]

"wind too high to go either back or forward, and we have nothing to eate but a little Pounded fish which we purchasd. at the Great Falls, This is our present situation! truly disagreeable. aded to this the robes of our selves and men are all rotten from being continually wet, and we cannot precure others, or blankets in these places. about 12 oClock the wind shifted . . . and blew with . . . such violence that I expected every moment to see trees taken up by the roots, some were blown down. Those squals were suckceeded by rain O! how Tremendious is the day."

29 November 1805.

[CLARK]

"The Shore below the point at our camp is formed of butifull pebble[s] of various colours. I observe but fiew birds of the Small kind, great numbers of wild fowls of Various kinds, the large Buzzard with white wings, grey and bald eagle's, large red taled Hawks, ravens & crows in abundance, the blue Magpie, a Small brown bird which frequents logs & about the roots of trees, Snakes, Lizards, Small bugs, worms, Spiders, flyes & insects of different kinds are to be Seen in abundance at this time."

•

The "large buzzard" was the condor (*see* 30 October 1805), the "blue magpie" a Steller's jay, and the "small brown bird" the winter wren. The beautiful, raucous Steller's jay, *Cyanocitta stelleri carbonacea*, inhabits the coast country west of the Cascades and is named after the German naturalist Georg Wilhelm Steller, who reported the first sighting of this bird while in Alaska as a member of the Bering-Chirikov expedition in 1741 (*see* Stejneger, *Georg Wilhelm Steller*, 270–71). Sportsmen despise the jay for its habit of loudly scolding the intruder from the nearest tree, warning all game within hearing. Farmers resent its theft of berries and fruit, and it can clear a filbert tree of every nut. The other two sub-species are *C.s. frontalis*, or blue-fronted jay, from the eastern slopes of the Cascades, and *C.s. annectens*, from the Blue Mountains eastward to

"I observe . . . the blue Magpie"
Steller's jay.

the Rockies; Lewis is credited with the first description of the latter (*see* 20 September 1805).

This day Lewis set out with five men in the small canoe to hunt for a place to winter.

30 November 1805.

[CLARK]

"Several men Complain of a looseness and griping which I contribute [attribute] to the diet, pounded fish mixed with Salt water. . . . The Squar gave me a piece of bread made of flour which She had reserved for her child and carefully Kept untill this time, which unfortunately got wet, and a little Sour. this bread I eate with great satisfaction, it being the only mouthful I had tasted for Several months past. . . . The Chinnooks [,] *Cath láh máh* & others in this neighbourhood bury their dead in their Canoes. for this purpose 4 pieces of Split timber are Set erect on end, and sunk a fiew feet in the ground, each brace . . . sufficiently far assunder to admit the width of the Canoe in which the dead are to be deposited; through each of those perpindicular posts, at a hight of 6 feet a mortice is cut, through which two bars of wood are incerted, on those cross bars a Small canoe is placed, in which the body is laid after beaing Carefully roled in a robe of Some dressed Skins; a paddle is also deposited with them; a large Canoe is now reversed, overlaying and imbracing the Small one, and resting with its gunnals on the cross bars; one or more large mats . . . are then rold. [rolled] around the Canoe and the whole securely lashed with a long cord usially made of the bark of the *arbar. vita* or cedar bark. on the cross bars which support the Canoes is frequently hung or laid various articles of Clothing culinary utensils &c. we cannot understand them Sufficiently to make any enquiries relative to ther religious opinions, from their depositing Various articles with their dead, [they] beleve in a State of future ixistence."

•

Canoe burial was a favorite method of interment below the Cascades and along the coast. Sometimes, instead of being deposited in a canoe, the bodies were placed in a tree. From the Cascades to The Dalles, vault burial was usual. At The Dalles and above there were rock-slide burials, vaults, cremations, and underground interment, because native groups came from far and near to fish and trade there, and each followed their respective customary practices.

This day Lewis and his party explored the country around Youngs Bay, seeking signs of game. They saw a great abundance of waterfowl and shore birds, but no deer or elk.

1 December 1805.

[CLARK]

"The emence Seas and waves which breake on the rocks & Coasts to the s.w. & nw roars like an emence fall at a distance, and this roaring has continued ever Since our arrival in the neighbourhood of the Sea Coast which has been 24 days Since we arrived in Sight of the Great West-

"bury their dead in their Canoes"
Painting by Henry Warre, 1845.

ern; (for I cannot Say Pacific) Ocian as I have not Seen one pacific day Since my arrival in its vicinity, and its waters are forming [foaming] and petially [perpetually] breake with emence waves on the Sands and rocky coasts, tempestous and horiable."

2 December 1805.
[CLARK]

"I feel verry unwell, and have entirely lost my appetite for the Dried pounded fish which is in fact the cause of my disorder at present. . . . Joseph Field came in with the Morrow bones of a elk which he killed at 6 miles distant, this welcome

"Jo. fields gives me an account of a great deal of Elk"
Pictograph, Columbia River.

news to us. I dispatched Six men in a empty Canoe with Jo: imediately for the elk. . . . Jo. fields gives me an account of a great deel of Elk Sign & says he Saw 2 Gangs of those animals on his rout, but it rained So hard that he could not Shoot them."

3 December 1805.

[CLARK, FIRST DRAFT]

"the men sent after an Elk yesterday returnd. with an Elk which revived the Sperits of my men verry much, I am unwell and cannot eate, the flesh. O! how disagreeable my situation, a plenty of meat and incap[ab]le of eateing any"

"200 yards to a spring, where we encamped"

[CLARK]

"an Indian Canoe of 8 Indians Came too, those Inds. are on their way down to the *Clát-sops* with *Wap pa to* to barter with that Nation, I purchasd a fiew of those roots for which I gave Small fish hooks, those roots I eate with a little Elks Soupe which I found gave me great relief. . . . the Squar choped the bones fine boiled them and extracted a pint of Grease, which is Superior to the tallow of the animal. . . . I marked my name on a large pine tree imediately on the isthmus[:] William Clark December 3rd. 1805. By Land from the U. States in 1804 & 1805."

4 December 1805.

[CLARK]

"I Se[n]t out Sergiant Pryor and 6 men to the Elk he had killed with directions to carry the meat to a bay which he informed me was below . . . and I should proceed on to that bay as soon as the wind would lay a little. . . . the waves [were] too high for me to proceed in Safty. . . . no account of Capt. Lewis. I fear Some accident has taken place in his craft or party."

5 December 1805.

[CLARK]

"Capt. Lewis returned with 3 men in the Canoe and informs me that he thinks that a Sufficient number of Elk may be pr[o]cured convenient to a Situation on a Small river which falls into a Small bay a Short distance below. . . . This was verry satisfactory information to all the party. we accordingly deturmined to proceed on to the Situation . . . as Soon as the wind and the weather should permit and Comence building huts &c."

6 December 1805.
[CLARK]

"The high tide of today is 13 inches higher than yesterday, and obliged us to move our Camp which was in a low Situation, on higher ground. Smoke exceedingly disagreeable."

7 December 1805.
[CLARK, FIRST DRAFT]

"we set out at 8 oClock down to the place Capt. Lewis pitched on for winter quarters"
[CLARK]

"we proceeded on around the point [Smith] into the bay [Youngs] and landed to take brackfast. . . . here all the party of Sergt. Pryors joined us except my man York, who had stoped to rite his load and missed his way. . . . I delayed about half an hour before York Came up, then proceeded around this Bay which I call Meriwethers Bay the Cristian name of Capt. Lewis. . . . we assended a river [Lewis and Clark] which falls in on . . . the bay 3 miles to the first point of high land on the West Side, the place Capt. Lewis had viewed. . . . this is certainly the most eligable Situation for our purposes."

•

In 1792 Lieutenant William Broughton explored the area, and named Youngs Bay and River after Sir George Young of the Royal Navy. The Lewis and Clark River, originally called Netul, was renamed some time before 1844, when the present name first appeared in print.

Gass wrote: "Unloaded our canoes and carried our baggage about 200 yards to a spring, where we encamped." This spring may still be seen near the Fort Clatsop National Historical Monument headquarters.

VII

PREPARING FOR WINTER

8 TO 29 DECEMBER 1805

8 December 1805.

[CLARK]

"We haveing fixed on this Situation as the one best Calculated for our Winter quarters I deturmin'd to go as direct a Course as I could go to the Sea Coast which we could here roar. . . . my principal object is to look out a place to make Salt, blaze the road or rout that they [the] men out hunting might find the direction to the fort if they Should get lost in cloudy weather—and See the probility of game in that direction. . . . passed the heads of 2 brooks . . . crossed 2 Slashes [swamps] and arrived at a open ridgey prarie covered with Sackacomma [*see* 20 December 1805]. . . . discovered a large gange of Elk . . . and we prosued them . . . about 3 miles, Killed one and camped."

•

Robert Stuart wrote of Fort Clatsop in 1812: "It was very disagreeably situated, being surrounded with swamps and quagmires, but the immense number of Elk and wild fowl which resort thither in winter for food more than compensates for the inconvenience" (*On the Oregon Trail,* 27–28). However, he continues, because of the heavy brush and rugged terrain "the utmost efforts of the hunter are seldom crowned with success, besides from the middle of Octr. to the middle of March no man in the woods can possibly keep his arms in order, on account of the unceasing rains" (ibid., 29). When a flintlock gun is fired, sparks from the flint ignite a bit of powder in a pan on the side of the lock, which sets off the charge. It was very difficult to keep the priming powder dry in the rain.

The Roosevelt's or Olympic elk, *Cervus canadensis rooseveltii,* is one of the finest of game animals; a large bull can weigh as much as fifteen hundred pounds. The horns are dropped in late winter, but by September the new growth is ready for combat to acquire females or to guard them, thus ensuring that the issue will inherit characteristics from only the most vigorous.

9 December 1805.

[CLARK]

"Set out on a Westerly direction. . . . met 3 Indians . . . [who] made Signs that they had a town on the Seacoast at no great distance, and envited me to go to their own which envitation I axcepted. . . . proceeded on to the mouth of the creek [Necanicum River] which makes a great bend[.] above the mouth of this Creek or to the s. is 3 houses and about 12 families of the Clatsop Nation. . . . those people treated me with extrodeanary friendship, one man attached himself to me . . . Spred down new mats for me to Set on, gave me fish berries rutes &c. on Small neet platters of rushes to eate which was repeated, all the Men of the other houses came and smoked with me[.] These people appeared much neeter in their diat than Indians are Comonly, and frequently wash theer faces and hands. in the eve[ni]ng an Old woman presented [in] a bowl made of a light coloured horn a kind of Surup made of Dried berries which is common to this Countrey which the natives Call *Shele wele* [salal, *see* 26 January 1806]. . . . they gave me Cockle Shells to eate a kind of Seuip [soup] made of bread of the Shele well berries Mixed with roots in which they presented in neet trenchers Made of wood. . . . those people have a Singular game which they are verry fond of and is performed with Something about the Size of a large been [bean] which they pass

from, one hand into the other with great dexterity [*see* 18 April 1806]. . . . this amusement has occupied about 3 hours of this evening, Several of the lodge in which I am in have lost all the beeds which they had about them. . . . when I was Disposed to go to Sleep the man who' had been most attentive named *Cus-ka lah* producd 2 new mats and Spred them near the fire. . . . I had not been long on my mats before I was attacked most Violently by the flees and they kept up a close Siege dureing the night[.]"

•

The light-colored horn was from the mountain sheep. After being scraped thin, it could be softened by being boiled and was then formed into useful shapes.

10 December 1805.

[CLARK]

"verry early I rose and walked on the Shore of the Sea coast [at what is now Seaside] and picked up Several curious Shells. . . . after amuseing my self for about an hour on the edge of the rageing Seas I returned to the houses, one of the Indians pointed to a flock of Brant Sitting in the creek at Short distance below and requested me to Shute one, I walked down with my Small rifle and killed two at about 40 yds distance, on my return to the houses two Small ducks Set at about 30 Steps from me[.] the Indians pointed at the ducks they were near together, I Shot at the ducks and accidently Shot the head of one off, this Duck and

"a bowl . . . of a light coloured horn"

"neet trenchers Made of wood"
This cedar mortar, made with stone tools, was found on Sauvie Island. Constant immersion under water had preserved it.

brant was carried to the house and every man came around examined the Duck look at the gun size of the ball which was 100 to the pound and Said in their own language *Clouch Musket, wake, com ma-tax, Musket* which is, a good Musket do not under Stand this kind of Musket &c. I entered the Same house I slept in, they imediately Set before me their best roots, fish and Surup, I attempted to purchase a Small Sea otter Skin for read [red] beads which I had in my pockets, they would not trade for those beeds not priseing any other Colour than Blue or White, I purchased a little of the berry bread and a fiew of their roots for which I gave Small fishing hooks, which they appeared fond of. I then Set out on my return by the Same rout I had Come out accompanied by *Cus-ka-lah* and his brother as far as the Second [3d.] Creek, for the purpose of Setting me across, from which place they returned, and I proceeded on through a heavy rain to the Camp at our intended fort. . . . found Capt. Lewis with all the men out Cutting down trees for our huts &c. . . . 4 men complaining of Violent Coalds."

•

The language that Clark heard was Chinook Jargon, a trade language used throughout the Northwest Coast. It consisted of words derived from several Indian tongues, the Chinook predominating because the Chinook were the chief traders. With the white invasion, some French and English words were added, such as "shan-tic" (from *chanter*, to sing) and "musket." John R. Jewitt, an armorer (blacksmith) aboard the American ship *Boston* and one of two survivors of an Indian attack upon the ship at Nootka Sound in 1803, discovered while he was held captive that the Nootkans had two languages. He considered one of them to be for poetic expression and the other for ordinary or everyday use. In Jewitt's account of his captivity, he illustrated this by citing a phrase that is the equivalent of "do not know" in English. His *Narrative*, first published in 1815, states: "*Ie-yee ma hi-chill*, Ye do not know. It appears to be a poetical mode of expression, the common one for [']do not know,['] being, *Wik-kum-atash*; from this, it would seem that they have two languages, one for their songs and another for common use" (166). Although Jewitt's spelling, *Wik-kum-atash*, is a slight variance of Clark's *wake, com ma-tax*, the two are clearly the same phrase. Lewis and Clark did not recognize that two tongues were used by the Clatsops and Chinook; when Indians spoke to whites they almost always used the Jargon, an expressive language, which, before the nineteenth century ended, was spoken by more than a hundred thousand people, many of whom were white.

11 December 1805.
[CLARK]

"we are all employed putting up huts or Cabins for our winters quarters, Sergeant Pryor unwell from a dislocation of his sholder, Gibson with the disentary, Jo. Fields with biles on his legs, & Werner with a Strained Knee."

12 December 1805.

[CLARK]

"The flees were so troublesom last night that I made but a broken nights rest. we find great difficulty in getting those trouble[some] insects out of our robes and blankets. In the evening two Canoes of *Clat Sops* Visit us they brought with them Wappato, a black Sweet root they call *Sha-na toe qua* [see 21 January 1806], and a Small Sea Otter Skin, all of which we purchased for a few fishing hooks and a Small Sack of Indian tobacco which was given [us] by the Snake Inds. Those Indians appear well disposed, we gave a Medal to the principal Chief named *Con-ny-au* or *Com mowol* [Coboway]. . . . I can readily discover that they are close deelers, & Stickle for a verry little, never close a bargin except they think they have the advantage[.]"

13 December 1805.

[CLARK]

"The *Clatsops* leave us today after a brackfast on Elk. . . . they Sold me two robes of the skins of a Small animal about the size of a cat [see 15 February 1806], and to Captain Lewis 2 Cat or Loucirvia [*Loup cervier*, Canadian lynx] Skins for the purpose of makeing a Coat. . . . We continue to put up the Streight butiful balsom pine on our houses, and we are much pleased to find that the timber Splits butifully and to the width of 2 feet or more."

Gass wrote the next day: "We completed the building of our huts, 7 in number, all but the covering, which I now find will not be so difficult as I expected; as we have found a kind of timber in plenty, which splits freely and makes the finest puncheons I have ever seen. They can be split 10 feet long and 2 broad, not more than an inch and an half thick" (*Journal*, 210–11).

Some fir trees can be split quite readily but none can match the western red cedar, *Thuja plicata*. The Indians used this handsome, durable wood for house planks, canoes, utensils, arrow shafts, and innumerable other things. Some early homesteaders built their houses and outbuildings entirely from split cedar, and Lewis and Clark probably roofed their huts with it. In using the term "puncheons," Gass was referring to split planks.

14 December 1805.

[CLARK]

"all employd in finishing a house to put meat into. all our last Supply of Elk has Spoiled in the repeated rains which has been fallen ever Since our arrival at this place, and for a long time before, Scerce one man in camp can bost of being one day dry Since we landed at this point, the Sick getting better, my man York Sick with Cholick and gripeing."

•

15 December 1805.

[CLARK, FIRST DRAFT]

"I set out early with 16 men and 3 canoes for the Elk [killed on the 13th] proced up the 1st right hand fork 4 miles & pack the meat from the woods to the canoes from 4 mile to 3 miles distance. . . . all hands pack not one man exempted from this labour[.] 5 did not join us tonight[.]"

•

The five men lost in the woods were Ordway, Colter, Collins, Whitehouse, and McNeal. Ordway comments the next day, "we suffered with wet and cold, all last night, and could not make a fire for everything we had was wet. We soon found ourselves this morning and went to camp."

16 December 1805.

[CLARK, FIRST DRAFT]

"I had the two canoes loaded with 11 Elk which was brought to the canoes. . . . the winds violent Trees falling in every direction, whorl winds, with gusts of rain, Hail & Thunder, this kind of weather lasted all day, Certainly one of the worst days that ever was!"

17 December 1805.

[CLARK]

"all the men at work about the houses, some Chinking, Dobbing Cutting out dores &c. &c. . . . a Mountain [Saddle] S E about 10 miles distant, has got snow on its top which is ruged and uneavin."

•

"Dobbing" means daubing mud between the logs of the walls or on the interior and exterior of the fireplaces to stop up cracks.

Saddle Mountain is a weather-resistant volcanic intrusion into softer marine rocks. It has withstood the forces of erosion and now dominates the countryside, the centerpiece of a state park, famous for the beauty and profusion of wildflowers that carpet its summit in early summer. Along the path, one may still see elk trails like those followed by Lewis and Clark's hunters, and even occasionally one of the herds feeding on the lush grass and herbs of the rolling hills below, long since denuded of their virgin forest cover.

18 December 1805.

[CLARK, FIRST DRAFT]

"rained and snowed alturnetely all the last night and the gusts of snow and hail continue untill 12 oClock, cold and a dreadfull day . . . we continue at work at our huts, the men being but thinly dressed, and no shoes causes us to doe but little[.]"

19 December 1805.

[CLARK]

"we dispatched Sjt. Pryor with 8 men in 2 canoes across Meriwethers Bay for the boards of an old Indian house which is vacant. . . . 2 Indians came and stayed a short time to day."

"A Mountain S. E. . . . which is ruged and uneavin"
Saddle Mountain viewed from the south (see entry for 17 December)

20 *December 1805.*

[C L A R K]

"3 Indians arrive in a Canoe. they brought with them mats, roots & Sackacome [*sac à commis*] berries to Sell for which they asked Such high prices that we did not purchase any of them. Those people ask generally double and tribble the value of what they have to Sell, and never take less than the real value of the article in Such things as is calculated to do them Service. Such as Blue & white beeds, with which they trade with the nativs above; files which they make use of to Sharpen their tools, fish hooks of different Sizes and tobacco. Tobacco and blue beeds they do prefur to every thing."

•

Sacacommis is the name the Coast Indians used for the kinnikinnick or bearberry, *Arctostaphylos uva-ursi*, a small creeping shrub that covers im-

"they brought Sackacome berries to Sell" Kinnikinnick or bearberry.

mense areas of the coast and the thinly forested interior. *Kinnikinnick* is a word of Algonquian origin meaning any smoking mixture. The bearberry leaves were used as a tobacco substitute or mix, and some enthusiasts still dry and smoke them. Clark wrote on 21 December: "dispatched two men to the open lands near the Ocian for Sackacome, which we make use of to mix with our tobacco to Smoke which has an agreeable flavour." The early French-Canadian voyageurs called it *sac à commis*, meaning "clerk's bag," because fur-trader clerks carried their smoking mixture in a pouch. The berries ripen in September and last on the bush all winter. The Indians gathered and dried them. Lewis wrote of them, "to me it is a very tasteless and insippid fruit."

21 December 1805.
[CLARK]

"rained as useal all the last night, and contd. moderately all day to day without any intermition, men employed at the houses. one of the indians was detected Stealing a horn Spoon, and leave the camp."

•

"one of the indians was detected Stealing a horn Spoon"
Spoons made from mountain goat horns were common on the Northwest Coast.

The Indians used horns from mountain sheep and goats for making spoons. The horns of the sheep are light colored, of the goats a jet black.

22 December 1805.

[CLARK, FIRST DRAFT]

"we finish dobbing 4 huts which is all we have covered, the Punchin [puncheon] floor & bunks finished [.] Drewyer go out to trap. beaver. Sjt. Ordway, Gibson and my servent sick. . . ."

[CLARK]

"We discover that part of our last Supply of meat is Spoiling from the womph [warmth] of the weather notwithstanding a constant Smoke kept under it day and night."

23 December 1805.

[CLARK]

"Capt. Lewis and my self move into our hut to day unfinished. two canoes with Indians of the *Clát sop* nation came up to day. I purchased 3 mats and bags all neetly made of flags and rushes, those bags are nearly square of different sizes open on one Side."

[CLARK, FIRST DRAFT]

"I also gave a string of wompom to a chief, and

sent a small pice of Sinimon to a sick Indian [Cuscalah] in the town who had attached himself to me."

•

The Biddle-Allen edition of the journals says that a medal was given to the chief along with the wampum (Allen, *History of the Expedition*, 2:99). Sending the stick of cinnamon to his sick friend Cuscalah was one of the thoughtful courtesies that helped Clark maintain good relations with the Indians with whom he dealt.

Ordway completes his daily record: "nothing extraordinary hapened more than common this day" (Quaife, *Journals*, 318).

24 December 1805.
[CLARK]

"Cuscalah . . . come up in a canoe with his young brother & 2 Squars he laid before Capt. Lewis and my self each a mat and a parcel of roots. . . . Some time in the evening two files was demanded for the presents of mats and roots, as we had no files to spare we returned the presents which displeased Cuscalah a little. He then offered a woman to each of us which we also declined axcepting of, which displeased the whole party verry much—the female part appeared to be highly disgusted at our refusing to axcept of their favours &c."

25 December 1805.
[CLARK, FIRST DRAFT]

"This morning at day we were saluted by all our party under our winders, a Shout and a Song. after brackfast we divided our tobacco . . . one half we gave to the party who used Tobacco those who did not we gave a Handkerchief as a present. . . . I rcvd a present of a Fleesh Hoserey [fleece hosiery] vest draws and socks of Capt. Lewis, pr. Mockersons of Whitehouse, a small Indian basket of Guterich, and 2 doz weasels tails of the Squar of Shabono, & some black roots of the Indians[.]"

[CLARK]

"we would have Spent this day the nativity of Christ in feasting, had we any thing either to raise our Sperits or even gratify our appetites, our Diner concisted of pore Elk, so much Spoiled that we eate it thro' mear necessity, Some Spoiled pounded fish and a fiew roots."

•

Gass adds: "and we are without salt to season that" (*Journal*, 213). Thus was spent Christmas Day, 1805.

26 December 1805.
[CLARK, FIRST DRAFT]

"The rain continued as usial all day. . . . Joseph Fields finish a Table & 2 seats for us. we dry our wet articles and have the blankets fleed, hut smoke[s] verry bad."

•

Fleas were an indigenous calamity in Northwest Indian country. The warm dirt floors made an ideal breeding habitat and the hardy vermin were impossible to eradicate. Gass wrote on 15 April 1806, while passing the "Friendly village" three miles above Lyle, Washington: "Passed a place where there was a village in good order last fall when we went down; but has been lately torn down, and again erected at a short distance from the old ground where it formerly stood. The reason of this removal I cannot conjecture, unless to avoid the fleas which are more numerous in this country than any insects I ever saw" (*Journal*, 241–42).

27 December 1805.
[CLARK]

"*Co-ma wool* the Chief and 4 men of the *Clatsop* nation . . . presented us a root which resembles the licquirish in Size and taste, which they rost like a potato which they call *Cul ho-mo* [*see* 17 November 1805], also a black root which is cured in a kill [kiln] like the *pash-a-co* above; this root has a Sweet taste and the nativs are verry fond of it[.] they call this root *Shaw-na-táh-que* [*see* 21 January 1806]. also a dried berry about the size of a cherry which they Call *Shell well* [*see* 26 January 1806] all those roots those Indians value highly and give them verry Spearingly. . . . Those roots and berries are timely and extreamly great-full to our Stomachs, as we have nothing to eate but Spoiled Elk meat[.]"

•

The Clatsop chief, Coboway, called by Lewis and Clark Comawool, has a niche in Oregon history because of his three daughters, Yainast, Kelapotah, and Celiast. Yainast married Joseph Gervais, who came to the Oregon Country with Wilson Price Hunt in 1811. The first school in Oregon was built at his home. He was a justice of the peace and prominent in local politics. Kelapotah married Louis LaBonte, also of the Hunt party. He started the first farm on the Yamhill River and was influential in securing Oregon for the United States. Celiast married Solomon Howard Smith, who came to Oregon with Nathaniel Wyeth in 1832; she taught school in Fort Vancouver and later at the Gervais home. He had a farm on the Clatsop Plains as well as other interests, including the first ferry on the Columbia River. One of the Smiths' seven children was Silas B. Smith, a lawyer and an authority on the culture of his mother's people (*see* Corning, *Dictionary of Oregon History*, 98, 138, 228; and Dobbs, *Men of Champoeg*, 30–35, 182).

28 December 1805.
[CLARK]

"Derected Drewyer, Shannon, Lebeach, Ruben Field, and Collin to hunt; Jos. Fields, Bratton, Gibson to proceed to the Ocean at some conveneint place form a Camp and Commence makeing Salt with 5 of the largest Kittles, and Willard and Wiser to assist them in carrying the

"his Hat . . . was made with a double cone"

Kittles to the Sea Coast. all the other men employed about putting up pickets & makeing the gates of the *fort*. My Man Y[ork] verry unwell from a violent coald and Strain by carrying meet from the woods and lifting the heavy logs on the works &c."

29 December 1805.
[CLARK, FIRST DRAFT]

"a young Chief 4 Men and 2 womin of the War-ci-a-cum tribe came in a large canoe with *Wapto* roots, Dressed Elk skins &c. to sell, the Chief made me a present of about a half a bushel of those roots[.] we gave him a medal of the small size and a piece of red ribin to tie around the top of his Hat which was made with a double cone, the diameter of the upper about 3 Inches the lower about 1 foot."

[CLARK]

"the Nations above carry on a verry considerable interchange of property with those in this neighbourhood. they pass altogether by water, they had no roads or paths except portages from one creek to another, all go litely dressed ware nothing below the waste in the Coaldest of weather[.]"

•

The "double cone" hat was supposed to be worn only by chiefs; the greater the chief, the more cones. Originally each cone represented a potlatch, and thus this style of hat was peculiar to the Northwest Coast Indians, where the potlatch was customary. The one illustrated here we saw being made by Lily Belle Williams, a Quinault Indian of Queets, Washington. They are sometimes called pagoda hats because the shape resembles those worn by Chinese laborers.

"our fortification is completed this evening"
Fort Clatsop reconstructed.

VIII

AT FORT CLATSOP

30 DECEMBER 1805 TO 22 MARCH 1806

30 December 1805.

[CLARK]

"Drewyer . . . killed 4 Elk at no great distance off. . . . we had a Sumptious Supper of Elks tongues & morrow bones which was truly gratifying. our fortification is completed this evening and at Sun set we let the nativs know that our Custom will be in the future, to Shut the gates at Sun Set at which time all Indians must go out of the fort and not return into it untill next morning."

•

A replica of Fort Clatsop has been constructed on the original location, now Fort Clatsop National Memorial. The plans were prepared from sketches and descriptions in the journals. A "Living History" museum near the fort includes displays, illustrated lectures, and demonstrations of equipment used on the journey, such as the flintlock gun. A portion of the Lewis and Clark trail to the coast has been restored.

31 December 1805.

[CLARK]

"With the party of *Clátsops* who visited us last was a man of much lighter Coloured than the nativs generaly, he was freckled with long duskey red hair, about 25 years of age. . . . this man appeared to understand more of the English language than the others but did not Speak a word of English, he possessed all the habits of the indians[.]"

•

This freckled, red-headed Indian was later noted by other visitors to the region. Ross Cox, a member of the Astor party in 1811, wrote: "An Indian belonging to a small tribe on the coast, to the southward of the Clatsops, occasionally visited the fort [Astoria]. He was a perfect *lusus naturae* [freak of nature], and his history is curious. His skin was fair, his face partially freckled, and his hair quite red. He was about five feet ten inches high, was slender, but remarkably well made; his head had not undergone the flattening process; and he was called Jack Ramsay, in consequence of that name having been punctured on his left arm. The Indians allege that his father was an English sailor, who had deserted from a trading vessel, and had lived many years among their tribe, one of whom he married" (*Columbia River*, 1:286–87).

Alexander Henry wrote on 8 December 1813: "There came . . . a man about 30 years of age, who has extraordinary dark red hair and is much freckled—a supposed offspring of a ship that was wrecked within a few miles of the entrance of this river [Columbia] many years ago. Great quantities of beeswax continue to be dug out of the sand near this spot, and the Indians bring it to trade with us" (*Journals*, 2:768).

Pieces of beeswax are still occasionally found on Nehalem Spit. They may have come from a castaway Spanish galleon named the *San Francisco Xavier*, lost in 1705 en route from Manila to Acapulco. Carbon-14 analysis of the wax indicates that it dates from some time in the mid-seventeenth century.* A piece has been found bearing the numerals 67, which are interpreted by some to be the middle two numerals in 1679 (*see* Cook, *Flood Tide of Empire*, 33).

---

*A more recent radiocarbon test indicates that dates for the beeswax could range between A.D. 1485 and 1655 (*see* John A. Woodward, "Prehistoric Shipwrecks on the Oregon Coast?" *Contributions to the Archaeology of Oregon* 3 [1986]:221).

1 January 1806.
[LEWIS]

"This morning I was awoke at an early hour by the discharge of a volley of small arms, which were fired by our party in front of our quarters to usher in the new year; this was the only mark of rispect which we had in our power to pay this celebrated day. our repast of this day . . . consisted principally in the anticipation of the 1st. day of January 1807, when in the bosom of our friends we hope to participate in the mirth and hilarity of the day, and when with the zest given by the recollection of the present, we shall completely . . . enjoy the repast which the hand of civilization has prepared for us."

•

The fort now being finished, Lewis posted regulations for the conduct of the party. A sentinel was to be on duty at all times of day and night; Indians should be treated in a firm but friendly manner; only the sentinel could open the gate at night; the meat house and canoes should be visited regularly; and each guard on being relieved must bring in two loads of wood for the commanding officers. No man would be exempt from carrying meat from the woods, and any tools must be checked in and out except those loaned to John Shields.

A list of thirteen traders who had come into the Columbia was recorded in the expedition's journals, including "1 Ey'd Skellie, in a large ship, long time gorn" and "Callallamet. Visits them in

Beeswax found on Nehalem Sand Spit.

a 3 masted Vessle. Trader has a wooden leg."
This information was obtained from the Indians.

Gass and Ordway say the newly completed fort was named Fort Clatsop, but neither of the captains mentions the christening, although both later call the fort by that name.

2 January 1806.
[CLARK]

"we are infestd. with sworms of flees already in our new habitations. . . . The large, & small or whistling swan, Sand hill Crane, large and Small Gees, brown and white brant, Cormorant, Duckanmallard, Canvisback duck, and Several other species of Ducks Still remain with us; tho' I doe not think that they are as plenty as on our first arrival in this neighbourhood."

3 January 1806.
[LEWIS]

"At 11 A.M. we were visited by our near neighbours Cheif or Tiá. Co-mo-wool, alias Conia and six Clatsops. the[y] brought for sale some roots buries and three dogs also a small quantity of fresh blubber. this blubber they informed us they had obtained from their neighbours the Callamucks [Tillamooks] who inhabit the coast to the s.e. near whose village a whale had recently perished. . . . our party from necessaty having been obliged to subsist some length of time on dogs have now become extreemly fond of their flesh; it is worthy of remark that while we lived principally on the flesh of this anamal we were much more healthy strong and more fleshey than we had been since we left the Buffaloe country. for

"Sand hill Crane . . . Still remain with us"

my own part I have become so perfectly reconciled to the dog that I think it an agreeable food
and would prefer it vastly to lean Venison or
Elk."

•

Clark's journal reads the same, except for the
penultimate line, where he writes: "for my own
part I have not become reconsiled to the taste of
this animal as yet." Tiá in Chinook Jargon is today
spelled tyee. In Lewis and Clark's time it meant
"chief" only, although it subsequently came to
mean anything superior.

4 January 1806.
[CLARK]

"Comowool and the Clatsops . . . left us in the
morning. Those people the *Chinnooks* and
others residing in this neighborhood . . . have
been verry friendly to us; they appear to be a
Mild inoffensive people, but will pilfer if they
have an oppertunity. . . . They are great higlers in
trade. . . . I . . . beleive this treat [trait] in their
charecter proceeds from an avericious all grasp-
ing disposition. in this respect they differ from
all Indians I ever became acquainted with, for
their dispositions invariably lead them to give
whatever they possessed off no matter how use-
full or valueable, for a bauble which pleases their
fancy, without consulting its usefullness or
value."

•

The Chinooks were the middlemen on the river,
bartering with local tribes for furs and other merchandise, in turn trading with the sea peddlers
who came into the river. Slaves, procured in
trade from such places as the great trade mart on
the Long Narrows, were bartered with other
Northwest tribes for canoes, dentalium shells,
and furs.

The natives' desire to possess any trinket that
struck their fancy led to fierce competition between trading ships in setting the fashion for a
particular item. Fortunate was the vessel that had
an ample supply of Jew's harps—if that were the
fad of the moment—while its competitors had
none. In 1791 Captain Joseph Ingraham of the
American brig *Hope* had his armorer make ornamental iron collars, which became objects greatly
esteemed by the Haida. The demand became so
great that it kept the armorer busy seven days a
week, and enabled Ingraham to reap a handsome
profit in furs (*see* Ingraham, *Voyage to the Northwest Coast*, 105–6).

5 January 1806.
[LEWIS]

"At 5 P.M. Willard and Wiser returned. . . . they
informed us that it was not untill the fifth day . . .
that they could find a convenient place for making salt; that they had at length established themselves on the coast about 15 Miles S.W. . . . near
the lodge of some Killamuck families; that the
Indians were very friendly and had given them a
considerable quantity of the blubber of a whale

which perished on the coast some distance S.E. of them; part of this blubber they brought with them, it is white & not unlike the fat of Poork. . . . I had a part of it cooked and found it very pallitable and tender. . . . they commenced the making of salt. . . . they brought with them a specemine of the salt. . . . this was a great treat to myself and most of the party, having not had any since the 20th Ultmo. [of the preceding month]. I say most of the party, for my friend Capt. Clark declares it to be a mear matter of indifference with him whether he uses it or not. . . . the want of bread I consider as trivial provided I get fat meat, for as to the species of meat I am not very particular, the flesh of the dog the horse and the wolf, having from habit become equally formiliar with any other, and I have learned to think that if the chord be sufficiently strong, which binds the soul and boddy together, it dose not so much matter about the materials which compose it. . . . Capt. Clark determined this evening to set out early tomorrow with two canoes and 12 men in quest of the whale."

6 January 1806.
[CLARK]

"The last evening Shabono and his Indian woman was very impatient to be permitted to go with me, and was therefore indulged; She observed that She had traveled a long way with us to See the great waters, and now that monstrous fish was also to be Seen, She thought it verry hard that She could not be permitted to See either

(She had never yet been to the Ocian). after an early brackfast I Set out with two Canoes down the *Netel* [Lewis and Clark] R into Meriwether [Youngs] Bay. . . . Soon after . . . the wind Sprung up from the N.W. and blew So hard and raised the waves so high that we were obliged to put into a Small creek Short of the Village. . . . I deturmined to assend this Creek as high as the canoes would go; which from its directions must be near the open lands in which I had been on the 10th. ulto., and leave the Canoes and proceed on by land. at the distance of about 3 miles up this creek I observed Some high open land, at which place a road set out and had every appearance of a portage, here I landed drew up the canoes and Set out by land. . . . from the top of a ridge . . . we Saw a large gange of Elk. . . . I divided the party So as to be certain of an elk, Several Shot[s] were fired only One Elk fell. . . . we proceeded on to . . . a little river 70 yards wide which falls into the Ocian near the 3 Clat Sop houses which I visited on the 9th. ulto. . . . the evening a butiful Clear moon Shiney night, and the 1st. fair night which we have had for 2 months[.]"

7 January 1806.
[CLARK]

"Some frost this morning. I[t] may appear somewhat incredible, but So it is that the Elk which was killed last evening was eaten except about 8 pounds, which I directed to be taken along with the Skin. . . . I proceeded on . . . to near the base of [a] high Mountain where I found our Salt makers . . . had made a Neet close camp, convenient to wood Salt water and the fresh water of the Clátsop [Necanicum] river which at this place was within 100 paces of the Ocian. they wer also Situated near 4 houses of the Clatsops & Killamox. . . . I hired a young Indian to pilot me to the whale for which Service I gave him a file in hand and promised Several other small articles on my return. . . . we proceeded on the round Slipery Stones under a high hill. . . . after walking 2½ miles . . . my guide made a Sudin halt, pointed to the top of the mountain and uttered the word *Pe shack* which means bad. . . . I . . . view this emence mountain [Tillamook Head] the top of which was obscured in the clouds, and the assent appeard. to be almost perpindecular. . . . I soon found that the [path] became much worst as I assended, and at one place we were obliged to Support and draw our selves up by the bushes & roots for near 100 feet, and after about 2 hours labour and fatigue we reached the top of this high mountain, from the top of which I looked down with estonishment to behold the hight which we had assended. . . . In the face of this tremendeius precipic[e] imediately below us, there is a *Stra(tar)* of white earth . . . the neighbouring indians use to paint themselves. . . . we left the top of the precipice and proceeded on a bad road and encamped on a small run passing to the left [Canyon Creek]: all much fatiagued[.]"

Alexander Henry mentions the clay in 1813: "They also bring bags of a beautiful white clay which they collect a few miles s. on the coast. Being found only at the base of a steep bank, the method of obtaining it is necessarily hazardous. To reach it a person is lowered down from the top with a strong cord around his body, and hauled up when he has filled his bag" (*Journals*, 2:768).

The saltmakers' cairn, a pile of boulders used by Fields, Bratton, and Gibson to support the evaporating kettles, has long been a historical landmark at Seaside. Located early in this century by a committee from the Oregon Historical Society, it was authenticated by local residents and a stout iron fence was erected to guard it. This site, one of the few remaining geographical mementos of the expedition, is now part of Fort Clatsop National Memorial. The original cairn has been replaced with a restoration.

8 January 1806.
[CLARK]

"Set out early and proceeded to the top of the mountain. . . . from this point I beheld the grandest and most pleasing prospects which my eyes ever surveyed, in my frount a boundless Ocean; to the N. and N.E. the coast as far as my sight could be extended, the Seas rageing with emence wave[s] and brakeing with great force from the rocks of Cape Disapointment as far as I could See to the N.W. The Clatsops Chinnooks and other villagers on each Side of the Columbia

"In the face of this tremendeius precipic[e] . . . there is a Strai(tar) of white earth"
Tillamook Head, viewed from the south.

river and in the Praries below me, the meander-ings of 3 handsom Streams heading in Small lakes at the foot [of] the high Country; The Co-lumbia River for some distance up, with its Bays and Small rivers: and on the other side I have a view of the coast for an emence distance to the S.E. by S. the nitches and points of high land which forms this corse for a long ways aded to the inoumerable rocks of emence Sise out at a great distance from the shore and against which the Seas brak with great force gives this coast a most romantic appearance. from this point of View My guide pointed to a Village at the mouth of a Small river [Ecola Creek] near which place he Said the whale was, he also pointed to 4 other places where the Villages of the *Killamox* were Situated, I could plainly See the houses of 2 of those Villages & the Smoke of a 3rd. . . . I pro-ceeded on down a Steep decent to a Single house the remains of an old *Kil a mox* Town in a nitch imediately on the Sea Coast. . . . I observed large Canoes of the neetest kind on the ground. . . . I examoned those canoes and found that [they] were the repository of the dead. . . . The coast in the neighbourhood of this old village is slipping from the Sides of the high hills, in emence masses; fifty or a hundred acres at a time give way and a great proportion of [in] an instant precipi-tated into the Ocean. . . . we passed over 3 of these dismal points and arived on a butifull Sand Shore on which we continued for 2 miles, crossed a Creek [Ecola] near 5 Cabins, and pro-ceeded on to the place the whale had perished, found only the Skelleton of this Monster on the Sand. . . . The whale was already pillaged of every Valuable part by the Kilamox Inds. . . . this Skele-ton measured 105 feet. I returned to the Village of 5 Cabins . . . which I shall call *E co-la* or Whale Creek, found the nativs busily engaged boiling the blubber, which they performed in a large Squar wooden trought by means of hot stones. . . . although they possessed large quantities of this blubber and oil . . . they disposed of it with great reluctiance. . . . with the Small Stock of merchandize I had taken with me I was not able to precure more blubber than about 300 lb. and a fiew gallons of oil; Small as this stock is I prise it highly; and thank providence for directing the whale to us; and think him much more kind to us that he was to jonah, having Sent this Monster to be *Swallowed by us* in Sted of *Swallowing of us* as jonah's did. . . . I enquired of those people . . . by Signs the Situation, mode of liveing & Strength of their nation. They informed me that the bulk of their nation lived in 3 large villages Still further along the Sea coast to the S.S.W. at the enterence of 3 Creek[s] which fell into a bay . . . and a Small river which fell into the Bay . . . (which I call *Kil a mox* River)[.] they crossed over to the (*Wap pato I.*) on the *Shock. ah lil con* (which is the Indian name for the Columbia River) and purchaced Wappato &c. [*see* 2 April 1806]. . . . The *Kil á mox* in their habits cus-toms manners dress & language differ but little from the Clatsops, Chinnooks and others in the neighbourhood."

"an old Kil a mox *Town in a nitch imediately on the Sea Coast"*
The village was at Indian Beach on top of the bank on the right.

●

In 1961 a landslide did extensive damage to installations and roads in Ecola State Park. The coast continues to slip.

9 January 1806.
[CLARK]
"last night . . . about 10 oClock I was alarmed by a loud Srill voice from the cabins on the opposite side. . . . my guide . . . made signs that Some one's throat was Cut. . . . I found that one man Mc.-

176

Spoon carved from whalebone in the shape of a whale.

Neal was absent. . . . I imediately Sent off Sergt. Pryor & 4 men in quest of Mc.Neal, who' they met comeing across the Creak in great hast. . . . the people were alarmed on the opposite side at Something but what he could not tell."

•

A supposedly friendly Indian had taken McNeal to a lodge where he was given some blubber, then to another where, in Clark's words, he was promised "Something better." But a woman held him by his blanket and, when shaken off, started to scream, being quickly joined by others, all fearing that McNeal was destined to be murdered for his few possessions. The screaming, Clark wrote, "allarmed the men of the village who were with me in time to prevent the horred act." Ordway notes that this creek was named by Captain Clark "McNeal's folley" (Quaife, *Journals*, 321). Coues, Thwaites, Bakeless, and other students of the expedition identify the creek as Nehalem River and place the scene of this inci-

dent at Nehalem Bay. But it was almost certainly at what is today Cannon Beach, on the banks of Ecola (formerly Elk) Creek.

At sunrise this day the party shouldered the oil and blubber and set out upon what the Captain termed "the dreaded road on which we have to return 35 miles to Fort Clatsop." Late in the evening they arrived at the salt works, where they camped for the night, much fatigued.

10 January 1806.
[CLARK]

"I set out at Sunrise. . . . I thought it a favourable time to go on to the fort at which place we arrived at 10 oClock PM, found Several indians of the Cath-láh-máh nation the great Chief *Sháh-hár-wáh cop* who resides not far above us on the South Side of the Columbia River, this is the first time I have Seen the Chief. . . . we gave him a medal of the Smallest Size, he presented me with a basquet of Wappato."

Cannon Beach,
where Clark saw
the whale.
Tillamook Head,
top; Ecola
(formerly Elk) or
"McNeal's folley"
Creek, top center.
The whale
beached near
Haystack Rock,
left center.

11 January 1806.

[CLARK]

"This morning the Sergt. of the guard reported that our Indian Canoe had gone a Drift. . . . we Sent a party down to the bay in Serch of her, they returned unsecksessfull. . . . this will be a verry considerable loss to us if we do not recover her, She is so light that 4 men can carry her on their Sholders a mile or more without resting, and will carry four men and from 10 to 12 hundred pounds. The Cathlamahs left us this evening on their way to the Clatsops, to whome they perpose bartering their Wappato for the blubber & Oil of the whale, which the latter purchased for Beeds &c. from the Kilamox; in this Manner there is a trade continually carried on by the nativs."

12 January 1806.

[CLARK]

"This morning Sent out Drewyer and one man to hunt, they returned in the evening Drewyer haveing killed 7 Elk; I scercely know how we Should Subsist, I beleive but badly if it was not for the exertions of this excellent hunter; maney others also exert themselves, but not being acquainted with the best method of finding and killing the elk and no other wild animals is to be found in this quarter, they are unsucksessfull in their exertions. . . . We have heretofore devided the Meat when first killed among the four messes, into which we have divided our party, leaveing to each the care of preserving and distribution of useing it; but we find that they make such prodigal use of it when they happen to have a tolerable Stock on hand, that we are determined to adopt a Different System with our present stock of Seven Elk; this is to jurk it and issue it to them in Small quatities."

•

George Drouillard (called "Drewyer" in the journals) was the most valuable man to the leaders of the expedition. Besides being an expert woodsman and hunter, his knowledge of Indians and his dexterity with the universal sign language enabled him to converse with all the Plains Indians, and he apparently had some success in conversing with the natives on western waters. He was employed as a civilian interpreter and his wages were twenty-five dollars a month, while the enlisted men received five dollars each.

Drouillard's father was a French Canadian, his mother a Shawnee. He was between twenty-five and thirty years old when he signed on with the Corps of Discovery at Fort Massac. After the journey he became a trapper with the fur trader Manuel Lisa. Under Lisa's orders, he shot and killed a deserter, for which he was tried for murder and acquitted. In 1810, while trapping on the Jefferson River near Three Forks, Montana, he was killed by a party of Blackfoot Indians (*see* Skarsten, *George Drouillard*, 18, 27–31, 271–79, 281–313).

13 January 1806.
[LEWIS]

"this evening we exhausted the last of our candles, but fortunately had taken the precaution to bring with us moulds and wick, by means of which and some Elk's tallow in our possession we do not yet consider ourselves destitute of this necessary article."

14 January 1806.
[CLARK]

"From the best estermate we were enabled to make as we descended the columbia we conceived that the nativs inhabiting that noble stream . . . From Towarnehiooks [Deschutes] River . . . to the grand rapids [Cascades] annually prepare about 30,000 lbs. of pounded fish . . . for Market. . . . The persons who usually visit the enterance of this river for the purpose of traffic or hunting, I believe is either English or Americans; the Indians inform us that they Speak the Same language with ourselves, and gave us proofs of their veracity by repeating maney words of English, *Sun of a pitch,* &c. *(heave the lead & many blackguard phrasses).* . . . This traffic on the part of the whites consist in vending, guns, principally old British or American Musquets, powder, balls and shote, brass tea kittles, Blankets from two to three points, scarlet and blue Cloth (Coarse), plates and Strips of Sheet Copper and brass, large brass wire Knives Beeds & Tobacco with fishing hook buttons and Some other Small articles; also a considerable quantity of Salors Clothes. . . . The Nativs are extravigantly fond of the most common cheap Blue and white beeds, of moderate size, or Such that from 50 to 70 will way one pennyweight, the blue is usially preferred to the white."

•

The estimate of "30,000 lbs. of pounded fish" would be only a small portion of the total harvest along the upper Columbia River where the salmon were dried in the sun, a process not suitable to the lower river. Although difficult to quantify, vastly greater amounts of salmon must have been taken annually from the Columbia and its tributaries in prehistoric times.

Salmon once ascended the Columbia in immense numbers. The Indians could net or spear as many as they wished with little effort, especially at the falls and rapids, where the fish would rest briefly in the pools and eddies while battling their way through the swift water. Ordway wrote while on the upper River: "this morning passd several Small villages the Savages all hid themselves in their flag loges untill we passed them. the Indians are numberous along the River. the villages near each other and great quantitys of Sammon drying" (Quaife, *Journals,* 301). We have been on every sandbar, every island on the Columbia below its junction with the Snake, and many of those above, and not one failed to produce evidence of occupancy; some were deep with the accumulated debris of centuries. There were few permanent residents on the Columbia above The Dalles, for there was no wood for fuel; they came to the river only to fish, trade, and gamble, returning to the sheltered valleys to winter.

Five species of salmon ascend the Columbia River, fanning out into the tributaries to spawn and die. The largest is the Chinook, *Oncorhynchus tshawytscha*, also called king or tyee, the "common salmon" of the journals. In prehistoric times they averaged about thirty pounds, and have reached one hundred. They are among the tastiest of all fish. The coho or silver, *O. kisutch*, average about eight pounds. The sockeye or blueback, *O. nerka*; the chum, *O. keta*; and the pink, *O. gorbaucha*, were of minor importance on the Columbia. From April to late September the river abounded with fish from runs of one or another of these species. In the journals, the "red charr" was the sockeye or blueback; the "white salmon trout" was the coho and sometimes the steelhead.

It is difficult now to visualize the hordes of salmon that entered the Columbia at the time of the invasion by whites. Seines, traps and fish wheels harvested them by the thousands of tons. Traps were eventually outlawed, but the seines and fish wheels still took fish in vast numbers. Fish wheels were anchored or constructed in a channel where the salmon passed, and were turned by the current. They would scoop up the fish as a shovel does coal, and slide them into a waiting barge. One such barge on the Long Narrows reportedly caught sixty-eight thousand pounds in eight hours; there were many wheels along the river until they were outlawed in the 1920s.

15 January 1806.
[LEWIS]

"The implyments used by the Chinnooks Clatsops Cuthlahmahs &c in hunting are the gun the bow & arrow, deadfalls, pitts, snares, and spears or gigs. . . . The bow and arrow is the most common instrument among them, every man being furnished with them whether he has a gun or not. . . . Their bows are extremely neat and very elastic, they are about two and a half feet in length, and two inches in width in the center. . . . they are very flat and thin . . . the back of the bow being thickly covered with sinews of the Elk laid on with a Gleue which they make from the sturgeon; the string is made of sinues of the Elk also. The arrow is formed of two parts usually tho' sometimes entire; those formed of two parts are unequally divided[.] that part on which the feathers are placed occupyes four fifths of it's length and is formed of light white pine. . . . the lower extremity of this is a circular mortice secured by sinues. . . . this mortice receives the one end of the second part which is . . . about 5 inches long, in the end of this the barb is fixed and confined with sinue, 2nd. this barb is either stone, iron or copper . . . forming at it's point a greater angle than those of any other Indians I have observed. . . . maney of the Elk we have killed . . . have been wounded with these arrows, the short piece with the barb remaining the animal. . . . pits are em-

"[The] barb is either stone, iron or copper"

ployed in taking the Elk, and of course are large and deep."

16 January 1806.
[LEWIS]

"no occurrence worthy of relation took place today. we have plenty of Elk beef for the present and a little salt, our houses dry and comfortable. . . . The Clatsops Chinnooks &c. in fishing employ the common streight net, the scooping or diping net with a long handle, the gig, and the hook and line. . . . their nets and fishing lines are made of the silk-grass or white cedar bark. . . . before the whites visited them they made hooks of bone and other substances. . . . these are flattened and leveled off of their extremities . . .

where they are firmly attached together with sinues and covered with rosin."

The gig or spear had a bone point that was released from a socket when the fish was struck. A short cord anchored the point to the pole, so that the fish would not break the pole in its struggles. The nets were usually made from the fibers of nettle, wild iris, or Indian hemp. The "straight net," which might be over one hundred feet long, was kept upright in the water by wooden floats and stone sinkers fastened to the net with cedar-bark rope. Perforated, banded, and notched stone sinkers are found in great numbers along the Columbia River. Occasionally one is discovered with the cord binding still in place, preserved by constant immersion in water.

Types of net weights used by natives to fish on the Columbia River. Left to right, top row—banded, girdled and perforated; second row—perforated pendant, double notch and quadruple notch cobble; bottom row—single notch cobble and single notch with original lashing of bark.

17 January 1806.

[CLARK]

"This morning we were visited by Comowool and 7 of the Clatsops. . . . one of the party was dressed in three verry elegant Sea otter Skins which we much wanted. . . . he would not dispose of them for any other Consideration but Blue beeds. . . . these Coarse blue beeds are their favorite Merchandize and are Called by them *Tia com ma shuck* or chief beeds. . . . The Culinary articles of the Indians in our neighbourhood consists of wooden bowls or troughs, Baskets, Shell and wooden Spoons and wooden Scures [skewers] or Spits, their wooden Bowles are of different forms and Sizes, and most generally dug out of the solid piecies. . . . those are extreemly well executed and maney of them neetly covered, the larger vessels with handholes to them; in these vessels they boil their fish and flesh by means of hot Stones. . . . Their baskets are formed of Cedar bark and bargrass So closely interwoven . . . that they are watertight. . . . Some of those are highly ornimented with the Strans of bargrass which they dye of Several Colours. . . . this grass grows only on their mountains near the Snowey region. . . . their meat is roasted with a Sharp Scure, one end of which is incerted in the meat while' the other is Set erect in the ground. The spit for roasting fish . . . is incerted in the fish with its head downwards. . . . the Side[s] of the fish . . . are expanded by means of Small Splinters of wood which extend Crosswise the fish. a small mat of rushes or flags is the usual plate."

18 January 1806.

[LEWIS]

"Two of the Clatsops who were here yesterday returned today for a dog they had left; they remained with us a few hours. . . . no further occurrence worthy of relation took place. the men are still much engaged in dressing skins in order to cloath themselves and prepare for our homeward journey."

19 January 1806.

[LEWIS]

"two Clatsop men and a woman . . . brought for sale some Sea Otter skins of which we purchased one, giving in exchange the remainder of our blue beads consisting of 6 fathoms and about the same quantity of small white beads and a knife. we also purchased a small quantity of train oil. . . . Several families of these people usually reside together in the same room. . . . their provision seems to be in common and the greatest harmoney appears to exist among them. . . . These families when associated form nations . . . each acknowledging the authority of it's own chieftain who dose not appear to be heriditary, nor his power to extend further than a mear repremand. . . . the creation of a chief depends upon the upright deportment of the individual & his ability and disposition to render service to the community; and his authority or the deference paid him is in exact equilibrio with the popularity or voluntary esteem he has acquired among the individuals of his band or nation. Their laws like those of all uncivilized Indi-

"The Culinary articles . . . consists of wooden bowls . . . Baskets . . .wooden Spoons"

ans consist of a set of customs which have grown out of their local situations."

•

This discussion of authority is an accurate analysis of Clatsop chieftainship. In contrast to the warlike Plains tribes, the Indians along the Columbia River did not have powerful ruling chiefs. Since they lacked dominant leadership, formal or protracted war was difficult for them to wage, although they made sporadic raids on weaker tribes to capture women or slaves.

Later white invaders—perhaps for their own convenience—either failed to recognize the lack of autocratic social organization among the Indians of the West or chose not to do so. When Indian lands were being confiscated, the signature of an "acknowledged chief" of the tribe on the treaty was considered sufficient authority for the seizure of a vast domain.

Train oil is extracted from whale blubber, but the term is frequently applied to oil from any fish or sea mammal.

20 January 1806.
[LEWIS]

"The Indians who visited us today understood us sufficiently to inform us that the whites did not barter for the pounded fish. . . . The native roots which furnish a considerable proportion of the subsistence of the indians in our neighbourhood are those of a specicies of Thistle, fern, and rush; the Liquorice, and a small celindric root the top of which I have not yet seen, this last resembles the sweet pittatoe very much in it's flavor and consistency."

21 January 1806.

[L E W I S]

"The root of the thistle, called by the natives *Shan-ne-tah-que* is [a] perpendicular fusiform and possesses from two to four radicles; it is from 9 to 15 Inc[h]es in length and about the size [of] a mans thumb; the rhind somewhat rough and of a brown colour. . . . when prepared for uce . . . it becomes black, and is more shugary than any f[r]uit or root that I have met with in uce among the natives."

•

The edible thistle, *Cirsium edule*, is the tallest of the thistles of this area, and in rich soil can reach a height of ten feet. The leaves and flower heads are woolly, the bloom light purple, and the flower heads droop downward, a characteristic that helps identify the plant. It is no longer abundant.

22 January 1806.

[L E W I S]

"There are three species of fern in this neighborhood the root of one which the nat[i]ves eat; this grows very abundant in the open uplands and praries where the latter . . . consist of deep loose rich black lome. the root is horizontal sometimes a little deverging or obliquely descending, frequently dividing itself as it procedes into two equal branches and shooting up a number of stems. . . . the center of the root is divided into two equal parts by a strong flat & white ligament like a piece of thin tape on either side . . .

there is a white substance which when the root is roasted in the embers is much like wheat dough."

•

The bracken fern, *Pteridium aquilinum*, is as common to the west of the mountains as the sagebrush is to the east. The young "fiddleneck" shoots were gathered in the spring for greens by both Indians and pioneers. The bracken is one of the most beautiful ferns, often unappreciated because it is so common.

23 January 1806.

[L E W I S]

"dispatched Howard and Warner to the Camp of the Salt-make[r]s for a supply of salt. The men of the garison are still busily dressing Elk's skins for cloathing, they find great difficulty for the want of branes; we have not soap to supply the deficiency, nor can we procure ashes to make the lye; none of the pines which we use for fuel affords any ashes; extrawdinary as it may seem, the greene wood is consoomed without leaving the residium of a particle of ashes. The root of the rush used by the natives is a sollid bulb about one inch in length and usually as thick as a man's thumb. . . . the pulp is white and brittle. . . . this root is reather insipid in point of flavour, it grows in greatest abundance along the sea coast in sandy grounds."

[C L A R K]

"The instruments used by the nativs in digging their roots is a Strong Stick of three feet and a

"a specicies of Thistle"

*"species of fern . . . the
root of one which the
nat[i]ves eat"*

half long Sharpened at the lower end and its upper inserted into part of an Elks or buck's horn which Serves as a handle; standing transvirsely in the stick."

•

Brain tissue was one of the necessary ingredients in tanning. Lye, had it been available, could have been used for making soap as a substitute.

The "rush" was *Equisetum*, a diminished relict of the giant trees that flourished during the Carboniferous period, long before the age of mammals. This plant bursts in great abundance from the damp soil early in the spring. First to emerge are the reproductive stems, which may be eaten raw like celery or boiled like greens. Later the sterile fronds emerge, growing a tall spire encircled by rows of wispy leaves resembling long pine needles, after which the roots may be dug. The sterile stems are overlain with silica and may be used for polishing, for which reason the plant is sometimes called "scouring rush."

Swan, writing in the 1850s, states: "The root of a species of rush [*E. telmateia*], found on the seashore, of the size of a walnut, is eaten either raw or baked; its taste raw is similar to the Jerusalem artichokes, and baked resembles a mealy potato" (*Northwest Coast*, 88).

24 January 1806.
[LEWIS]
"The Indians witnissed Drewyer's shooting some . . . Elk, which has given them a very exalted opinion of us as marksmen and the superior excellence of our rifles compared with their guns; this may probably be of service to us, as it will deter them from any acts of hostility if they have ever meditated any such. My Air-gun also astonishes them very much; they cannot comprehend it's shooting so often and without powder; and think that it is great *medicine*. . . . the most valuable of all their roots is foreign to this neighbourhood I mean the *Wappetoe*, or the bulb of the Sagitifolia or common arrow head, which grows in great abundance in the marshey grounds of that beatifull and firtile valley on the Columbia commencing just above the entrance of Quicksand River, and extending downwards for about 70 miles. this bulb forms a principal article of traffic between the inhabitants of the valley and those of this neighbourhood or sea coast."

•

A gun and a rifle have this difference: the gun has a smooth bore like a shotgun, while the rifle has spiral grooves within the barrel that cause the bullet to spin and stabilize its flight. It is much more accurate than a gun, which shoots a round lead slug like a small marble. A musket is a long-barreled gun. The air gun was an impractical weapon but a great curiosity to all the Indians. It had a reservoir that by vigorous pumping could be raised to an air pressure of over a thousand pounds per square inch. The air could be released in bursts, propelling several successive missiles through the barrel.

"The instrument used by the nativs in digging their roots is a Strong Stick"
Sketch from the journals, and digging stick handle from the Multnomah village site.

25 January 1806.
[LEWIS]
"Commowooll and the Clatsops departed early this morning. . . . In the evening Collins one of the Saltmakers returned and reported that they had mad[e] about one bushel of salt & that himself and two others had hunted from the salt camp for five days without killing any thing and they had been obliged to subsist on some whale which they procured from the natives. I have lately learned that the natives whome I have heretofore named as distinct nations, living on the sea coast s.e. of the Killamucks, are only bands of that numerous nation, which continues to extend itself much further on the coast than I have enumerated them, but of the particular appellations of those bands I have not yet been enabled to inform myself."

Among the tribes recognized as living south of the Tillamooks were the Siletz, Yaquina, Alsea, Siuslaw, lower Umpqua, and Coos.

26 January 1806.
[LEWIS]
"Werner and Howard who were sent for salt on the 23d. have not yet returned, we are apprehensive that they have missed their way; neither of them are very good woodsmen, and this thick heavy timbered pine country added to the constant cloudy weather makes it difficult for even a good woodsman to steer for any considerable distance the course he wishes. The Shallon or deep purple berry [see 8 February 1806] is in form much like the huckkleberry and terminates

189

"The root of the rush . . . is a sollid bulb"
Equisetum. Left, young flowering stalk. Right, root stock showing bulbs.

bluntly with a kind of cap or cover at the end like that fruit; they are attached separately to the sides of the boughs of the shrub by a very short stem hanging underneath the same and are frequently placed very near each other on the same bough; it is a full bearer."

[CLARK]

"the nativs either eat these berries ripe immediately from the bushes, or dryed in the Sun or by means of the Sweating Kiln; verry frequently they pound them and bake them in large loaves of 10 or 15 pounds weight; this bread keeps verry well dureing one Season and retains the moist

"My Air-gun . . . astonishes them very much"

jouicies of the frute Much better than by any other method of preservation. The bread is broken and stured [stirred] in cold water untill it be sufficiently thick and then eaten, in this way the nativ's most generally use it."

•

The "Shallon" was the salal, *Gaultheria shallon*, one of our most beautiful shrubs. It thrives in cool coastal country, often forming impenetrable thickets. The plant's leaves are thick and glossy, the flowers strung like little bells along the stems. A common perch for the plant is on top of a decayed stump or log. Nowadays the berries are seldom gathered except by birds and squirrels.

The salal fruit was not baked, as Clark says, but simply dried and pressed into cakes (see Gunther, *Ethnobotany*, 43).

27 January 1806.

[CLARK]

"This morning Collins Set out to the Saltmakers[.] Shannon returned and reported that himself and party had killed 10 Elk. . . . two of those . . . at the distance of 9 miles from this place near the top of a mountain . . . the rout . . . at least 5 miles by land thro' a countrey almost inexcessable, from the fallen timber brush, and Sink holes, which were now disguised by the Snow; we therefore concluded to relinquish those two Elks for the present, and ordered every man who could be speared from the Fort to go early in the morning in Serch of the other eight, which is at no great distance from the *Ne tul* [Lewis and Clark] river, on which we are. Goudrich has recovered from the louis veneri which he contracted from a amorous contact with a chinnook damsel. . . . I cannot lern that the Indians have any Simples sovereign specifics in the cure of this disease; indeed I doubt verry much whether any of them have any means of effecting a perfect cure. . . . Notwithstanding that this disorder does exist among the indians on the Columbia yet it is witnessed in but fiew individuals. . . . The berry which the nativs call *Sol me* is the production of a plant about the Size and much the Shape of that common to the atlantic States which produces the berry commonly called the *Sollomons Seal berry*. . . . the berry when grown and unripe is not Specked as the [eastern] Solomon's Seal berry is. . . . the *Sol me* grows in the woodlands amonge the moss . . . and is an annual plant to all appearance."

•

The berry called "solme" by the Indians was the wild cranberry, *Vaccinium oxycoccos*, not the false solomon seal, *Smilacina*, species.

28 January 1806.
[LEWIS]

"Howard and Werner returned with a supply of salt. . . . they inform us that the salt makers are still much straitened for provision . . . and that there are no Elk in their neighbourhood. . . . The light brown berry, is the fruit of a tree about the size shape and appearance . . . [of] the wild crab apple. . . . The wood of this tree is excessively hard when seasoned. the natives make great uce of it to form their wedges with which they split their boards . . . for the purpose of building houses. These wedges they also employ in splitting their fire-wood and in hollowing out their ca-

noes. I have seen the natives drive the wedges of this wood into solid dry pine which it cleft without fracturing or injuring the wedg[e] in the smallest degree. . . . the natives also have wedges made of the beams of the Elk's horns which appear to answer extremely well."

•

The western crabapple, *Pyrus fusca*, grows up to thirty feet high (but usually less) in thickets along the coast. The flowers are white and sweet scented, the fruit is yellow turning to purple, oblong, one-half to three-quarters of an inch long. The Indians were very fond of the fruit, and enriched it with oil or grease. The bark was prized by men of the expedition, who chewed it as a substitute for tobacco.

A few wooden wedges have been found along the Columbia, preserved by their constant immersion in mud or water. Antler wedges occur in great numbers in old village sites, as well as slabs of scoria and sandstone on which they were ground to shape. Sometimes wedges were made from bone rather than antler.

For driving wedges a bottle-shaped stone was used; it was wielded like a rubber stamp, not like a mallet. Hafted mauls were unknown. The girdled stones found in great numbers on western rivers are weights for fish nets, not hammer stones fitted with a handle.

"berry commonly called the Sollomon Seal*"*
False Solomons seal, flower and fruit.

29 *January 1806.*
[L E W I S]

"Nothing worthy of notice occurred today. our fare is the flesh of lean elk boiled with pure water, and a little salt. the whale blubber . . . is now exhausted. on this food I do not feel strong, but enjoy the most perfect health; a keen appe-tite supplys in a great degree the want of more luxurious sauses or dishes, and still renders my ordinary meals not uninteresting to me, for I find myself sometimes enquiring of the cook whether dinner or breakfast is ready."

Crabapple, flower and fruit.

"the natives make great uce of it [wood of the western crabapple] *to form their wedges"*
Wood wedge from the Columbia River.

30 January 1806.
[LEWIS]

"The dress of the Clatsops and others in this neighbourhood differs but little from that discribed of the skillutes; they never wear leggins or mockersons. . . . they wear a hat of a conic figure without a brim confined on the head by means of a stri[n]g. . . . these hats are made of the bark of cedar and beargrass. . . . on these hats they work various figures of different colours. . . . these figures are faint representations of whales the canoes and the harpoonneers striking them. sometimes squares diamonds triangles &c. The form of a knife which seems to be preferred by these people is a double edged and double pointed daggar; the handle being in the middle, and the blades of unequal lengths. . . . these knives they carry with them habitually and most usually in the hand."

•

Basket hats with the whale motif were not made on the Columbia River, being endemic to the Northwest Coast from Cape Flattery northward. These hats, beautifully made and sometimes richly painted, were a valuable trade item. Alexander Ross wrote: "All classes wear the *cheapool*, or hat, which is made of a tough, strong kind of grass, and is of so close a texture as to be waterproof. The crown is of a conic form, terminating generally in a point at the top, and the rim so very broad as to screen the shoulders from the rain. The *cheapool* is checkered or diversified with the rude figures of different animals, particularly the dog and deer, not painted but ingeniously interwoven" (*Adventures of the First Settlers*, 96–97).

The basket hats were sturdy as well as colorful. On 8 August 1806, while Lewis was trying to overtake Clark on the Missouri, he saw the remains of a camp on shore and there Sergeant Ordway "found at this place a part of a Chinnook hat which my men recognized as the hat of Gibson."

31 January 1806.
[LEWIS]

"Joseph Fields arrived this evening . . . he had been hunting . . . for the last five days . . . and had been unsuccessfull untill yesterday evening when he had fortunately killed two Elk. . . . Charbono found a bird dead lying near the fort this morning. . . . I immediately recognized it to be of the same kind of that which I had seen in the Rocky mountains on the morning of the 20th. of September last. this is a beatifull little bird. . . . and I beleive is rare even in this country, or at least this is the second time only that I have seen it."

•

Lewis described the Pacific varied thrush, *Ixoreus naevius*, in great detail. Sometimes called the Alaskan robin, it is a handsome winter visitor to the lowlands; by early May it has disappeared from western valleys to nest in the coniferous forests. It is robin-size, with an eye stripe and wing bars of orange and a distinctive dark crescent on its breast. The mountain hiker knows its song as a part of the enchantment of the wilderness—a single, eerie, quavering note followed after a pause by another of lower or higher pitch.

1 February 1806.
[LEWIS]

"the natives inhabiting the lower portion of the Columbia River make their canoes remarkably neat light and well adapted for riding high waves.

I have seen the natives . . . riding waves in these canoes with safety and apparently without concern where I should have thought it impossible for any vessel of the same size to [have] lived a minute. they are built of white cedar. . . . cut out of a solid stick of timber, the gunwals at the upper edge foald over outwards and . . . stand horrizontally forming a kind of rim to the canoe to prevent the water beating into it. they are all furnished with more or less crossbars in proportion to the size of the canoe. these bars are round sticks about half the size of a man's arm, which are incerted through holes made in either side of the canoe just below the rim of the gunwall and are further secured with strings of waytape; these crossbars serve to lift and manage the canoe on land. when the natives land they invariabley take their canoes on shore. . . . some of the large canoes are upwards of 50 feet long and will carry from 8 to 10 thousand lbs. or from 20 to thirty persons and some of them . . . are waxed painted and ornimented with curious images at bough and Stern; these images sometimes rise to the hight of five feet, the pedestals on which these immages are fixed are sometimes cut out of the solid stick with the canoe, and the imagary is formed of seperate small pieces of timber firmly united with tenants [tenons] and mo[r]tices without the assistance of a single spike of any kind. one sets in the stern and steers with a paddle the others set by pears and paddle over the gunwall next to them, they all set on their feet. their paddles are of a uniform shape. . . . They have but few axes among them, and the only tool usually imployed in felling the trees or forming the canoe . . . is a chissel. . . . with sometimes a large block of wood for a handle; they grasp the chissel just below the block with the right hand while the left they take hold of the top of the block and strike backward against the wood with the edge of the chissel."

•

The best canoes were made by the Nootka and other tribes on Vancouver Island and above. The manufacture of a canoe with metal tools is difficult enough; with only stone and shell utensils the task would seem insurmountable. Some forty-seven years after Lewis and Clark's visit, James Swan saw and described the process: "A suitable tree is first selected, which in all cases is the cedar, and then cut down. This job was formerly a formidable one, as the tree was chipped around with stone chisels, after the fashion adopted by beavers, and looks as if gnawed off. At present, however, they understand the use of the axe, and many are expert choppers. When the tree is down, it is first stripped of its bark, then cut off into the desired length, and the upper part split off with little wedges, till it is reduced to about two thirds of the original height of the log. The bow and stern are then chopped into rough shape, and enough cut out of the inside to lighten it so that it can be easily turned. When all is ready, the log is turned bottom up, and the Indian goes to work to fashion it out. This

he does with no instrument of measurement but his eye, and so correct is that, that when he has done his hewing no one could detect the least defect. When the outside is formed and rough-hewn, the log is again turned, and the inside cut out with the axe. This operation was formerly done by fire, but the process was slow and tedious. During the chopping the Indian frequently ascertains the thickness of the sides by placing one hand on the outside and the other on the inside. The canoe is now again turned bottom up, and the whole smoothed off with a peculiar-shaped chisel, used something after the manner of a cooper's adze. This is a very tiresome job, and takes a long time. Then the inside is finished, and the canoe now has to be stretched into shape. It is first nearly filled with water, into which hot stones are thrown, and a fire at the same time of bark is built outside. This in a short time renders the wood so supple that the center can be spread open at the top from six inches to a foot. This is kept in place by sticks or stretchers, similar to the method of a boat's thwarts. The ends of these stretchers are fastened by means of withes made from the taper ends of cedar limbs, twisted and used instead of cords. When all is finished, the water is emptied out, and then the stem and head-pieces are put on[.] These are carved from separate sticks, and are fastened on by means of withes and wooden pegs or treenails. After the inside is finished to the satisfaction of the maker, the canoe is again turned, and the charred part, occasioned by the bark fire, is

"their paddles are of a uniform shape"
Clark's sketch of a paddle, top, and an effigy four inches long carved from
antler, bottom, found on the Shoto village site.

rubbed with stones to make the bottom as smooth as possible, when the whole outside is painted over with a black mixture of burned rushes and whale oil. The edges all around are studded with little shells, which are the valve joint of the common snail. This description I give is of the making of a canoe near my house, and I saw the progress every day, from the time the tree was cut down till the canoe was finished. This was a medium sized canoe, and took three months to finish it" (*Northwest Coast*, 80–82).

In 1811 Gabriel Franchère observed that "Their oars, or paddles, are of ash and are about five feet long; the top end has a grip very much like the top of a crutch. The blade is cut in a half-moon shape, having two sharp points (*Adventures at Astoria*, 113–14).

2 February 1806.
[L E W I S]
"Not any occurrence today worthy of notice; but all are pleased, that one month of the time which binds us to Fort Clatsop and which separates us from our friends has now elapsed. . . . These people are excessively fond of their games of risk and bet freely every species of property of which they are possessed."

•

The bone or hand game was universal with the Indians and is still played on the reservations; for a detailed description, *see* 18 April 1806.

3 February 1806.

[LEWIS]

"late in the evening the four men who had been sent to assist the saltmakers in transporting meat . . . returned, and brought with them all the salt which had been made, consisting of about one busshel only. with the means we have of boiling the salt water we find it a very tedious opperation . . . notwithwstanding we keep the kettles boiling day and night."

4 February 1806.

[LEWIS]

"the Elk are in much better order in the point near the praries [Clatsop Plains] than they are in the woody country arround us or up the Netul [Lewis and Clark]. in the praries they feed on grass and rushes, considerable quantities of which are yet green and succule[n]t. in the woody country their food is huckle berry bushes, fern, and an evergreen shrub which resembles the lorel in some measure; the last constitutes the greater part of their food and grows abundantly through all the timbered country, particularly the hillsides and more broken parts of it."

•

Elk do browse on salal, especially in winter (*see* 8 February 1806), but it is not their principal food.

"the only tool usually imployed . . . is a chissel"
Stone adze blade and antler handle found on Sauvie Island.

5 *February 1806.*

[LEWIS]

"Late this evening one of the hunters fired his gun over the swamp of the Netul [Lewis and Clark] opposite to the fort and hooped. I sent Sergt. Gass and a party over; the tide being in, they took advantage of a little creek which makes up in that direction nearly to the highlands [probably Green Slough], and in their way fortunately recovered our Indian Canoe, so long lost and much lamented. The Hunter proved to be Reubin Fields, who reported that he had killed six Elk on the East side of the Netul a little above us; and that yesterday he had heard Shannon and Labuishe fire six or seven shots after he had seperated from them and supposed that they had also killed several Elk. Filds brought with him a phesant which differed but little from those common to the Atlantic States; it's brown is reather brighter and more of a redish tint. it has eighteen feathers in the tale of about six inches in length. this bird is also booted as low as the toes."

•

Lewis and Clark were the first to describe the ruffed grouse, *Bonasa umbellus sabini*, a brown, strikingly marked resident of the coast and the western Cascades. The male announces his domination of his selected territory with a pulsating throb that intensifies the mystery of the forest. In mating season the beat gradually increases in tempo until it becomes a muffled roar.

6 *February 1806.*

[LEWIS]

"Sent Sergts. Gass and Ordway this morning with R. Fields and a party of men to bring in the Elk which Fields had killed. Late in the evening Sergt. Pryor returned with the flesh of about 2 Elk and 4 skins the Indians having purloined the ballance of seven Elk which Drewyer killed the other day. I find that there are 2 vilages of Indians living on the N. side of the Columbia near the Marshey Islands [Marsh, Woody, Welch, etc.] who call themselves Wach-ki-a-cum. These I have her[e]tofore considered as Cath-láh-máhs. they speak the same language and are the same in every other rispect."

7 *February 1806.*

[LEWIS]

"This evening Sergt. Ordway and Wiser returned with a part of the meat which R. Fields had killed; the ballance of the party with Sergt. Gass remained in order to bring the ballance of the meat to the river at a point agreed on where the canoe is to meat them again tomorrow morning. This evening we had what I call an excellent supper it consisted of a marrowbone a piece and a brisket of boiled Elk that had the appearance of a little fat on it. this for Fort Clatsop is living in high stile. In this neighbourhood I observe the honeysuckle common in our country. I first met with it on the waters of the Kooskooske near the Chopunnish nation, and again below the grand rapids In the Columbian Valley on tide-water.

"I observe the honeysuckle"

The Elder also common to our country grows in great abundance in the rich woodlands on this side of the rocky Mountains; tho' it differs here in the colour of it's berry, this being of a pale sky blue while that of the U'States is a deep perple. . . . The small pox has distroyed a great number of the natives in this quarter. it prevailed about 4 years since among the Clatsops and destroy[ed] several hundred of them, four of their chiefs fell victyms to it's ravages. those Clatsops are deposited in their canoes on the bay a few miles below us. I think the late ravages of the small pox may well account for the number of remains of vilages which we find deserted on the river and Sea coast in this quarter."

•

The honeysuckle was the common orange variety, *Lonicera ciliosa*. Some tribes used the bark for medicinal purposes. According to the ethnobotanist Erna Gunther, "It is remarkable that in every tribe the plant is associated with the crow" (*Ethnobotany*, 48).

The elder was *Sambucus coerulea*, the com-

*"The Elder . . . grows
in great abundance"*
Blue elderberry.

mon blue elderberry, gathered in great quantities by the Indians, and later by the whites for pies and wine. Another elderberry, *S. arborescens*, is a glowing red when ripe. The berries are reported to be poisonous and we have never known them to be eaten, but Gunther writes that all the Indians gathered and ate them. Elderberries are members of the honeysuckle family (*see* Gunther, *Ethnobotany*, 47).

Smallpox epidemics probably occurred on the lower Columbia in 1775 and 1801 (*see* 3 April 1806; and Boyd, "Demographic History," 137–

38). A disastrous epidemic broke out between 1830 and 1835 among the Indians of the lower Columbia Valley and its branches; some records indicate that their decimation was almost total. The Rev. Samuel Parker wrote in 1835: "I have found the Indian population in the lower country, that is, below the falls of the Columbia, far less than I had expected, or what it was when Lewis and Clark made their tour. Since the year 1829 probably seven-eights, if not as Doct. Mc-Laughlin believes, nine-tenths, have been swept away by disease, principally by fever and ague.

. . . So many and so sudden were the deaths which occurred, that the shores were strewed with the unburied dead. Whole and large villages were depopulated; and some entire tribes disappeared, the few remaining persons, if there were any, uniting themselves with other tribes" (*Journal of an Exploring Tour*, 192).

Even yet, along the shores of the Columbia, the annual spring freshets occasionally erode from the banks a fragmentary skeleton or two, victims of the pestilence who lay where they died to be covered by silt from floods of long ago. Whites as well as Indians were stricken, but, with better care and more resistance, almost all the whites recovered. The prevailing opinion is that the sickness was malaria, although others contend it was a virulent form of influenza (*see* Boyd, "Demographic History," 139; and Cook, "Epidemic of 1830–1833," 303–26).

8 February 1806.
[CLARK]

"late in the evening Serjt. Pryor returned with Shannon Labieshe his party down the Netul [Lewis and Clark]. they brought with them the flesh of 4 Elk which those two hunters had killed. we have both Dined and suped on Elks tongues and marrowbones, a great Luxury for Fort Clatsop. The *Shallon* is a production of shrub which I have taken heretofore to be a species of Loral and mentioned as abounding in this neighbourhood, and that the Elk feed much on its leaves. it generally rises to the hight of 3 feet, and not un-

usially attain to that of 5 feet. . . . This shrub is a evergreen. the frute is a deep purple berry about the size of a buck shot or common black cherry."

•

Some authors credit Lewis and Clark with the discovery of *G. shallon*, but that honor belongs to Archibald Menzies, the naturalist with Vancouver's exploring expedition in 1792. David Douglas wrote on 8 April 1825: "On stepping on the shore *Gaultheria Shallon* was the first plant I took in my hands. So pleased was I that I could scarcely see anything but it. Mr. Menzies correctly observes that it grows under thick pine-forests in great luxuriance and would make a valuable addition to our gardens" (*Journal*, 102).

9 February 1806.
[CLARK]

"This morning Collins and Wiser set out on a hunting excurtion; in the evening Drewyer returned; had Killed nothing but one Beaver. he saw one black Bear, which is the only one which has been seen in the neighbourhood since our arrival. the Indians inform us that they are abundant but are now in their holes. . . . The stem of the Black Alder is simple branching and defuse. the bark is smoth of a light colour with white coloured spredding spots or blotches, resembling that of beech. the leaf is procisely that of the common alder of the United States or Virginia."

•

"*The* Shal lon [or] . . . *deep purple berry*"
Sketch from the journals, top; shrub in blossom, middle; and in fruit, bottom.

The red alder (Lewis called it black; others have named it Oregon alder), *Alnus rubra* and its close relative, the Sitka alder *A. sinuata*, inhabit North Pacific coastal regions from California to Alaska. Every new opening in the forest is quickly covered with a carpet of alder seedlings sprouting thick as wheat. Old logging roads, after being abandoned for years, may be traced over the hillsides by lanes of dense alder growth. The red alder's mottled, ashy-gray or whitish bark would seem to belie its name until a shallow scratch of the surface reveals its underlying red-brown color. Clark's mention of "white coloured spredding . . . blotches" may refer as much to lichens, *Ochrolechia parella* and *Graphis scripta*, as to the natural color of the bark.

After cedar, alder was the most important wood to the Indians. From the bark they made a reddish dye to color basketry, or boiled it down to a decoction for curing sundry ills. Alder makes excellent firewood even when green. But its greatest use was for carving bowls, spoons, and platters; the nearly grainless wood acquires a beautiful glossy patina from use.

10 February 1806.
[Lewis]

"Drewyer visited his traps today but caught no beaver. Collins and Wiser returned had killed no Elk. Willard arrived late in the evening from the Saltworks, had cut his knee very badly with his tommahawk. He had killed four Elk not far from the Salt works the day before yesterday, which he had butch[er]ed and took a part of the meat to camp. but haveing cut his knee was unable to be longer uceful at the works and had returned. he informed us that Bratton was very unwell, and that Gibson was so sick that he could not set up or walk alone and had desired him to ask us to have him brought to the Fort. Coalter also returned this evening. continue the operation of drying our meat. There is a tree common to the Columbia river below the entrance of cataract [Klickitat] river which in it's appearance when divested of it's foliage, much resembles the white ash; the appearance of the wood and bark is also that of the ash. . . . the leaf 8 inches in length and 12 in bredth. . . . In the same part of the country there is also another growth which resembles the white maple in it's appearance, only it is by no means as large; seldom being more than from 6 to 9 inches in diameter, and from 15 to 20 feet high, they frequently grow in clusters as if from the same bed of roots spreading and leaning outwards."

•

The Oregon bigleaf maple, *Acer macrophyllum*, is one of the state's most splendid trees, much branched, ascending some fifty to seventy feet, though it may reach higher. It seldom grows in pure stands. The leaf is large, a foot or more wide; the seed is winged. Lewis and Clark first saw this tree on 30 October 1805, near what was later called Wind River.

The vine maple, *Acer circinatum*, is more a shrub than a tree. It grows prostrate and ex-

"the leaf 8 inches in length and 12 in bredth"
Oregon bigleaf maple.

tremely crooked, and quickly covers logged-over lands outside the range of alder. In the fall the leaves turn a brilliant scarlet, the most spectacular of all western colors.

Both these maples were new to science. The type specimens collected by Lewis near the Cascades are in the Lewis and Clark Herbarium at the Academy of Natural Sciences in Philadelphia.

11 February 1806.
[L E W I S]

"sent Sergt. Pryor with a party of four men to bring Gibson to the fort. also sent Colter and Wiser to the Salt works to carry on the business with Joseph Fields; as Bratton had been sick we desired him to return to the Fort also if he thought proper. . . . There is a shrub which grows commonly in this neighborhood which is precisely the same with that in Virginia sometimes called the quill-wood. also another near the water in somewhat moist grounds & rises to the hight of 5 or 6 feet with a large, peteolate spreading, plane, crenate and somewhat woolly leaf like the rose raspberry. it is much branched the bar of a redish brown colour and is covered with a number of short hooked thorns which renders it extreemly disagreeable to pass among; it dose no[t] cast it's foliage untill about the 1st. of December. . . . The[re] is also found in this neighbourhood an evergreen shrub which . . . rises to the hight of from four to five feet, the stem simple branching. . . . the bark is of a redish dark brown. . . . the fruit a small deep perple berry like the common huckleberry of a pleasent flavor. the natives eat this berry when ripe but seldom collect it in such quantities as to dry it for winter uce."

•

The shrub with the hooked thorns was probably the wild blackcap raspberry, *Rubus leucodermis*. The description quite nicely fits the evergreen blackberry, but this unlovely intruder, now covering vast areas of rich western bottom lands with impenetrable thickets, post-dates Lewis and Clark. The one with the purple berry is the coast or evergreen huckleberry, *Vaccinium ovatum*, a plant that in some years yields an extravagant harvest. The branches of this attractive shrub are gathered for floristry greens. Swan wrote of it: "The cranberry, which is very plentiful, and forms quite an article of traffic between the whites and Indians, is next in season, and is followed by a species of whortleberry, called by the Indians shotberries, which last till December, when the rains beat the fruit off the bushes. The berries grow in clusters. The leaf is small, of oval shape, with finely serrated edges. It is also an excellent berry, and, if kept dry and cool, can be preserved fresh for several months. It is, how-

ever, usually dried by the Indians, and eaten early in spring, before the other berries begin to ripen" (*Northwest Coast*, 89).

The specimen collected by Lewis and Clark at Fort Clatsop is still in the Lewis and Clark herbarium at the Academy of Natural Sciences.

12 February 1806.

[L E W I S]

"This morning we were visited by a Clatsop man who brought with him three dogs as a remuneration for the Elk which himself and nation had stolen from us some little time since, however the dogs took the alarm and ran off; we suffered him to remain in the fort all night. There are two species of ever green shrubs which I first met with at the grand rappids of the Columbia and which I have since found in this neighbourhood also; they grow in rich dry ground not far usually from some watercourse. the roots of both species are creeping and celindric. the stem of the 1st. is from a foot to 18 inches high and as large as a goosqu[i]ll. . . . each point of their crenate margins of the leaves armed with a subulate thorn or spine. . . . The stem of the 2nd is . . . abo[u]t the same size as the former, joined and unbranched."

•

The two species of Oregon grape are *Mahonia aquifolium* and *M. nervosa*. The Indians gathered the pungent berries (which are not grapes, but are kin to the barberry) for food; from the roots they made a handsome yellow dye and a vil-

"the fruit is a small deep perple berry" Coast or evergreen huckelberry.

lainous medicine. The Oregon grape is the state flower of Oregon.

13 February 1806.
[CLARK]

"The Clatsops left us this morning. . . . yesterday we completed the opperation of drying the meat, and think we have a sufficient stock to last us this month. the Indians inform us that we shall have great abundance of small fish in March which from the discription must be the Herring [*see* 24 February 1806]. Those people have also informed us that one Moore who sometimes touches at this place and trades with the nativs of this coast, had on board his ship 3 Cows. . . . I think this (if those cows were not Coats [Goats]) strong circumstantial proof that their is a settlement of white persons at Nootka Sound or some place to the NW of us on the coast."

[LEWIS]

"There is a species of bryer which is common in this neighbourhood of a green colour which grows most abundant in the rich dry lands. . . . the fruit is a berry . . . much esteemed by the natives but is not dryed for winter consumption. . . . There are also two species of firn which are common to this country beside that formerly discribed [bracken] of which the natives eat the roots."

"there are two species of ever green shrubs"
Oregon grape, *Mahonia aquifolium*, left, and *M. nervosa*.

•

The berry was the wild blackberry, *Rubus macropetalus*. It is not to be confused with the plebeian evergreen blackberry of commerce and restaurant pies, by comparison a drab and insipid fruit.

The ferns were the sword fern, *Polystichum munitum*, and the deer fern, *Blechnum spicant*. The root of the sword fern was baked or boiled for food while the leaves were used in making mattresses, lining baking pits, and covering drying racks. The deer fern seems to have been used as food only in an emergency.

Oregon grape type specimen collected by Lewis at the Cascades.

"a berry . . . much esteemed by the Indians"
Wild blackberry

14 February 1806.
[L E W I S]

"We are very uneasy with rispect to our sick men at the salt works. Sergt. Pryor and party have not yet returned nor can we conceive what causes their delay. Drewyer visited his traps today and caught a very fine fat beaver on which we feasted this evening. on the 11th. inst. Capt. Clark completed a map of the country through which we have been passing from Fort Mandan to this place."

•

A copy of this testimonial to Clark's cartographic and geographic skill is included in the atlas of the Thwaites edition of the original journals. From celestial observations, daily courses and sketches, information from the natives, and skillful reasoning, all the main watercourses and mountains were laid down, as well as rapids, woodlands, Indian villages, and the camping places of the party. This was the first map drawn of a vast part of the present western United States, and became a source for many subsequent maps.

The beaver, *Castor canadensis*, is an irrevocable part of western history. Until about 1840 it was the most valuable resource of the wilderness, but was trapped so extensively that its numbers were vastly reduced. The slightly barbed hairs of its pelt are ideal for felting, and for many years in

*"There are . . . two species of fern . . . of which
the natives eat the roots"*
Sword fern, right, and deer fern

the nineteenth century no gentleman was well dressed without a beaver hat. Slow and clumsy on land, in water the beaver is a powerful swimmer. Its powerful jaws and sharp incisors enable it to fall large trees, cut them up, and drag the logs to the water, where it uses them for building and for food. It eats the bark and the tender twigs, as well as roots, leaves, and grass. The beaver lodge is made of branches, peeled logs, and mud; sometimes it is merely a burrow in the bank. To discourage enemies, the entrance is always under water, and a tunnel leads to the living quarters above water level. Beaver dams contributed to water control and helped prevent erosion, while the artificial pools the beavers formed gradually filled with humus over the centuries, creating rich soil that became known as beaver-dam land.

15 February 1806.
[L E W I S]

"Drewyer and Whitehouse set out this morning on a hunting excurtion towards the praries of Point Adams. . . . about 3 P.M. Bratton arrived from the salt works and informed us that Sergt. Pryor and party were on their way with Gibson who is so much reduced that he cannot stand alone and that they are obliged to carry him on a litter. . . . the s.w. winds are frequently very violent on the coast when we are but little sensible of them at Fort Clatsop. in consequence of the lofty and thickly timbered fir country which surrounds us. . . . after dark Sergt. Pryor arrived with Gibson. we are much pleased in finding him by no means as ill as we had expected. we do no[t] conceive him in danger by any means, tho' he has yet a fever and is much reduced. We beleive his disorder to have orriginated in a violent cold. . . . We gave him broken dozes of diluted nitre and made him drink plentifully of sage tea, had his feet bathed in warm water and at 9 P.M. gave him 35 drops of laudanum. . . . The horse is confined principally to the nations inhabiting the great plains of Columbia. . . . the Sosone or snake Indians, the Chopunnish, Sokulks, Cutssahnims, Chymnapums, E[c]helutes & Chilluckkittequaws. all of whom enjoy the bennefit of that docile, generous and valuable anamal the horse, and all of them except the three last have immence numbers of them. . . . an eligant horse may be purchased of the natives . . . for a few beads or other paltry trinkets which in the U'-States would not cost more than one or two dollars. This abundance and cheapness of horses will be extremely advantageous to those who may hereafter attemp[t] the fir trade."

•

The horse was the most abundant of animals on the quaternary plains a few million years ago. With its eyes set far up on its head, it could see predators while it was feeding, and—as anyone knows who has ridden one—it has an astonishing ability to make a quick start when alarmed. It was able to survive the change from browsing to grazing as the forests and brush-covered plains became grasslands after periods of geological up-heaval. The horse disappeared some seven thousand years ago from the North American continent, not to return until it was reintroduced by the Spaniards. The Indians of the prairies obtained the horse about 1720, thereby dramatically changing their culture.

Lewis's prediction of cheap horses for the fur traders proved unfounded, because the Indians quickly learned their value and charged what the traffic would bear.

16 February 1806.
[L E W I S]

"Sent Shannon Labuish and Frazier this morning on a hunting excursion up the Kil-haw-a nak-kie [Youngs] river which discharges itself into the head of the bay. . . . Bratton is still very weak and complains of a pain in the lower part of his back when he moves which I suppose proceeds from dability. I gave him barks [and saltpeter, adds Clark]. Gibson's fever still continues obstenate tho' not very high, I gave him a doze of Dr. Rush's [pills] which in many instances I have found extreemly efficatious in fevers which are in any measure caused by the presence of boil. the nitre has produced a profuse perspiration this evening and the pills operated late at night after which his fever abated almost entirely and he had a good night's rest. The Indian dog is usually small or much more so than the common cur. they are party coloured; black white brown and brindle are the most usual colours. the head is

long and the nose pointed eyes small, ears erect and pointed like those of the wolf, hair short smooth except on the tail where it is as long as that of the curdog and streight. The natives do not eat them nor appear to make any other use of them but in hunting the Elk."

•

The "barks" refer to Peruvian bark or cinchona, a source of quinine. Fifteen pounds of pulverized bark were in the medical supplies. Rush's pills were commonly called "Rush's Thunderbolts" for the speed and violence with which they acted. Fifty dozen were in the medicine chest, each contained fifteen grains of jalap—a potent cathartic—and ten of calomel. They were prescribed for nearly every ailment. Gass wrote: "Captain Clarke gave all the sick a doze of Rush's Pills, to see what effect they would have" (*Journal*, 170).

Dr. Benjamin Rush was a prominent physician in Philadelphia who was one of the signers of the Declaration of Independence. President Jefferson had sent Lewis to take a short medical course from him before the start of the expedition, but Clark seems to have been the favorite doctor on the journey.

17 February 1806.
[L E W I S]

"Collins and Windsor were permitted to hunt today towards the praries in Point Adams with a view to obtain some fresh meat for the sick. . . .

continue the barks with Bratton, and commenced them with Gibson his fever being sufficiently low this morning to permit the use of them. I think therefore that there is no further danger of his recovery. at 2 P.M. Joseph Fields arrived from the Salt works and informed us that they had about 2 Kegs of salt on hand which with what we have at this place we suppose will be sufficient to last us to our deposits of that article on the Missouri. we there[fore] directed a party of six men to go with Fields in the morning in order to bring the salt and kettles to the fort."

•

John Collins was recruited by Lewis in Pittsburgh, from Carlisle Barracks. Like Whitehouse, he assigned the land grant he received after the expedition to Drouillard. Clark writes "dead" after Collins's name in his 1825–28 list. Practically nothing else is known about this valuable member of the party. Others who emerged from obscurity and sank into oblivion were Gibson, Goodrich, Hall, McNeal, Thompson, Labiche, Lepage, Werner, and Windsor.

18 February 1806.
[CLARK]

"we were visited by a Clatsop and seven Chinnooks from whome I purchased a sea otter's skin and two hats made of waytape and silk grass and white cedar bark. they remained untill late in the evening and departed for their village. . . . Whitehouse brought me a roab [robe] which he pur-

chased of the Indians formed of three skins of the *Tiger Cat*, this Cat differs from any which I have ever seen. it is found on the borders of the plains and woody Country lying along the Pacific Ocean. this animale is about the size or reather larger than the wild cat of our countrey and is much the same in form, agility and ferosity. . . . the nativs of this Country make great use of the skins of this cat, to form the robes which they wear; three whole skins is the complement usually employed and sometimes four in each roab."

•

The Oregon bobcat, *Lynx rufus fasciatus*, and the much-maligned coyote between them limited the number and preserved the vigor of the rodent population by consuming the halt, the infected, and the excess. The bobcat has a preference for rocky, open country, and loves to doze in the sun by its den in the rimrocks. It is seldom seen now, for vigorous hunting has nearly obliterated this stealthy predator, to the advantage of the rabbits, mice, squirrels, and gophers.

19 February 1806.
[CLARK]

"Sergt. Ordway set out again with a party to the Salt works by land. in the evening Sergt. Gass returned with the flesh of Eight Elk, and seven skins haveing left one with Shannon and Labiesh who remained over the Netul [Lewis and Clark] to continue the chase. we divided the skins between the messes in order that they might be

"the Tiger Cat . . . *differs from any which I have ever seen"*
Oregon bobcat

prepared for covering the baggage when we set out in the spring. our sick appear to strengthen but slowly I gave Bratten 6 of Scotts pills which did not work him. he is very weak and complains of his back."

•

The party was divided into three "messes," each under a sergeant. Each mess had a set of cooking vessels and a cook. The organization was strictly military, and held to military discipline.

20 February 1806.
[LEWIS]

"This forenoon we were visited by *Tah-cum* a principal Chief of the Chinnooks and 25 of his nation. we had never seen this chief before he is a good looking man of about 50 years of age reather larger in statu[r]e than most of his nation; as he came on a friendly visit we gave himself and party something to eat and plyed them plentifully with smoke. we gave this chief a small medal with which he seemed much gratified. in the evening at sunset we desired them to depart as is our custom and closed our gates. we never suffer parties of such number to remain within the fort all night; for notwithstanding their apparent friendly disposition, their great avarice and hope of plunder might induce them to be treacherous. at all events we determined always to be on our guard as much as the nature of our situation will permit us, and never place ourselves at the mercy of any savages."

21 February 1806.
[LEWIS]

"Visited this morning by 3 Clatsop who remained with us all day; they are great begers; I gave one of them a few nedles with which he appeared much gratifyed. . . . Sergt. Ordway returned with the party from the salt camp which we have now evacuated. they brought with them the salt and eutensils. our stock of salt is now about 20 Gallons; 12 gallons of which we secured in 2 small iron bound kegs and laid by for our voyage. gave Willard and bratton each a doze of Scotts pills; on the former they operated and on the latter they did not. Gibson still continues the barks three times a day and is on the recovery fast."

22 February 1806.
[LEWIS]

"We were visited today by two Clatsop women and two boys who brought a parsel of excellent hats made of Cedar bark and ornamented with beargrass. two of these hats had been made by measures which Capt. Clark and myself had given one of the women some time since with a request to make each of us a hat; they fit us very well, and are in the form we desired them. we purchased all their hats and distributed them among the party. the woodwork and sculpture of these people as well as these hats and their waterproof baskets evince an ingenuity by no means common among the Aborigenes of America. in the evening they returned to their village and Drewyer accompanied them in their canoe in order to get the dogs which the Clatsops have agreed to give us in payment for the Elk they stole from us some weeks since. these women informed us that the small fish began to run which we supposed to be herring from their description. they also informed us that their Chief, Conia or Comowooll, had gone up the Columbia to the valley in order to purchase wappetoe, a part of which he intended trading with us on his return."

23 February 1806.
[LEWIS]

"not anything transpired during this day worthy of particular notice. our sick are all on the recovery, except Sergt. Ordway who is but little wo[r]se and not very ill tho' more so than any of the others. the men have provided themselves very amply with mockersons and leather cloathing, much more so indeed than they ever have since they have been on this voige."

[CLARK]

"The Sea Otter is found only on the sea coast and in the salt water. Those animals which I took to be the sea otter from the Great Falls of the Columbia to the mouth, proves to be the Phosia or Seal which at a little distance has every appearance of the sea otters."

[LEWIS]

"This animal when fully grown is as large as a common mastive dog. . . . the colour is a uniform dark brown and when in good order and season perfectly black and glossey. it is the riches[t] and

I think the most delicious fur in the world at least I cannot form an idea of any more so."

24 February 1806.
[LEWIS]

"This evening we were visited by Commowooll the Clatsop Chief and 12 men women and children of his nation. Drewyer came a passenger in their canoe, and brought with him two dogs. The chief and his party had brought for sail a Sea Otter skin some hats, stergeon and a species of small fish which now begin to run, and are taken in great quantities in the Columbia R. about 40 miles above us [Cowlitz River] by means of the skimming or scooping nets. on this page I have drawn the likeness of them as large as life; it [is] as perfect as I can make it with my pen and will serve to give a general idea of the fish. the rays of the fins are boney but not sharp tho' somewhat pointed. the small fin on the back next to the tail has no rays or bone being a thin membranous pellicle. the fins next to the gills have eleven rays each. those of the abdomen have eight each, those of the pinna-ani are 20 and 2 half formed in front. that of the back has eleven rays. all the fins are of a white colour. the back is a bluish duskey colour and that of the lower part of the sides and belley is of a silvery white. no spots on any part. the first bone of the gills next behi[n]d the eye is of a bluis[h] cast, and the second of a light goald colour nearly white. the puple of the eye is black and the iris of a silver white. the under jaw exceeds the uper; and the mouth opens to great extent, folding like that of the herring. it has no teeth. the abdomen is obtuse and smooth; in this differing from the herring, shad, anchovey &c. of the Malacopterygious Order & Class Clupea, to which however I think it more nearly allyed than to any other altho' it has not their accute and serrate abdomen and the under jaw exceeding the upper. the scales of this little fish are so small and thin that without minute inspection you would suppose they had none. they are filled with roes of a pure white colour and have scarcely any perceptable alimentary duct. I find them best when cooked in the Indian stile, which is by roasting a number of them together on a wooden spit without any previous preperation whatever. they ar so fat they require no additional sauce, and I think them superior to any fish I ever tasted, even more delicate and lussious than the white fish of the lakes which have heretofore formed my standard of excellence among the fishes. I have heard the fresh anchovey much extolled but I hope I shall be pardoned for beleiving this quite as good. the bones are so soft and fine that they form no obstruction in eating this fish."

•

Lewis was the first to describe the eulachon or smelt, *Thaleichthys pacificus*. The description is here taken verbatim from the journals to show the care and detail he took in this important duty. Most of his descriptions of plants, trees, birds, and animals are complete and precise—a re-markable accomplishment for one with only a few months' training, and at a time when there were few professional scientists.

25 February 1806.
[LEWIS]

"It continued to rain and blow so violently that there was no movement of the party today. the Indians left us in the morning on their return to their village. Willard somewhat worse, the other Invalledes on the ricovery. I am mortifyed at not having it in my power to make celestial observations since we have been at Fort Clatsop, but such has been the state of the weather that I have found it utterly impracticable. The Rackoon is found in the woody country on this coast in considerable quantities. the natives take a few of them in snars and deadfalls; tho' appear not to vallue their skins much, and but seldom prepare them for robes."

26 February 1806.
[CLARK]

"This morning we dispatched Drewyer and two men in our indian canoe up the Columbia River to take sturgion and anchovey. . . . we also sent Shields Jo. Fields and Shannon up the Netul to hunt Elk. and directed Ruebin Field and some other men to hunt in the point towards the Praries & Point Adams. thus we hope shortly to replenish our stock of provisions which is now reduced to a mear minnamum. we have three days provisions only in store and that of the most inferior dried Elk a little tainted. *what a prospect for good living at Fort Clatsop at present! Sewelel* is the Clatsop and Chinnook name for a small animal found in the timbered country on this coast. . . . the nativs make great use of the skins of this animal in forming their robes, which they dress with the fur on them and attached together with the sinears [sinews] of the Elk or Deer. I have never seen the animale and can therefore only describe it from the skin and a slight view which some of our party have obtained of the liveing animal silky. . . . we have purchased several of the roabs made of those skins to loin [line] a westcoat of the sea otter, which I have made, and Capt. Lewis a Tiger cat skin coat loined with them also, they make a very pleasant light lighting [lining]."

•

The *"sewelel"* was the Pacific mountain beaver, *Aplodontia rufa*, first described by Lewis and Clark. The Chinook word seh-was-wel actually means a robe made from the skins; the creature itself was called o'gwoolal. Not to be confused with the more familiar and larger, paddle-tailed beaver, *Castor canadensis*, the mountain beaver (really not a beaver at all) is a small animal about the size of a cat. It is blocky and compact, wide of snout and broad of hip like a diminutive hippopotamus. The legs and ears are short, the eyes small and weak, the tail stubby and almost invisible. Its feet, strong and unusually large, are as fit for excavating as a trenching machine.

The mountain beaver is the most primitive of all living rodents; fossils found in upper formations show that it has survived practically unchanged for as much as fifty million years. Another peculiarity of the *Aplodontia* is that it is a family with only one species. Vegetarian and nocturnal, it will eat almost any green plant or shrub. It cuts grass, which turns to hay, around the entrance of burrows, but uses it mostly for bedding and nest material rather than food. Mountain beavers make extensive runways throughout their range, infuriating lumbermen and stockmen, who would like to eliminate them.

27 February 1806.
[LEWIS]

"Reubin Fields . . . reports that there are no Elk towards point Adams. C[o]llins who had hunted up the Netul on this side returned in the evening having killed a buck Elk. Willard still continues very unwell and the other sick men have nearly recovered. Gutridge and Mc.Neal who have the pox are recovering fast, the former nearly well."

[CLARK]

"The Braro so called by the French engages is an animal of the civit genus and much resembles the common badger. this is an enhabitent of the open plains of the Columbia as they are of those of the Missouri, but are sometimes also found in the woody country. they burrow in the hard Grounds in the Plains with surprising ease and dexterity and will cover themselves in the Ground in a very few minits. . . . it is very clumsy

"Sewelel . . . *is a small animal*"
Mountain beaver and burrow.

and runs very slow, depending more on burr[y]-ing to secure itself than running. I have in several instances out run and caught this animal."

•

The badger, *Taxidea taxus*, was unknown to science as a native of North America until Lewis and Clark sent a specimen to Jefferson from the Mandan villages. This member of the weasel family delights in dry, open, treeless country, and with its powerful legs and claws roots out squirrels, mice, and gophers from their dens. Far from fastidious, it will eat anything it can catch, from marmots to grasshoppers and even roots and herbs. It is fierce and pugnacious, and dogs quickly learn to give it a wide berth.

28 February 1806.
[CLARK]

"*Kus-ke-lar* a Clatsop man his wife and a small boy . . . visited us today. They brought some anchovies, sturgeon, a beaver robe, and some roots for sale tho' they asked such high prices for every article that we purchased nothing but a part of a sturgeon for which we gave a fiew fishing hooks. we suffered them to stay all night. . . . the hunters informed us that the Elk is tolerable plenty near the mountains about nine or ten miles distant. Kuskalaw brought a dog which Peter Crusat had purchased with his capo[t] which this fellow had on."

1 March 1806.
[LEWIS]

"Kuskelar and wife left us about noon. he had a good looking boy of about 10 years of age with him who he informed us was his slave. this boy had been taken prisoner by the Killamucks from some nation on the Coast to the s. East of them at a great distance. like other Indian nations they adopt their slaves in their families and treat them very much as their own children."

[CLARK]

"The Prarie Hen sometimes called the Grouse is peculiarly the inhabitant of the Great Plains of Columbia. . . . the tails of which is pointed or the feathers in its center much longer than those on the Sides. . . . in winter season this berd is booted even to the first joint of it's toes. . . . they associate in large flocks in autumn & winter and are frequently found in flocks of from five to six even in summer."

•

The Columbian sharp-tailed grouse, *Pedioecetes phasianellus columbianus*, was first described by Lewis and Clark. Once excessively numerous, it had disappeared from Oregon by the late 1950s, although efforts are being made to reintroduce it. On one occasion, while we were quietly resting on the Lewis and Clark trace near Lemhi Pass, a small flock passed within a few feet of us, sweeping every inch of the ground for anything edible.

2 March 1806.

[CLARK]

"The diet of the sick is so inferior that they recover their strength but slowly. none of them are now sick but all in a state of convelessence with keen appetites and nothing to eate except lean Elk meat. The nativs of this neighbourhood eate the root of the cattail or cooper's flag. It is pleasantly tasted and appears to be very nutricious. the inner part of the root which is eaten without any previous preperation is composed of a number of capellary white flexable strong fibers among which is a mealy or starch like substance which readily disolves in the mouth and separates from the fibers which are then rejected. it appears to me that this substance would make excellent starch, nothing can be of a purer white than it is. This evening late Drewyer, Crusat & Wiser returned with a most acceptable supply of fat sturgeon, fresh anchoves and a bag containing about a bushel of *Wappato*. we feasted on Anchovies and wappetoe."

•

The cattail, *Typha latifolia*, gave up not only its edible root but its fruiting stalk, gathered in enormous quantities for making mats. Mats were essential to Northwest Coast Indians and there were never enough of them. They were used for partitions, bedding, covers, bags—in short, everything for which we would use textiles. The stalks were gathered in midsummer and carefully dried, then laid away until an opportunity presented itself to work on them, usually during bad weather. Then they were trimmed and laid side by side, the small and large ends alternating, and stitched together with long wooden or bone needles and fiber thread. The stitches were about four inches apart and, to prevent the stalks from splitting, were compressed by passing a grooved tool over the seams. Mat creasers were domestic objects upon which the Native Americans frequently lavished their artistic ability.

Swan wrote of mats: "Some are very prettily ornamented round the edges with colored grasses, neatly worked and woven in. These mats are so well made that they shed water like a duck's back, and, when set on their edge, as affectually exclude rain as the best shingle roof.... The newly-made ones have a very fragrant smell, which makes them pleasant and healthy to sleep upon" (*Northwest Coast*, 162).

3 March 1806.

[LEWIS]

"Two of our perogues have been lately injured very much in consequence of the tide leaving them partially on shore. they split by this means of their own weight.... Our convalessents are slowly on the recovery. Lapage is taken sick, gave him a doze of Scots pills which did not operate. ... we are counting the days which seperate us from the 1st of April and which bind us to fort Clatsop. The large black and white pheasant is peculiar to that portion of the Rocky Mountain watered by the Columbia river.... they are about

"The nativs . . . eate the root of the cattail"

Cattail in flower.

Mat needle and creaser, Sauvie Island.

the size of a well grown hen. . . . the feathers of the body are of a dark brown black and white . . . irregularly intermixed. . . . this mixture gives it very much the appearance of that kind of dunghill fowl which the hen-wives of our country call *dommanicker* [Dominique]. . . . they have a narrow stripe of vermillion colour above each eye. . . . it is booted to the toes."

•

Franklins grouse, *Canachites canadensis franklinii*, another first for Lewis and Clark, is a variant of the spruce grouse. These grouse are quite rare even in their natural upland habitat. They are so unwary that they can sometimes be knocked down with a stick, hence their other name, "fool hen."

4 March 1806.

[LEWIS]

"Not any occurence today worthy of notice. we live sumptuously on our wappetoe and Sturgeon. the Anchovey [smelt] is so delicate that they soon become tainted unless pickled or smoked. the natives run a small stick through their gills and hang them in the smoke of their lodges, or kindle a small fire under them for the purpose of drying them. they need no previous preperation of gut-ing &c. and will cure in 24 hours. the natives do not appear to be very scrupelous about eating them when a little feated [fetid]. the fresh sturgeon they keep many days by immersing it in water. they cook their sturgeon by means of vapor or steam. the process is as follows. a brisk fire is kindled on which a parcel of stones are la[i]d. when the fire burns down and the stones are sufficiently heated, the stones are so arranged as to form a tolerable level surface, the sturgeon which had been previously cut into large fletches is now laid on the hot stones; a parsel of small boughs . . . is next laid on and a second course of the sturgeon thus rep[e]ating alternate layers of sturgeon and boughs untill the whole is put on which they design to cook. it is next covered closely with matts and water is poared in such a manner as to run in among the hot stones and the vapor arrising being confined by the mats, cooks the fish. the whole process is performed in an hour, and the sturgeon thus cooked is much better than either boiled or roasted."

•

The Columbia River white sturgeon, *Acipenser transmontanus*, once abounded in the Columbia and Snake rivers, and grew to astonishing size. Alexander Ross wrote: "Sturgeon also are very abundant and of uncommon size, yet tender and well flavoured, many of them weighing upwards of 700 pounds, and one caught and brought to us measured thirteen feet nine inches in length, and weighed 1,130 pounds" (*Adventures of the First Settlers*, 101). They are bottom feeders, and their favorite diet is the lamprey eel, which still ascends the Columbia River to spawn. From about 1880 sturgeon were slain in large numbers by commercial fishermen because they destroyed nets and raised havoc with fish wheels. Later the fish grew popular with the consuming public, and by the end of the nineteenth century as many as six million pounds a year were being harvested.

5 March 1806.
[L E W I S]

"This morning we were visited by two parties of Clatsops. they brought some fish a hat and some skins for sale most of which we purchased. they returned to their village in the evening. . . . the hunters returned from the *kil-haw-á-nack-kle* River. . . . they informed us that the Elk had all gone off to the mountains a considerable distance from us. this is unwelcome information and reather allarming we have only 2 days provisions on hand, and that nearly spoiled. we made up a small assortment of articles to trade with the Indians and directed Sergt. Pryor to set out early in the morning in a canoe with 2 men, to ascend the Columbia to the resort of the Indian [sturgeon] fishermen and purchase some fish; we also directed two parties of hunters to renew the Chase tomorrow early. . . . if we find that the elk have left us, we have determined to ascend the river slowly and indeavour to procure subsistence on the way, consuming the Month of

March in the woody country. earlyer than April we conceive it a folly to attempt the open plains where we know there is no fuel except a few small dry shrubs."

6 March 1806.
[L E W I S]

"at 11 A.M. we were visited by Comowoll and two of his children. he presented us with some Anchovies which had been well cured in their manner. we fou[n]d them excellent. they were very acceptable particularly at this moment."

[C L A R K]

"we gave the old mans sones a twisted wire to ware about his neck, and I gave him a par of old glovs which he was much pleased with. this we have found much the most friendly and decent Indian that we have met with in this neighbourhood."

[L E W I S]

"Hall had his foot and ankle much injured yesterday by the fall of a large stick of timber; the bones were fortunately not broken and I expect he will be able to walk again shortly. Bratton is now weaker than any of the convalessants, all of whom recover slowly in consequence of the want of a proper diet, which we have it not in our power to procure."

•

Usually Clark copies Lewis's entries verbatim, but here where Lewis writes "decent savage" Clark uses "decent Indian."

7 March 1806.
[L E W I S]

"The wind was so high that Comowol did not leave us untill late this evening. . . . Bratton is much wo[r]se today, he complains of a violent pain in the small of his back and is unable . . . to set up."

[C L A R K]

"I applied a bandage of flanel to the part and rubed it well with some volatile linniment which was prepared with sperits of wine, camphire, castile soap, and a little laudinum. he felt himself better in the evening at which time I repeated the linniment and bathed his beet [feet] to restore circulation which he complained of in that part. . . . John Shields Reuben Fields & Robert frasure [Frazer] measured 2 trees of the fur kind one 37 feet around, appears sound, has but fiew limbs for 200 feet it is East of the Netul [Lewis and Clark] abt. 280 feet high."

•

William Bratton was one of nine young men from Kentucky recruited by Captain Clark at Mulberry Hill, Kentucky. He was a blacksmith and gunsmith, both of which skilled trades were essential to the expedition. After the death of Sergeant Floyd on the Missouri, he was a candidate for the vacant position, losing to Patrick Gass by a narrow margin in the voting. Bratton fought in the War of 1812. He was married in Ohio and lived there for a time, later moving to Waynetown, Indiana, where he died in 1841. His

"measured 2 trees of the fur kind one 37 feet around"

grave there has a commemorative marker, one of the few known graves of Corps of Discovery members.

Private Robert Frazer so impressed the captains that he was transferred from the extra work force, used only as far as the Mandan villages, to the permanent party. He kept a journal that is now lost; only a prospectus and a map of the West that he drafted have survived. After the expedition he was sent to Louisiana to uncover evidence concerning the Aaron Burr episode. Records show that he had to appeal twice to Clark for help after being arrested for fighting. He died in Franklin County, Missouri, in 1837.

8 March 1806.
[LEWIS]

"Bratton is much better today, his back gives him but little pain. . . . The white brant is very common in this country particularly below tidewater where they remain in vast quantities during the winter. they feed like the swan gees &c on the grass roots and seeds which they find in the marshes. . . . The small goose of this country is reather less than the brant; it's head and neck like the brant are reather larger than that of the goose in proportion; their beak is also thicker and shorter, their notes are more like those of our tame gees; in all other rispects they are the same with the large goose with which, they so frequently associate that it was some time after I first observed this goose before I could determine whether it was a distinct species or not. I have now no hesitation in declaring them a distinct speceis. the larger goose is the same of that common on the Atlantic coast, and known by the appellation of the wild, or Canadian goose."

•

The "white brant" was the lesser snow goose, *Chen hyperborea*. It breeds in the arctic and winters west of the Mississippi River Valley from Canada to Mexico. This rather small goose is sleek and tidy, white with black wing tips.

The Canada goose, *Branta canadensis*, is the most common of the geese and is familiarly known as the honker; it is this goose, during the spring and fall migrations, that animates the night with its majestic cry of the wild. The "small goose" was the lesser Canada goose, *B. canadensis leucopareia*. It is not a separate species but a subspecies, very common in the Oregon Country.

9 March 1806.
[LEWIS]

"This morning the men set out at daylight to go in qu[e]st of the Elk which Collins had killed, they returned with it at eleven A.M. Bratton complains of his back being very painfull to him today; I conceive this pain to be something of the rheumatism. we still apply the linniment and flannel; in the evening he was much better. . . . visited by 3 Clatsop men who brought a dog some fish and a Sea Otter for sale. . . . We set Shields to work to make some sacks of Elk skin to contain various articles. The Large Swan is precisely the same

"The white brant is very common in this country"

common to the Atlantic States. the small swan differs only from the larger one in size and it's note. it is about one fourth less and it's note entirely different. the latter cannot be justly immetated by the sound of letters nor do I know any sounds with which a comparison could be pertinent. it begins with a kind of whistleing sound and terminates in a round full note which is reather louder than the whisteling, or former part; this note is as loud as that of the large swan. from the peculiar whistleing note of this bird I have called it the *whistleing swan."*

•

Canada geese.

Lewis mistakenly wrote that the large swan, or trumpeter, *Olor buccinator*, was the same as that common to the eastern states, it should have been the small or whistling swan, *Olor columbianus*. Lewis is credited with originating the popular name "whistling swan" for this graceful fowl.

The trumpeter is the largest and most impressive of North America's water birds. Its numbers have now decreased significantly. The whistling swan still populates the lower Columbia River Valley in winter, where we have seen flocks ranging from a few up to a hundred or more. A

great migration takes them from their Arctic breeding grounds on the tundra to their winter range as far south as California. Every year they alight at places along the Columbia they have known since the glacial age.

10 March 1806.
[CLARK]

"we sent out two parties of hunters on this side of the Netul [Lewis and Clark], one above and the other below, we also directed a party to set out early in the morning and pass Meriwethers Bay

Lesser Canada geese.

and hunt beyond the Kilhowanakkle. From the last we have considerable hope, as we have as yet hunted but little in that quarter."

11 March 1806.
[CLARK]

"Early this morning Sergt. Pryor arrived with a small Canoe loaded with fish which he had obtained from the *Cath-lah-mah's* for a very small part of the articles he had taken with him. . . . The dogs of the Cathlamah's had bitten the throng assunder which confined his canoe and she had gorn adrift; he borrowed a Canoe from the Indians in which he has returned. he found his canoe on the way and secured her, untill we return the Indians their canoe. . . . we once more live in *clover*; anchovies, fresh sturgeon and Wappatoe. . . . The *Mule Deer* we have never found except in rough country. . . . when met in the wood lands or river bottoms and pursued, they imediately run to the hills or open country as the Elk do, the contrary happens with the common Deer. there are several differences between the Mule and common deer as well as in form as in habits. they are fully a third larger in general. . . . the Ears are peculiarly large. I measured those of a large Buck which I found to be *eleven* inches long and 3½ in width."

"from the peculiar whistleing note of this bird I have called it the Whistleing swan"

"The reptiles of this country are the rattlesnake garter snake and the common brown Lizzard. . . . The garter snake so called in the United States is very common in this country. . . . they differ not at all from those of the U'States. . . . There is a speceis of water lizzard of which I saw one only just above the grand rapids of the Columbia. it is about 9 inches long. . . . the belley and under part of the neck and head were of a brick red, every other part of the colour of the upper part of the body a dark brown."

•

Lewis and Clark were the first to describe the warty salamander, *Diemyctylus torosus*. The description here of the mule deer, *Odocoileus hemionus*, is by Clark, but copies Lewis's journal for 10 May 1805, when the expedition members were on the Missouri. Apparently they did not see any mule deer on the Columbia River system below the Clearwater. This deer, however, was then widespread over the semi-arid plains and forested hills east of the Cascades and is still found in the mountains, where it is a favorite hunting trophy. It can maneuver with astonishing agility through and over the cut-rock canyons and slopes despite weighing two hundred or

"the Ears are peculiarly large"
Mule deer.

three hundred pounds. Like the black-tailed deer, it prefers browsing fodder to grass. The first description of this ungulate, as well as the name "mule deer," is credited to Lewis and Clark.

12 March 1806.
[L E W I S]
"I beleive the Callaumut Eagle is sometimes found on this side of the rocky mountains from the information of the Indians in whose possession I have seen their plumage. these are the

"There is a species of water lizard"
Warty salamander.

same with those of the Missouri, and are the most beatifull of all the family of the Eagles of America. it's colours are black and white with which it is beatifully variagated. . . . this eagle is fared by all carniverous birds, and on his approach all leave the carcase instantly on which they are feeding. . . . with these feathers the natives decorate the stems of their sacred pipes or callaumets. . . . the natives . . . who can procure these feathers attach them to their own hair and mains and tails of their favorite horses by way of ornament. The Whale is sometimes pursued harpooned and taken by the Indians of this coast, tho' I beleive it is much more frequently killed by runing fowl [foul] on the rocks of the coast in violent storms and thrown on shore by the wind and tide. in either case the Indians prese[r]ve and eat the blubber and oil as has been before mentioned. the whale bone they also carefully preserve for sale. Our party are now furnished with 358 pair of mockersons exclusive of a good portion of dressed leather. They are also provided with shirts overalls capoes of dressed Elk skins for the homeward journey."

[C L A R K]

"The horns of some of the Elk . . . have Grown to the length of six inches. the latter are in the best order, from which it would seem that the pore Elk retain their horns longer."

•

The whale was hunted by the Makah, Nootka, and others about Vancouver Island, but not by the Indians of the Columbia. They did hunt the seal and sea lion.

Lewis and Clark had seen both the bald and

"The reptiles . . . [include] the rattlesnake"

golden eagle on the Columbia; here they are speaking of the Northern bald eagle, *Haliaeetus leucocephalus alascanus*. Tradition and legend cloak the habits of the majestic and fierce bald eagle. A clumsy fisher, it seldom captures its own prey but demands tribute from the osprey and other aggressive raptorial birds, or devours carrion on the beach.

The observation that unhealthy animals retained their antlers was a remarkably astute one by Clark. We once saw a mule deer still bearing a trophy rack in late March and, on inquiring, found that deer or elk that are unhealthy drop their antlers late or not at all. The "pore elk" with horns that Clark saw were diseased or aged; such animals are the usual prey of carnivores.

13 March 1806.
[LEWIS]

"We sent Drewyer down to the Clatsop village to purchase a couple of their canoes if possible. Sergt. Pryor and a party made another surch for the lost perog[u]e but was unsuccessfull. . . . The Porpus is common on this coast and as far up the river as the water is brackish. the Indians sometimes gig them and always eat the flesh of this fish when they can procure it; to me the flavor is disagreeable."

14 March 1806.
[LEWIS]

"late in the evening Drewyer arrived with a party of the Clatsops who brought an indifferent canoe some hats and roots for sale. the hats and roots we purchased, but could not obtain the canoe without giving more than our stock of merchandize would lisence us. I offered him my laced uniform coat but he would not exchange."

[CLARK]

"we are informed by the Clatsops that they latterly seen an Indian from the *Quin-na-chart* [Quinault] Nation who reside six days march to the N.W and that four vessles were there and the owners Mr. Haley, Moore, Callamon & Swipeton were tradeing with that numerous nation, whale bone oile and skins of various discription."

15 March 1806.
[CLARK]

"We wer visited this Afternoon in a canoe 4 feet 2 I. wide by *De-lash-hel-wilt* a Chinnook Chief his wife and six women of his Nation, which the Old Boud his wife had brought for Market. this was the same party which had communicated the venereal to several of our party in November last,

and of which they have finally recovered. I therefore gave the men a particular charge with respect to them which they promised me to observe. Late this evening we were also visited by Ca-tel a Clatsop man and his family. he brought a Canoe and a sea otter skin for sale neither of which we could purchase of him. . . . Bratten is still very weak and unwell. [The sorrel with an oval obtuse and ternate leaf has now put forth it's leaves. some of them have nearly obtained their growth already. the birds are singing very agreably this morning particularly the common robin].* There is a third species of Brant in the neighbourhood of this place which is about the size and much the form of the bided brant. . . . the breast and belly are white with an irregular mixture of black feathers which give that part a pided appearance. . . . the note of this brant is much that of the common pided brant from which in fact they are not to be distinguished at a distance, but they certainly are a distinct species of brant."

•

The mountain sorrel, *Oxalis oregona*, covers the forest floor of the Oregon Country. It looks sufficiently like some Irish shamrocks for them to be mistaken for one another. The flowers, white

---

*The bracketed text is from an entry for 15 March 1806 in "Scientific Data Accompanying the Original Journals of Lewis and Clark" (Thwaites, *Journals*, 6:210).

with purple veins, are borne singly on slender stems. Country boys call it sheep sorrel and eat it like lettuce in the spring.

The white-fronted goose, *Anser albifrons*, was first described by Lewis and Clark. This widely distributed goose breeds in the far north and occasionally winters on or near the Columbia River.

16 March 1806.

[LEWIS]

"the Indians remained with us all day, but would not dispose of their canoes at a price which it was in our power to give. . . . two handkerchiefs would now contain all the small articles of merchanize which we possess; the ballance of the stock consists of 6 blue robes one scarlet do. one uniform artillerist's coat and hat, five robes made of our large flag, and a few old cloaths trimed with ribbon. on this stock we have wholy to depend for the purchase of horses and such portion of our subsistence from the Indians as it will be in our power to obtain. a scant dependence indeed, for a tour of the distance of that before us. . . . The *white Salmon Trout* which we had previously seen only at the great falls of the Columbia has now made it's appearance in the creeks near this place. one of them was brought us to day by an Indian who had just taken it with his gig. . . . it was 2 feet 8 Inches long, and weighed 10 lbs."

[CLARK]

"[they] now begin to run &c. &c."

17 March 1806.

[LEWIS]

"Catel and his family left us this morning. Old Delashelwilt and his women still remain. they have formed a ca[m]p near the fort and seem to be determined to lay close s[i]ege to us but I beleive notwithstanding every effort of their wining graces, the men have preserved their constancy to the vow of celibacy which they made on this occasion to Capt. C. and myself. we have had our perogues prepared for our departure, and shal set out as soon as the weather will permit. the weather is so precarious that we fear by waiting untill the first of April that we might be detained several days longer before we get from this point to the Cathlahmahs as it must be calm or we cannot accomplish that part of our rout. Drewyer returned late this evening from the Cathlahmahs with our canoe which Sergt. Pryor had left some days since, and also a canoe which he had purchased from those people. for this canoe he gave my uniform laced coat and nearly half a carrot of tobacco. it seems that nothing excep[t] this coat would induce them to dispose of a canoe which in their mode of traffic is an article of the greatest val[u]e except a wife, with whom it is equal, and is generally given in exchange to the father for his daughter. I think the U'States are indebted to me another Uniform coat for that of which I disposed on this occasion was but little woarn."

•

"they certainly are a distinct species of brant"
White-fronted goose.

A "carrot of tobacco" was a twist of fifteen to twenty leaves or from one to two pounds. The meaning of the term has changed over the years and now is used only in Louisiana, where Perique tobacco is grown.

18 March 1806.
[LEWIS]

"Drewyer was taken last night with a violent pain in his side. Capt. Clark bled him. Several of the men are complaining of being unwell. It is truly unfortunate that they should be sick at the moment of departure. . . . Comowooll and two Cathlahmahs visited us today; we suffered them to remain all night. this morning we gave Delashelwilt a certificate of his good deportment &c. and also a list of our names, after which we dispatched him to his village with his female band. These lists of our names we have given to several of the natives and also paisted up a copy in our room. . . . on the back of some of these lists we added a sketch of the connection of the upper branches of the Missouri with those of the Columbia . . . on which we also delineated the track we had come and that we meant to pursue on our return."

•

One of these papers was given by the Indians to Captain Samuel Hill of the American brig *Lydia*, which according to one account had entered the Columbia River to obtain wood to replace some damaged spars. Four months earlier, in July 1805, Captain Hill had rescued John R. Jewitt and John Thompson, the sole surviving crew members of another American ship, the *Boston*, who had been held in captivity at Nootka Sound since March 1803. In an account of his captivity and rescue, published in 1815 with assistance from a ghostwriter named Richard Alsop, Jewitt wrote: "We proceeded about ten miles up the [Columbia] river to a small Indian village where we heard from the inhabitants, that Captains Clark and Lewis, from the United States of America; had been there about a fortnight before, on their journey over-land, and had left several medals with them, which they showed" (*Narrative*, 161).

Jewitt states that this encounter occurred "after a period of nearly four months from our leaving Nootka" (*Narrative*, 161). This would place the *Lydia* on the Columbia River in the last half of November 1805. Since Jewitt's account was written many months after the fact, it is possible he was unable to recall exactly when this incident occurred.° If the correct date is some time in November 1805, the *Lydia* was on the lower Columbia at the same time Lewis and Clark were there, and for some reason they failed to make

---

° Jewitt kept a daily journal during his captivity, but his entries cease with his release on 19 July 1805 and shed no light about the *Lydia* on the Columbia (*see* Jewitt, *Journal*, 115–18). Captain Hill's unpublished autobiography fails to mention this encounter (*see* Large, "The Empty Anchorage.")

contact with one another. Whatever the case, the document given to Captain Hill sailed with him to Canton and a copy of it eventually reached the United States, where its contents became known to Nicholas Biddle, the first editor of the Lewis and Clark journals (*see* Allen, *History of the Expedition*, 2:204–5; Large, "The Empty Anchorage," 4–11; and 14 November 1805).

Ross Cox commented: "We also visited Fort Clatsop, the place where Captains Lewis and Clark spent the winter of 1805–1806; an accurate description of which is given in the journal of those enterprising travelers. The logs of the house were still standing, and marked with the names of several of the party" (*Columbia*, 1:106).

19 March 1806.
[LEWIS]

"It continued to rain and hail today in such manner that nothing further could be done to the canoes. a party sent out early after the Elk which was killed yesterday. . . . we gave Comowooll alias Connia, a cirtificate of his good conduct and the friendly intercourse which he has maintained with us during our residence at this place; we also gave him a list of our names."

•

This paper suffered the fate of so many priceless historical documents. On 18 May 1814, Alexander Henry, stationed at Astoria with the North West Company, wrote in his journal: "Coniah, the Clatsop chief, showed me his writing from Captains Lewis and Clark, dated Fort Clatsop, 19th March, 1806; a list of men accompanying the American Party." And on 21 May: "Coniah and other Clatsops brought back some of our stolen things. We clothed the chief, and gave him a writing in lieu of the American one, which I threw in the fire before him" (*Journals*, 2:915).

The next day, 22 May 1814, Henry was drowned with six others while crossing the Columbia during a gale.

20 March 1806.
[LEWIS]

"It continued to rain and blow so violently today that nothing could be done towards forwarding our departure. we intended to have Dispatched Drewyer and the two Fieldses to hunt near the bay on this side of the Cathahmahs untill we jounded [joined] them from hence, but the rain rendered our departure so uncertain that we declined this measure for the present. nothing ramarkable happened during the day."

•

It was impossible to repair the canoes while they were wet, and the rains were so incessant that they could not be dried even with the assistance of fires. Repairs were made by caulking the cracks and seams with pitch, gathered from fir trees. The hunt was to be in the bay at the mouth of the John Day River.

21 March 1806.

[L E W I S]

"As we could not set out we thought it best to send out some hunters and accordingly dispatched Sheilds and Collins on this side of the Netul [Lewis and Clark] for that purpose with orders to return in the evening or sooner if they are successfull. The hunters returned late in the evening unsuccessfull. . . . we directed Drewyer and the Fieldses to set out tomorrow morning early, and indevour to provide us some provision on the bay beyond point William. . . . our sick men Willard and Bratton do not seem to recover. . . . Bratton is now so much reduced that I am somewhat uneasy with rispect to his recovery."

22 March 1806.

[L E W I S]

"about 10 A.M. we were visited by 4 Clatsops and a killamucks; they brought some dried Anchoveis and a dog for sale which we purchased. the air is perefectly temperate, but it continues to rain in such a manner that there is no possibility of geting our canoes completed. at 12 OCk. we were visited by Commowooll and 3 of the Clatsops. to this chief we left our houses and fu[r]niture. he has been much more kind an[d] hospitable to us than any other indian in this neighbourhood."

IX

THE START FOR HOME
FORT CLATSOP TO THE GREAT SHUTE
23 MARCH TO 9 APRIL 1806

23 March 1806.

[LEWIS]

"the wind is pretty high but it seems to be the common opinion that we can pass point William [Tongue Point]. we accordingly distributed the baggage and directed the canoes to be launched and loaded for our departure. at 1 P.M. we bid a final adieu to Fort Clatsop."

[CLARK]

"at this place we had wintered and remained from the 7th of Decr. 1805 to this day and have lived as well as we had any right to expect, and we can say that we were never one day without 3 meals of any kind either pore Elk meat or roots, notwithstanding the repeated fall of rain which has fallen almost constantly since we passed the long narrows."

[LEWIS]

"at a 1/4 before three we had passed Meri-wethers bay and commencd. coasting the difficult shore; at 1/2 after five we doubled point William, and at 6. arrived at the mouth of a small creek [Mill Creek] where we found our hunters. we . . . encamped on the Stard. side of the Creek."

•

On this momentous occasion, homeward bound at last, Ordway noted only that "the rain Seased and it became fair. about meridian at which time we loaded our canoes & at 1 P.M. left Fort Clatsop on our homeward bound journey" (Quaife, *Journals*, 331). Gass wrote: "We were employed this forenoon in dividing and packing up our loading; and distributing it among the canoes, which were five in number, three large and two small. At noon we put it on board; and at 1 o'-clock left Fort Clatsop" (Gass, *Journal*, 230).

24 March 1806.
[LEWIS]

"we breakfasted and Set out at 1/2 after. 9 A.M. . . . [The brown bryery shrub with a broad pinnate leaf has begun to put forth its leaves. the polecat Colwort is in blume.]° at 1 P.M. we arrived at the Cathlahmah village where we halted and purchased some wappetoe, a dog for the sic, and a hat for one of the men. on one of the Seal Islands opposite to the village of these people they have scaffolded their dead in canoes elivating them above the tidewater mark. these people are very fond of sculpture in wood of which they exhibit a variety of specemines about their houses. the board peices supporting the center of the roof and those through which the doors are cut, seem to be the peices on which they most display their taist. I saw some of these which represented human figures setting and supporting the burthen on their sholders."

[CLARK]

"at this village I saw two very elegant canoes inlaid with shells. those shells I took to be teeth at first view, and the nativs informed . . . the men that they [were] the teeth of their enemies which they had killed in war. in examining them closely . . . we found that [they] were sea shells [operculum of the sea snail]. Capt. Cook may have mis-

taken those shells verry well for human teeth without a close examination. . . . we proceeded on through some difficult and narrow channels between the Seal Islands, and the South Side . . . opposit to the lower Warkiacom village, and Encamped. . . . a very considerable deposit of the dead at a short distance below. . . . Soon after we encamped 2 Indians visited us from the opposit side, one of them spoke several words of English and repeated the names of traders, and many of the salors. Made 16 miles."

•

The "brown bryery shrub" was probably the devils club, *Oplopanax horridum*, which grows profusely in the rain forests of the coast country. It is strange that this pugnacious plant did not receive more attention in the journals, for the hunters especially must have cursed such an obstruction to their progress through the thickets. It grows three to ten feet tall, and the leaves (the largest of any western shrub) and stems are well armed with long, sharp, stiff thorns. The flower is inconspicuous and the fruit a cluster of brilliant scarlet berries, as decorative as holly. The Indians burned the bark and mixed the ashes with grease for a brown face paint, or boiled it for medicine. Legend says that a fleeing hero or maiden threw bits of the plant on the ground, where they magically sprang into a bristling barrier to confound the pursuer.

The "polecat Colewort" was the skunk cabbage, *Lysichiton americanum*, an unjustly de-

---

°The bracketed text is from the entry for 24 March 1806 in "Scientific Data Accompanying the Original Journals of Lewis and Clark" (Thwaites, *Journals*, 6:210).

famed member of the arum family that from early March to May blankets its swampy habitat in the bottomlands with gold. The roots were eaten by bears in the spring despite their bitter, acrid taste, which increased their virtue for medicinal purposes. A charming legend concerns the polecat colewort. Long ago the people had to exist on berries and roots, principally skunk cabbage. Then Coyote invented the salmon, and there was plenty for all. Because he had fed the people for so long, Skunk Cabbage was rewarded with a blanket and a spiked war club and set in the rich soil by the river, where every spring he greets the returning salmon in his splendid golden uniform, holding aloft his club.

Wooden boxes and bowls were common on the Columbia River and the Northwest Coast. They were made from cedar or alder and frequently beautifully carved. Some were cut from the solid, others were made by bending, a method requiring great skill and patience. First the bottom was cut from a plank, then a board with a length equal to the perimeter of the bottom was made for the sides. Notches were cut across the board where the corners would be, after which the board was steamed and then bent around the bottom pieces. The meeting ends of the board were drilled and neatly sewn with spruce and cedar roots. Some boxes had lids made in the same fashion.

The village was the one Lewis and Clark had visited on 26 November 1805. Camp was made on Aldrich Point.

"The brown bryery shrub . . . has begun to put forth"
Devil's club.

"the polecat Colewort is in blume"
Skunk cabbage.

25 March 1806.
[L E W I S]

"we set out . . . along the South Coast of the river
against the wind and a strong current. . . . the red
willow and seven bark begin to put fourth their
leaves. after dinner we passed the river to a large
Island [Puget] and continued our rout along the
side of the same about a mile when we arrived at
a Cathlahmah fishing cam[p] of one lodge. . . .
they had ten or douzen very fine sturgeon which
had not been long taken. . . . we remained at this
place about half an hour. . . . it was with some difficulty that we could find a spot proper for an encampment, the shore being a swamp for several
miles back; at length late in the evening opposite
to the place we had encamped on the 6th. of November last; we found the entrance of a small
creek [Beaver Slough] which afforded us a safe
harbour from the wind, and encamped. . . . here
we found another party of cathlahmahs about 10
in number who had established a temperary residence here for the purpose of fishing and takeing seal. . . . They gave us some of the fleece
[flesh] of the seal which I found a great improve-
ment to the poor Elk. [The nettle and a variety of
other plants are now springing up.]"°

•

°The bracketed text is from the entry for March 25
1806 in "Scientific Data Accompanying the Original
Journals of Lewis and Clark" (Thwaites, *Journals,*
6:210).

*"those shells I took to be teeth at first
. . . [but] we found that [they] were
sea shells"*
Wooden bowl or box decorated with
operculum of the sea snail.

The "seven bark" was the nine bark, *Physocarpus capitatus*, a clustered shrub with a three-lobed leaf. The bark exfoliates in layers that festoon in thin strips, hence the name. The single flowers seem to huddle together, each projecting stamens tipped with red anthers, like colored bulbs in a miniature chandelier. The Indians apparently made no use of this shrub except to chew the peeled twigs occasionally for an emetic.

The nettle, *Urtica lyallii*, presents a path of fire to the unwary hiker in the rich alluvial flatlands along the Columbia River. Growing six to ten feet high, the profusion of slender stalks fences off the flood plains as effectively as barbed wire. Nettle stalks are the source of an excellent linen, and the plant was exploited by Europeans, Asians, and ab-

original Americans for centuries. To the Indians, it was second only to *Apocynum* as a source of fiber for twine, nets, and fishing lines. The young nettle shoots were boiled for greens, the roots steamed and eaten. Swan (*Northwest Coast*, 163) saw the roots being mixed with another plant to make a yellow dye. The nettle was believed to have powerful medicinal value, and the stalks were sometimes used for beating rheumatism out of those suffering from it.

In the old days, it is said, the people along the Great River were poor and hungry. Great numbers of fish lived in the stream but there was no way to catch them. Spider saw their plight and pitied them. Changing himself into a man, he married one of their maidens and taught

Bent and sewn wooden box found on Sauvie Island, preserved by constant immersion in water. Note the cameo design. Differential weathering shows it was once painted. The handle indicates the box may have been used for picking berries.

all the people to ret and spin nettle fibers and weave them into nets, a task none could do better than he. Now the people had food and prospered, for there were fish for all, and nettles grew in abundance.

26 March 1806.
[LEWIS]

"The wind blew so hard this morning that we delayed untill 8 A.M. we gave a medal of small Size to a man by the name of Wal-lál-le, a principal man among the Cathlahmahs, he appeared very thankfull for the honour conferred on him and presented us a large sturgeon. we continued our rout up the river to an old village on the Stard. side where we halted for dinner. . . . the two Wackiacums who have been pursuing us since yesterday morning with two dogs for sale, arrived[.] they wish tobacco in exchange . . . which we are not disposed to give as our stock is now reduced to a few carrots. . . . after dinner we proceeded on and passed an Elegant and extensive bottom on the South side and an island near it's upper point which we call Fanny's Island and bottom. . . . near the river towards the upper point we saw a fine grove of whiteoak trees. . . .

"seven bark begin to put fourth their leaves"

we continued our rout after dinner untill late in the evening and encamped on the next island above fanny's Island. [The humming bird has appeared. . . . found it the same with those common to the United States.]"°

●

The old village was near the mouth of Bradbury Slough, and opposite Abernethy Creek. It was noted by Ross (*Adventures of the First Settlers*, 113) in 1813: "passed Puget's Island and then the great Whill Wetz Village situated on Oak Point." Franchère (*Adventure at Astoria*, 47) called it by a different name: "We passed a large village, called Kreluit, and encamped . . . on a low point at the foot of an isolated rock." This name is the same as Lewis and Clark's "Skillute." George Gibbs called it Cooniac, and Verne Ray, Ka'naiak.°°

°The bracketed text is from an entry for 26 March 1806 in "Scientific Data Accompanying the Original Journals of Lewis and Clark" (Thwaites, *Journals*, 6:211).

°°The name, as now linguistically transcribed, is Qá-niak (*see* Silverstein, "Chinookans of the Lower Columbia," 534).

"The nettle and . . . other plants are springing up"

Alexander Henry, in 1814, records: "At eleven we embarked and passed the village at Oak Point, which stands on the s. side of the river, on an extensive low land. . . . The natives seated on the bank gazed at us as we passed; they appear numerous with an uncommon number of children. Captain [Nathan] Winship of the *Albatross* came here to build in 1810, but having cut wood and prepared timber, the water rose, obliging him to abandon the place, drift down the river, and put to sea" (*Journals*, 2:794–95). A month later Henry again passed the village and wrote: "At Oak Point village we put ashore again, where an immense number of sturgeon were strung and fastened to stakes in the river. They have one range of eight houses, measuring 120 paces (600 feet) and eight other detached houses, each 15 paces. The whole makes a pleasant appearance at a distance, but will not stand close inspection", (*Journals*, 2:832–33).

At the outlet of Abernethy Creek is a rocky mound used by the Kreluits for canoe burials. The village was across the river, on the Oregon shore. Fanny's Island, named for Captain Clark's sister Frances, is now Crims Island.

27 March 1806.
[LEWIS]

"We set out early this morning. . . . at 10 A.M. we arrived at two houses of this nation [the Skillutes] on the Stard. Side where we halted for breakfast. . . . the natives appeared extreemly hospitable,

Canoe burial site at the outlet of Abernethy Creek.

gave us dryed Anchovies, Sturgeon, wappatoe, quamash, and a speceis of small white tuberous roots. . . . these people are said to be numerous. in their dress, habits, manners and language they differ but little from the Clatsops, Chinnooks &c. . . . above the Skillutes on this river [the Coweliskee or Cowlitz] another nation by the name of the Hul-loo-et-tell reside who are said also to be numberous. at the distance of 2 m. above the village at which we breakfasted we passed the entrance of this river [Cowlitz]; we saw several fishing camps of the Skillutes on both sides of the Columbia. . . . late in the evening we . . . encamped about 4½ [miles] above the commencement of the bottom land on the stard. below Deer Island. . . . we were visited by a large canoe with eight men; from them we obtained a dryed fruit which resembled the raspburry and which I be[l]eive to be the fruit of the large leafed thorn frequently mentioned [salmonberry]. . . . before we set out from the Skillute village we sent on Gibson's canoe and Drewyer's . . . to Deer Island . . . to hunt and wait our arrival."

•

The Hul-loo-et-tell were the Toutle and lived on the Toutle River, on whose banks are numerous village sites. Camp was made on the Oregon shore a little below Goble and about one mile above Coffin Rock. On this small island and a nearby headland the Indians deposited their dead in canoes. As previously noted (*see* 6 November 1805), Lieutenant Broughton first saw this rocky isle on 28 October 1792. Concerning this locality, Alexander Henry wrote: "We soon came to a large village at the entrance of a small river [Kalama] on the N. A long range of houses runs parallel with the river, and the natives appear numerous. Opposite to this village, on the S., is a point of rocks on which their dead are deposited in wooden canoes; and immediately above this point is a rock island, on top of which are also dead bodies in canoes—one apparently that of a great chief, from the manner in which he is arranged. The island is called Coffin Rock" (*Journals*, 2:796).

The decommissioned Trojan nuclear power plant now overlooks this landmark where Columbia River Indians had brought their dead from time immemorial.

28 March 1806.
[LEWIS]
"This morning we set out very early and at 9 A.M. arrived at the old Indian village on the Lard. side of Deer Island where we found our hunters had halted. . . . by 10 A.M. they all returned to camp having killed seven deer. these were all the common fallow deer with the long tail [white-tailed deer]. I measured the tail of one of these bucks which was upwards of 17 inches long; they are very poor, tho' better than the black tailed fallow deer of the coast. these are two very distinct speceis of deer. the Indians call this large Island E-lal-lar or deer island which is a very appropriate name. . . . we have seen more waterfowl on this island than we have previously seen since we left Fort Clatsop. . . . one of the hunters killed a duck which appeared to be the male, it was a size less than the duckinmallard."

[CLARK]
"We had the canoes which wanted repareing hauled out and . . . dryed them sufficiently to receive the pitch which was immediately put on . . . them. . . . we saw a great number of snakes on this island. . . . The men who had been sent after the deer returned with four only, the other 4 having been eaten entirely by the Voulture except the skin."

[LEWIS]
"these birds had devoured 4 deer in the course of a few hours. the party killed and brought in three other deer a goose some ducks and an Eagle. Drewyer also killed a tiger cat. Joseph Fields informed me that the Vultures had draged a large buck which he had killed about 30 yards, had skined it and broken the back bone."

•

Coffin Rock, canoe burial island.

"one of the hunters killed a duck"
Ring-necked duck.

The duck killed by the hunter, according to Coues, was the ring-necked duck, *Aythya collaris*. Lewis meticulously describes this bird, heretofore unknown to science. The island is still called Deer Island. Samuel Parker, a Congregational missionary, wrote in 1835: "Among the many islands, with which the lower part of this river abounds, Deer Island, thirty miles below Fort Vancouver, is worthy of notice. It is large, and in the interior are several small lakes, the resort of swans, geese, and ducks. This island was formerly the residence of many Indians, but they are gone, and nothing is to be seen but the remains of a large village" (*Journal*, 152). Parker visited the island shortly after the malaria, influenza, and smallpox plagues of 1830–35.

One is inclined to consider Joseph Field's account of the gluttonous "Vultures" to be one of the tall tales for which the Mountain Men were so famous. But this scavenger must have been the same kind of bird Field's brother, Reuben, had shot on 18 November 1805. It was measured to have a wingspan of over nine feet. A bird so large could only have been the now endangered California condor, *Gymnogyps californianus*, a small number of which could have accomplished the feat of consuming so many deer carcasses (*see* Cutright, *Lewis and Clark*, 241).

29 March 1806.

[LEWIS]

"we set out early this morning and proceeded along the side of Deer Island; halted at 10 A.M. near its upper point and breakfasted. . . . the upper point of this island may be esteemed the lower side or commencement of the Columbian valley. . . . we proceeded on and at the distance of 14 miles from our encampment . . . passed a large inlet [Multnomah Channel] 300 yds. in width. . . . on the North side of the columbia a little above the entrance of this inlet a considerable river [Lewis] discharges itself. this stream the natives call the *Cah-wáh-na-hi-ooks*. . . . at the distance of three miles above the inlet on the N. side behind the lower point of an island [Bachelors] we arrived at the village of the Cath (*Quath*)-lah-poh-tle w[h]ich consists of 14 large wooden houses. . . . the floors of most of their houses are on a level with the surface of the earth tho' some of them are sunk two or 3 feet beneath. the internal arrangement . . . is the same with those of the nations below. they are also fond of sculpture. various figures are carved and painted on the peices which support the center of the roof, about their doors and beads [beds]. they had large quantities of dryed Anchovies [smelt] strung on small sticks by the gills and others which had been first dryed in this manner, were now arranged in large sheets . . . hung suspended by poles in the roofs of their houses; they also had an abundance of sturgeon and wappetoe; the latter they take in great quantities from the neighbouring ponds. . . . they have a number of large symeters of Iron from 3 to 4 feet long which hang by the heads of their beads [beds]; the blade of this weapon is thickest in the center tho' thin

Site of the village Quathlahpootle.

even there. . . . this is a formidable weapon. they have heavy bludgeons of wood made in the same form nearly which I presume they used for the same purpose before they obtained metal. . . . we gave the 1st. Cheif a small medal, which he soon transferred to his wife. after remaining at this place 2 hours we set out. . . . at the distance of 2 miles we encamped in a small prarie on the main shore. . . . heared a large hooting owl hollowing this evening, saw several of the crested fishers and some of the large and small blackbirds."

•

The midden of Quathlahpootle village can plainly be seen along the banks of Lake River just below Ridgefield, Washington. The journals give the village a population of nine hundred, more than that of the present town.

Gabriel Franchère saw the village in 1811 and wrote of it: "We left this beautiful place [Kalama] and proceeded to another large village that our guide told us was called Katlapootle. It was situ-

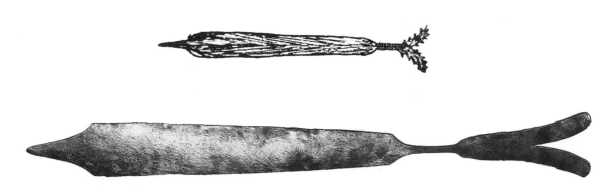

"this is a formidable weapon"
Sketch by Clark, top; and copper blade four feet long found near John Day River.

ated at the mouth of a small river that seemed to flow down from a snow-covered mountain [St. Helens]" (*Adventure at Astoria*, 50).

How the Columbia River Indians obtained the "large symeters of Iron" that Lewis observed at the village has long been debated. One possibility concerns the American fur-trading vessel *Jefferson*, whose captain, Josiah Roberts, ordered his ship's armorer to make a number of such sword blades, intended for use later to trade for *clemons* or elk hides at the mouth of the Columbia. Some four hundred of these blades were fabricated at Barkley Sound on the southwest coast of Vancouver Island in April 1794, many of them apparently being later exchanged for Columbia River elk hides (*see* Howay, "Yankee Trader," 87–88). Iron and copper swords of similar size

and shape, however, were seen and reported at Nootka, some six years earlier in the spring of 1788, by Joseph Ingraham, then an officer aboard the *Columbia Rediviva*. These blades, according to Ingraham, were "scarce among them," which could indicate that they had been made by the Indians themselves (*see* Ingraham to Martínez).

30 March 1806.
[LEWIS]

"We got under way very early in the morning. . . . at the distance of about 2 M. . . . we met a party of the Claxtars and Cathlahcumups in two canoes; soon after we were met by several canoes of the different nations who reside on each side of the river near this place. Wappatoe [Sauvie] Island is . . . high and extreemly fertile . . . with ponds which produce great quantities of the . . . bulb of which the natives call wappatoe. . . . we passed several fishing camps on Wappetoe island, and at the distance of 5 miles above quathlahpotle Island . . . we halted for breakfast [at Post Office Lake],. . . . here we were visited by several canoes which came off from two towns situated a little distance above us. . . . the 1st. call themselves Clan-nah-quah, the other about a mile above them call themselves Mult-no-mah. . . . we set out and had not proceeded far before we came to a landing place of the natives where there were several large canoes drawn out on shore and several natives seting in a canoe. . . . we halted a few minutes . . . and the Indians pointed to a village which was situated ab[o]ut 2 miles from the river behi[n]d a pond lying parallel with it on the N.E. side. . . . here they informed us that the Sho-toes resided. here we were joined by several other canoes. . . . most of these people accompanyed us untill 4 in the evening. . . . we continued . . . to the place we halted to dine on the 4th of Novembr. opposite to the center of Immage canoe island where the Indians stole Capt. Clarks tomahawk. here we encamped. . . . this valley . . . is about 70 miles wide on a direct line and it's length I believe to be very extensive, this valley would be competent to the maintenance of 40 or 50 thousand souls if properly cultivated."

[CLARK]

"discovered a high mountain S.E. covered with snow which we call Mt. Jefferson. [Saw a leather winged bat. . . . the frogs are abundant and crying in the swamps and marshes.]"°

•

The Multnomah village was at the present Reeder's Beach on Sauvie Island; the remains indicate it was once the largest and richest on the lower Columbia. The landing where the party stopped was the former outlet of Shillapoo Lake, now drained and farmed.

The so-called Shoto village was on Lake River, the outlet of Vancouver Lake. It is probable that the Indians tried to tell Lewis and Clark that "Soto" lived there, not that it was the name of the village. Reputedly the son of a Clatsop woman and a shipwrecked Spaniard known as Konapee to the Indians, in 1806 Soto was an old man, believed to be the "friendly chief" who met Lieutenant Broughton near this place in 1792. Alexander Henry wrote in January 1814, while near the Cascades: "At ten we were nearly abrest of the Soto village, where we saw the natives running into a low point of wood at the upper end of their village" (*Journals*, 2:799–800).

Franchère, approaching the Cascades in 1811, wrote: "We saw the hut of some Indian fishermen and we stopped for breakfast. Here we found an old, blind man who gave us a cor-

---

°The bracketed text is from the entry for 30 March 1806 in "Scientific Data Accompanying the Original Journals of Lewis and Clark" (Thwaites, *Journals*, 6:211).

Clay effigy from the Shoto village.

dial reception. Our guide said that he was a white man and that he was called Soto. We learned from the old man himself that he was the son of a Spaniard who had been wrecked at the mouth of the river; that some of the crew on this occasion got safely to land, but they had all been massacred by the Clatsops with the exception of four who were spared and who married native women. Disgusted with the savage life, four Spaniards, of whom the father of this man was one, had attempted, overland, to reach a settlement of white men, but had never been heard of again. When his father and companions left the country, Soto was quite young" (*Adventures at Astoria*, 50).

31 March 1806.
[LEWIS]
"We set out early and proceeded until 8 A.M. when we Landed on the N. side opposite one large wooden house of the *Sháh-ha-la* nation [*Ne-er-che-ki-po*] and took breakfast. when we descended the river in November last there were 24 other lodges formed of Straw and covered with bark near this house; these lodges are now distroyed and the inhabitants as the indians inform us have returned to the great rapids of this river which is their permanent residence. . . . These indians of the rapids frequently visit this valley at every season of the year for the purpose of collecting wappetoe which is abundant and appears never to be out of season. . . . at 10 A.M. we

Site of the Shoto village. The depressions are house pits.

resumed our march accompanyed by three men in a canoe; one of these fellows appeared to be a man of some note among them; he was dressed in a salor's jacket which was decorated in his own fashion with five rows of large and small buttons in front and some large buttons on the pocket flaps. they are remarkably fond of large brass buttons. . . . passed diamond [Government] Island and whitebrant [Lady] island to the lower point of a handsom prarie opposite to the upper en-trance of the Quicksand [Sandy] river; here we encamped having traveled 25 miles to day. a little below the upper point of Whitebrant Island Seal [Washougal] river discharges itself on the N. side. . . . we called it Seal river from the great abun-dance of those animals which we saw about it's entrance. we determined to remain at our pre-sent encampment a day or two for the several purposes of examining quicksand river, making some Celestial observations, and procuring some

"they are remarkably fond of large brass buttons"
Brass buttons from Columbia River village sites.

meat. . . . in the entrance of Seal river I saw a summer duck or wood duck as they are sometimes called."

[CLARK]

"three Indians encamped near us. . . . they informed us that . . . [the] quick sand river [Sandy] was short only headed in Mt. Hood which is in view. . . . distant from this place about 40 miles. this information if true will render it necessary to examine the river below on the South side behind the image canoe and Wappato islands for some river which must water the country weste of the western mountains to the waters of California."

•

The wood duck, *Aix sponsa*, one of the most beautifully colored of all birds, has a range of practically the entire continent. It nests in hollow trees near the water, and the nestlings can drop to the hard ground without sustaining the least injury. After landing, their bones and joints start to harden, and they are soon swimming about and fending for themselves.

The "lower point of a handsom prarie" would be about where the Washougal Woolen Mills now stand. Here the party camped for six days, hunting and drying meat for the journey ahead.

1 April 1806.
[LEWIS]

"This Morning early we dispatched Sergt. Pryor with two men in a small canoe up quicksand [Sandy] river with orders to proceed as far as he could and return this evening. we also sent a party of three hunters. . . . The Indians . . . informed us that the quicksand river is navigable a short distance only in consequence of falls and rapids; and that no nation inhabits it. Sergt Pryor returned in the evening and reported that he had ascended the river six miles. . . . We were visited by several canoes of natives in the course of the

"wappetoe which is abundant"

"Sergt Pryor . . . ascended the river six miles"
The Sandy River about where Pryor turned back.

day; most of whom were descending the river with their women and children. they informed me that they resided at the great rapids and were much streightened at that place for want of food . . . & that they did . . . not expect the Salmon to arrive untill the full of the next moon which happens on the 2d. of May. we did not doubt the varacity of these people who seemed to be on their way with their families and effects in surch of subsistence which they find it easy to procure in this fertile valley. . . . at 3 P.M. the hunters returned . . . having killed 4 Elk and two deer. . . . they informed us that game is very plenty. . . . I purchased a canoe from an Indian to day for which I gave him six fathoms of wampum beads; he seemed satisfied with his bargain and departed in another canoe but shortly afterward returned and canceled the bargain, took his canoe and returned the beads. this is frequently the case in their method of traiding and is deemed fair by them."

•

This day Lewis collected a type specimen of the slender toothwort, *Dentaria tenella*, "on the banks of the Columbia near the quicksand river." We have seen it flowering in profusion on the Washougal River and near Skamania; it blooms as early as 15 March.

2 April 1806.
[LEWIS]

"This morning we came to the resolution to remain at our present encampment . . . untill we had obtained as much dryed meat as would be necessary for our voyage as far as the Chopunnish. . . . we . . . dispatched two parteis consisting of nine men to the opposite side of the river. . . . we also sent out three others on this side, and those who remained in camp were employed in collecting wood making a scaffoald and cutting up the meat in order to dry it. about this time several canoes of the natives arrived at our camp and among others one from below which had on board eight men of the Shah-ha-la nation."

[CLARK]

"those men informed us that they reside on the opposit side of the Columbia near some pine trees which they pointed to in the bottom South of Dimond Island, they singled out two young men whome they informed us lived at the Falls of a large river which discharges into the Columbia on it's south side some miles below us. we readily provailed on them to give us a sketch of this river which they drew on a Mat with coal, it appeared that this river which they called *Multnó-mah* discharged itself behind the Island we call image canoe island. . . . I deturmined to take a small party and return to this river and examine its size. . . . I took with me six men, Thompson J. Potts, Peter P. Crusat, P. Wiser, T.P. Howard, Jos. Whitehouse & my man York in a large Canoe, with an Indian whome I hired for a Sun glass to accompany me as pilot. . . . I set out, and had not proceeded far eer I saw 4 large canoes . . . bending their course towards our Camp which at this time is very weak Capt. Lewis haveing only 10 men with him. I hesitated for a moment whether it would not be advisable for me to return and delay untill a part of our hunters should return to add more strength to our Camp. but on second reflection and reverting to the precautions always taken by my friend Capt. Lewis on those occasions banished all apprehensions and I proceeded on down. at 8 miles passed a village on the south side [near Blue Lake] at this place my Pilot informed me he resided and that the name of the tribe is *Ne-cha-co-lee*. . . . at 3 P.M. I landed at a large double house of the *Ne-er-che-ki-oo* tribe. . . . at this place we had seen 24 additional straw Huts as we passed last fall. . . . on the bank at different places I observed small canoes which the women make use of to gather wappato & roots in the Slashes. those canoes are from 10 to 14 feet long and from 18 to 23 inches wide . . . and about 9 inches deep. . . . I think 100 of these canoes were piled up and scattered in different directions in the woods, in the vicinity of this house. . . . I entered one of the rooms of this house and offered several articles to the nativs in exchange for wappato. they were sulkey and positively refused to sell any. I had a small pece of port fire match in my pocket, off of which I cut a pece one inch in length & put it into the fire and took out my pocket compas and set myself down on a mat on one side of the fire, and [also showed] a magnet which was in the top of my ink stand the port fire cought and burned vehemently, which changed the colour of the fire; with the magnit I turned the needle of the compas about very briskly; which astonished and alarmed these nativs and they laid several parsles of wappato at my feet, & begged of me to take out the bad fire; to this I consented; at this moment the match being exhausted was of course extinguished and I put up the magnet &c. this measure alarmed them so much that the womin and children took shelter in their beads [beds] and behind the men, all this time a very old blind man was speaking with great vehemunce, apparently imploring his god. I lit my pipe and gave them smoke, & gave the womin the full amount [value] of the roots which they had put at my feet. they appeared somewhat passified and I left them and proceeded on. . . . at a distance of 13 miles below the last village . . . I entered this river which the nativs had informed us of, called *Multnomah* [Willamette] River so called by the nativs from a nation who reside on Wappato Island a little below the enterance of this river. . . . I can plainly see Mt. Jefferson . . . S.E. Mt. Hood East, Mt. St. Helians [and] a high humped mountain [Mount Adams] to the East of Mt. St. Helians. thence 3 miles to a large Indian house on the Lard side below some high pine land. . . . 2 miles to a bend under the high lands on the Stard. Side passing a Larboard point. thence the river bends to the East of S East as far as I could see. at this place I think the width of the river may be stated as 500 yards and sufficiently deep for a Man of war or ship of any burthen."

•

Port fire is a slow-burning fuse used by the artillery and made from saltpeter, sulphur, and gunpowder wrapped in paper. Our guess is that Clark had it in his pocket for starting fires, a most difficult task in the wet season.

Clark was mistaken when he said the Indians called the river "*Multnomah*." The Indians of the West seldom, if ever, named rivers (only places), and the names were nearly always descriptive, such as "where the flax grows." Throughout their journals Lewis and Clark mention Indian names for rivers, a natural misunderstanding considering the prevalence with which non-Indians customarily give names to rivers, not to mention the usual difficulties that limit understanding be-

Remains of the eroded village Namuit on Sauvie Island. The gravel on the beach consists of rocks used by the native inhabitants for stone boiling.

tween different languages. On 8 January 1806, Clark noted that the Tillamooks called the Columbia River "Shock ah lil con," but what they really meant was that they bought wappato at a village where a chief of that name resided.

The Oregon historian Horace S. Lyman quotes Silas B. Smith, the son of Solomon Howard Smith and his Clatsop Indian wife, Helen (née Celiast Coboway; *see* 27 December 1805), as asserting that "the Indians in this northwest country as far east as the Rocky Mountains, never

name a river as a river. They name localities. . . . Some [whites] have even told me that they had found the name of the Columbia; but it is a mistake" (*History*, 2:201).

Where the word "nation" is used in the journals, as, for example, in "*Shah-ha-la* nation," it refers only to a separate group or village. All the Indians on the lower Columbia were Chinookan speakers and participants in essentially the same culture, except for a small band of Clatskanie who spoke Athapascan.

3 *April 1806.*

[C L A R K]

"The water had fallen in the course of last night five inches. . . . Being perfectly satisfyed of the size and magnitude of this great river which must water that vast tract of Country between the western range of mountains and those on the sea coast and as far s. as the Waters of Callifornia. . . . I deturmined to return. at 7 oClock A.M. set out on my return. . . . at 3 P.M. we arrived at the residence of our Pilot which consists of one long house with seven appartments or rooms in square form about 30 feet each room opening into a passage which is quit[e] through the house. those passages are about 4 feet in width and formed of wide boa[r]ds set on end in the ground and reaching to the Ruff [roof] which serves also as divisions to the rooms. . . . back of this house I observe the wreck of 5 houses remaining of a very large village. . . . I indeavored to obtain from those people of the situation of their nation, if scattered or what had become of the nativs who must have peopled this great town. an old man who appeared of some note among them and fa-ther to my guide brought forward a woman who was badly marked with the Small Pox and made signs that they all died with the disorder. . . . and which she was verry near dieing with when a girl. from the age of this woman this Distructive dis-order I judge must have been about 28 or 30 years past, and about the time the Clatsops in-form us that this disorder raged in their towns and distroyed their nation. . . . severall men and women whom I observed in this village had arived at a great age, and appeared to be helthy tho' blind. I provailed on an old man to draw me a sketch of the Multnomar River . . . which he readily done, and gave me the names of 4 nations who reside on this river two of them very nou-merous. The first is *Clark-a-mus* nation reside on a small river [Clackamas] which takes its rise in Mount Jefferson and falls into the Moltnomar about 40 miles up. this nation is noumerous and inhabit 11 Towns. the 2d. is the *Cush-hooks* who reside on the NE. side below the falls, the 3rd. *Char-cowah* who reside above the Falls on the SW. side neither of those two are noumerous. The fourth Nation is the *Cal-lar-po-e-wah* which is very noumerous & inhabit the country on each side of the Multnomar from its falls as far up as the knowledge of those people extend. they in-form me also that a high mountain passes the Multnomar at the falls, and above the country is an open plain of great extent. . . . at 4 P M left the village and proceeded on to Camp where I joind. Capt. Lewis."

•

The "open plain of great extent" was the Willa-mette River Valley, the rich soil of which lured thousands of emigrants across the plains in cov-ered wagons during the mid-nineteenth century.

The Nechacookee Village was just west of Blue Lake, near Troutdale. We have an old letter whose author says he saw it "when the farmer first cleared the land, with fireplaces quite distinct, about 12 in number. I have many fine carved artifacts from the site, arrow heads and elk bones were strewn all over." When a dike was built in that area, great masses of human bones were uncovered, victims of the smallpox or some other epidemic.

Apparently the village was abandoned soon after Clark's visit, for on 12 January 1814, Alexander Henry wrote: "One of our canoes fouled a stump, and tore two bits of bark from her bottom. . . . she was kept afloat for an hour, when we put ashore to repair her, at the remains of an old village on the s., below Seal Rock" (*Journals*, 2:797–98).

The Willamette is indeed a noble stream, with more than a thousand ocean vessels a year passing through the entrance between the islands Lewis and Clark called Image Canoe and Wappato, past Swan Island where Clark turned about, and on to what is today the heart of Portland. But it fails by a great distance to drain the vast area assigned to it by Captain Clark.

The map drawn by the old man and his description of the country were correct in every respect, and the names of the tribes are still used.

4 April 1806.
[LEWIS]

"Several parties of the natives visit us today as usual both from above and below; those who came from above were moving with their families, and those from below appeared to be impeled mearly by the curiossity to see us. About noon we despatched Gibson Shannon Howard and Wiser in one of the light canoes, with orders to proceed up the Columbia to a large bottom on the South side about six miles above us to hunt untill our arrival."

•

The "large bottom" is between Tunnel Point and Shepherds Dell, where Rooster Rock stands as the western gateway to the Columbia River Gorge.

5 April 1806.
[LEWIS]

"we were visited to day by several parties of the natives as usual; they behaved in a very orderly manner. . . . Saw the Log cock, the humming bird, gees ducks &c. today. the tick has made it's appearance it is the same with those of the Atlantic States. the Musquetoes have also appeared but are not yet troublesome."

[CLARK]

"The red flowering current is found here in considerable quantities on the upland, and the common Dog wood is found on either side of the river."

[LEWIS]

"it differs from that of the United States in the appearance of it's bark which is much smoother, it also arrives here to much greater size that I ever observed it elsewhere sometimes the stem is nearly 2 feet in diameter."

"The red flowering currant is found here"
Red currant, flower and fruit.

[CLARK]

"The country on either side is fertile."

[LEWIS]

"we measured a fallen tree of fir . . . which was 318 feet including the stump which was about 6 feet high. this tree was only about 3½ feet in diameter."

•

The "Log cock" was the Northern pileated woodpecker, *Dryocopus pileatus picinus*, a woodland inhabitant rendered vulnerable (particularly on the east side of the Cascades) by the destruction of its habitat. It is a somber black and has a brilliant red crest, much prized by the Indians for decorating their finery.

For sheer beauty, few plants can exceed the red flowering currant, *Ribes sanguineum*, as it stands lit by the sun on the edge of a wood. In late March it bursts into bloom, invariably greeted by the first hummingbirds. The hummingbird and the red currant are inseparable, and are as much a part of spring as the polecat colewort.

The fruit is tasteless and insipid, a disappointing progeny for so bright a promise. This shrub

"we measured a
. . . tree of fir"

was not unknown to science: Menzies had found it in 1787, but it was described and published by Frederick Pursh in 1814 from the Lewis and Clark specimen, leading some authors to attribute its discovery to them (*see* Pursh, *Flora Americae*, 1:164).

The flowering dogwood, *Cornus nuttallii*, grows up to sixty feet high, and its mass of white blossoms in early spring makes it stand out in the darkest wood. Frequently it blooms again in late fall. The bark is bitter. In pioneer times it was used as a substitute for quinine, and the Indians made an emetic or physic from it. The fine-grained wood is white and tough, useful for small articles like shuttles. Another species of the dogwood, *C. canadensis*, shares the same habitat but is only four to six inches tall, a miniature replica of a single twig of its great cousin.

6 April 1806.
[LEWIS]

"This morning we had the dryed meat secured in skins and the canoes loaded; we took breakfast and departed at 9 A.M. we continued up the N. side of the river. . . . passed the river to the south side in quest of the hunters. . . . from the appearance of a rock where we encamped on the 3rd. [2nd] of November last I think the flood of this spring has been about 12 feet higher than it was at that time. . . . at the distance of ten miles from our encempment we met with our hunters in the upper end of the bottom [Shepherds Dell]. . . . they had killed three elk this morning and

wounded two others so badly that they expected to get them."

[CLARK]

"formed a camp, near which we had a scaffold made ready to dry the meat. . . . Reubin Fields killed a bird of the quail kind or class which was whistleing near our camp. . . . this is a most butifull bird. . . . This supply of Elk I think by useing economey and in addition of roots and dogs which we may probably precure from the Nativs on Lewis's [Snake] river will be sufficient to last us to the Chopunnish where we shall meet with our horses. . . . we derected . . . th[at] Drewer and the two Fields proceed on to the next bottom [Warrendale] and hunt untill we should arive."

•

The picture of Rooster Rock (*see* 2 November 1805) plainly shows a high-water mark about twelve feet above the river level, similar to the line Clark saw.

The mountain quail, *Oreortyx pictus palmeri*, is indeed a beautiful bird. Lewis describes it in great detail, but it was officially recorded and named by David Douglas in 1829. The mountain quail has a long, straight plume and somewhat different markings from the California quail, *O.p. picta*.

7 April 1806.
[CLARK]

"This morning Drewyer & the two Fields set out agreeably to their orders of last evening, the re-

"this is a most butifull bird" The California quail, similar to the mountain quail that Fields brought to Lewis.

mainder of the party employed in drying the flesh of the five Elk . . . which we completed and we had it secured in dried shaved Elk Skins and put on board in readiness for our early departure. we were visited by several parties of Indians from a village about 12 miles above us of the *Shahalah* nation. . . . The day has been fair and weather exceedingly pleasent, we made our men exercise themselves in shooting and regulateing their guns. . . . I provaled on an old indian to mark the Multnomah R down on sand which hid [he did] and perfectly corisponded with the sketch given me by sundry others. . . . he also lais down the Clarkamos [Clackamas] . . . and . . . Mt. Jefferson which he lais down by raiseing the Sand as a very high mountain. . . . the Clarkamos nation . . . live principally on fish. . . . they build their houses in the same form with those of the Columbian Valley of wide split boa[r]ds and covered with bark of the white cedar which is the entire length of the one side of the roof and jut over at the eve about 18 inches. . . . transverse sp[l]inters of dried pine is inserted through the cedar bark in order to keep it smooth and prevent it's edge from colapsing [warping] by the heat of the sun; in this manner the nativs make a very secure light and lasting roof of thin bark. which we have observed in every vilege in this vally as well as those above."

8 April 1806.

[CLARK]

"This morning about day light I heard a considerable roreing like wind at a distance and in . . . a short time wav[e]s rose very high. . . . the winds swelded [swelled] and blew so hard and raised the waves so emensely high from the N.E. and tossed our canoes against the shore in such a manner as to render it necessary to haul them up on the bank. finding . . . that it is probable that we may be detained all day, we sent out Drewyer, Shennon, Colter & Collins to hunt. . . . we had the dried meat . . . exposed to the sun."

[LEWIS]

"I took a walk today of three miles down the river; in the course of which I had an opportunity to correct an errow [error] which I have heretofore made with rispect to the shrub I have hithertoo called the large leafed thorn. the leaf of this thorn is small being only ab[o]ut 2½ inches long [salmonberry, *see* 13 November 1805]. . . . the shrub which I have heretofore confounded with this grows in similar situations, has a stem precisely like it except the thorn and bears a large three loabed leaf."

[CLARK]

"John Shields cut out my small rifle & brought hir to shoot very well. The party owes much to the injinuity of this man, by whome their guns are repared when they get out of order which is very

often. [the goosburry has cast the petals of its flowers, and it's leaves obtained their full size]."°

•

Lewis had confused the salmonberry with the thimbleberry, *Rubus parviflorus*. The two shrubs are quite similar but easily differentiated: the thimbleberry has no thorns, its leaf is larger and smoother, its flower is white, its fruit red and more tasty. The Indians ate the young sprouts, as they did those of the salmonberry. The berries are too fragile and soft to dry satisfactorily, and are eaten fresh.

The gooseberry was *Ribes menziesii*, a rather uncommon shrub growing along shaded stream banks and roadsides, resembling the domestic variety. Blackberries were eaten fresh, but were of little importance.

To "cut out" a rifle is to clean and restore the rifling grooves with a special tool operated like a cleaning rod.

John Shields was one of the most valuable members of the expedition, frequently chosen by Lewis for special duty. In his report to the secretary of war in 1807, Lewis wrote of Shields: "Nothing was more peculiarly useful to us, in various situations, than the skill and ingenuity of this man as an artist, in repairing our guns, accoutrements, &c. and should it be thought proper to

---

°The bracketed text is from an entry for 8 April 1806 in "Scientific Data Accompanying the Original Journals of Lewis and Clark" (Thwaites, *Journals*, 6:213).

"bears a large three loabed leaf" Thimble berry, flower and fruit.

*"the goosburry has
cast the petals of its
flower"*

"passed several beautifull cascades"

Site of the Wahclellah village.

allow him some thing as an artificer, he has well deserved it" (Thwaites, *Journals*, 7:358).

Shields was born in Virginia and in October 1803 enlisted for the expedition in Kentucky. At the age of thirty-five, he may have been the old-est member of the party. During the winter of 1804–05 at the Mandan villages, he was kept busy making tomahawks and other ironwork to trade for corn. After the expedition he was a trap-per until his death in 1809.

Petroglyph near the
Wahclellah village site.

9 April 1806.
[LEWIS]
"We . . . continued our rout to the Wah-clel-lah
Village which is situated on the North side of the
river about a mile below the beacon rock; here
we halted and took breakfast. John Colter . . . observed the tomehawk in one of the lodges which
had been stolen from us on the 4th of November
last."

[CLARK]
"he took the tomahawk. . . . This village appears
to be the wintering station of two bands of the
Sha-ha-la Nation. One band has already moved
[to] the Falls of the Multnomah [at Oregon City]
which is the place where they take their Salmon.
The other band is now moveing a fiew miles
above to the foot of the first rapid. . . . 14 houses
only appear occupied. . . . 9 houses has been latterly abandened. . . . 10 or 12 others are to be
seen and appears to have been enhabited last fall.
soon after we arrived at this village the Grand
Chief and two others of the *Che-luck-kit-le-quaw*
Nation [*see* 28 October 1805] arived from below.
they had . . . been trading in the Columbia Vally
for Wappato, beeds and dried anchovies &c. in
exchange for which they had given pounded fish,

"The dogtoothed violet is in blume"—"also the bear claw"

shappalell, beargrass, acorns boiled berries &c. &c. and are now on their return to their village. as those people had been very kind to us as we decended the river we gave them smoke."

[LEWIS]

"on our way to this village we passed several beautifull cascades which fell from a great hight over stupendious rocks which closes the river on both sides nearly. . . . the most remarkable of these casscades falls 300 feet perpendicularly over a solid rock into a narrow bottom of the river on the south side.° it is a large creek, situated

---

°This may refer to today's Multnomah Falls, but its total height is actually some 620 feet (*see* McArthur, *Oregon Geographic Names,* 529).

about 5 miles above our encampment of last evening. several small streams fall from a much greater hight, and in their decent become a perfect mist which collecting on the rocks below again become visible and decend a second time in the same manner before they reach the base of the rocks."

[CLARK]

"at 2 o'Clock P.M. we set out and passed under Beacon rock on the North Side of two small Islds. [Pierce and Ives] situated nearest the N. side. at 4 P.M. we arived at the first rapid at the head of Strawberry island at which place on the N.W. Side of the Columbia here we found the nativs from the last village rebuilding their habitations of the bark of their old village 16 Huts are already compleated and appear only temporrary it is most probable that they only reside here dureing the season of the Salmon."

[LEWIS]

"we passed to the opposite side and entered the narrow channel which seperates brant [Bradford] Island from the South shore. . . . and encamped on the main shore. [the dogtoothed violet is in blume as is also the bears claw.]"*

•

The Wahclellah village was built on one of the most picturesque tracts on the Columbia, a handsome prairie flanked by massive basalt ramparts. The dog-tooth violet, *Erythronium sp.*, carpets the open woodlands with its colorful nodding blooms in April and May. There are several species, one of which is known as the avalanche lily, since it follows the receding snowbanks in early summer. Sometimes it bursts through the snow itself, the blossoms as white as their background.

The "bears claw" is the larkspur, *Delphinium menziesii*. It inhabits the dry hillsides, where its dark-blue flowers cloak its poisonous leaves and stem. Stockmen would gladly see the species extinguished.

---

*The bracketed text is from the entry for 9 April 1806 in "Scientific Data Accompanying the Original Journals of Lewis and Clark" (Thwaites, *Journals*, 6:213).

Trillium ovatum. Lewis collected the type specimen of this lily on 10 April 1806 at the Cascades.

X

HOMEWARD BOUND
GREAT SHUTE TO
THE WALLA WALLA RIVER
10 TO 29 APRIL 1806

10 April 1806.
[LEWIS]

"We set out early and droped down the channel to the lower end of brant Island from whence we drew [our canoes] up the rapid by a cord about a quarter of a mile which we soon performed. . . . we directed Sergt. Pryor to remain with the cord on the Island untill Gibson arrived and assist him . . . in geting his canoe up the rapid, when they wer to join us on the oposite side at a small village of six houses . . . where we halted for breakfast. in passing the river which is here about 400 yds. wide the rapidity of the currant was such that it boar us down a considerable distance notwithstanding we employed five oars. on entering one of these lodges, the natives offered us a sheepskin for sail, than which nothing could have been more acceptable except the animal itself. the skin of the head of the sheep with the horns remaining was cased in such manner as to fit the head of a man by whom it was woarn and highly prized as an ornament. we obtained this cap in exchange for a knife, and were compelled to give two Elkskins in exchange for the skin. this appeared to be the skin of a sheep not fully grown; the horns were about four inches long, celindric, smooth, black, erect and pointed. . . . these people informed us that these sheep were found in great abundance on the hights and among the clifts of the adjacent mountains. and that they had lately killed these from a herd of 36, at no great distance from their village. . . . we set out and continued our rout up the N. side of the river with great difficulty in consequence of the rapidity of the current and the large rocks which form this shore; the South side of the river is impassable. as we had but one sufficient toe-rope and were obliged to employ the cord in geting on our canoes the greater part of the way we could only take them one at a time which retarded our progress very much. by evening we arrived at the portage on the North side where we landed and conveyed our bagage to the top of the hill about 200 paces distant where we formed a camp. the small canoe got loose from the hunters and went a drift . . . the Indians caught her at the last village and brought her up to us this evening for which service we gave them a couple of knives."

•

The "sheepskin" was that of the mountain goat, *Oreamnos americanus* (*see* 29 October 1805). The original description and the naming of the animal were from data supplied by Captain Lewis, though he was not the first white man to record seeing it. The mountain goat was once common in the Cascade Mountains, but only north of the Columbia River. A few remnants of the great bands still exist in the Northern Cascades. The village where Lewis purchased the skin was a few hundred yards downstream from the north abutment of Bonneville Dam.

This day Lewis collected type specimens of the lovely western trillium, *Trillium ovatum*; the Oregon grape (*see* 12 February 1806); and, on Bradford Island, the graceful brown-and-green mission bell, *Fritillaria lanceolata*.

The white blossoms of the trillium are some of the earliest spring flowers and are sometimes called Easter lilies. The bulbs were used for medicine, either crushed for a poultice or soaked

in water for an eyewash. The bulbs of the mission bell were eagerly sought for food; the plant is sometimes called rice root.

11 April 1806.

[LEWIS]

"this portage is two thousand eight hundred yards along a narrow rough and slipery road. the duty of getting the canoes above the rapid was by mutual consent confided to my friend Capt. C. . . . by the evening Capt. C. took 4 of the canoes above the rapids tho' with much difficulty and labour. . . . the men complained of being so much fatiegued in the evening that we posponed taking up our 5th. canoe untill tomorrow. . . . the water appears to be considerably upwards of 20 feet higher than when we decended the river."

[CLARK]

"Great numbers of the nativs visited us and viewed us from the banks as we passed on with the canoes, maney of those people were also about our baggage and on the portage road. two of those fellows insulted John Shields. . . . one other Indn. stold an ax. . . . one other fellow attempted to steal Capt. Lewis's dog [Seaman], and had decoyed him nearly half a mile[.] we were informed of it by a man who spoke the Clatsop language and imediately sent three men with their guns who over took the Indians, who on their approach ran off and left the dog. . . . A Chief of the *Clah-clal-lahs* Tribe informed us that there was two very bad men who had been guilty of those mischevious acts. . . . this Chief

Mission bells and Lewis and Clark type specimen.

had a large fine pipe tomahawk which he informed me he got from a Trader he called Swippeton. I exchanged tomahawks with this Chief, as he appeared to be a man of consideration among the tribes of this neighbourhood and much conserned for the ingiries offered us, we gave him a medal of the small size which appeared to please him verry much, and will I hope . . . attach him to our interest, and he probably will harang his people in our favour, which may prevent any acts of violence being committed, on either side. nothing but the strength of our party has prevented our being robed before this time. . . . The inhabitents of the Wy-ach-hich Tribe village imedeately above those rapids on the N W. Side have latterly moved their village to the opposit side of the river, where they take their Salmon; they are now in the act of removeing and not only take their furniture and effects but also the bark and most of the boards which formed their houses."

[L E W I S]

"The salmon have not yet made their appearance, tho' the natives are not so much distressed for food as I was induced to believe. [What I have heretofore termed the broad leafed ash is now in blume. the fringe tree has cast the corolla and it's leaves have nearly obtained their full size.]"°

_____

°The bracketed text is from an entry for 11 April 1806 in "Scientific Data Accompanying the Original Journals of Lewis and Clark" (Thwaites, *Journals*, 6:213).

•

The medal given to the chief may be one of two in the Maryhill Museum's collection. They were owned by Mary Underwood Lane, a descendant of Chief Chenoweth of the Cascade tribe, who was hanged with eight others for their alleged participation in a massacre in 1856. The other is perhaps the one given to Tow-wale (*see* 21 November 1805).

Lewis had bought Seaman, a Newfoundland, for twenty dollars (a large sum) in Philadelphia. The dog endured with the humans all the hardships, privations, and joys of the entire trip. Ferocious grizzly bears were troublesome on the Missouri, and the expedition suffered several near-tragedies. The bears came close to camp at night, but Seaman gave timely warning of their visits. When a terrified bison charged through the sleeping camp on the Plains, the dog flew out and forced it to change course so that it passed without doing much damage. He would swim out to retrieve game shot in or over water, and once caught and drowned an antelope before bringing it ashore. On another occasion, he successfully chased down one of these swift creatures on land.

Seaman had his troubles, too. On the Missouri he became so exhausted that he had to be returned to camp, and he once got lost before eventually finding his way back—to Lewis's great relief. On the Plains the dog was tormented by barbed seeds in his fur, and suffered torture from

"we gave him a medal of the small size"
Washington "sowing" medals in Maryhill Museum.

clouds of mosquitoes. A beaver he seized in the water promptly sank its long teeth into the dog's leg, causing a wound from which he nearly bled to death. The Indians were astonished by Seaman, and the dog in turn seemed to enjoy displaying his talents to an appreciative audience.

The "fringe tree" was the osoberry, *Osmaronia cerasiformis*, also called Indian plum, bearberry, and (because of the unpleasant odor of the flowers) skunk bush. It grows in rich, moist soil in woods and open brushlands to a height of six feet. A more fitting name would be spring bush, for it is the earliest of the shrubs, conspicuous with its promise of winter's end. Every traveler must notice it by the roadside, yet few can call it by name. The fruit is a cluster of orange-colored, plum-shaped drupes, insipid but decorative. The Indians gathered and ate them, but not with enthusiasm.

"the broad leafed ash is now in blume"

12 April 1806.
[CLARK]

"rained the greater part of the last night and this morning untill 10 A.M. we employed all hands in attempting to take up the last canoe. in attempting to pass by a rock against which the current run with emence force, the bow unfortunately took the current at too great a distance from the rock, she turned broad side to the stream, and the exertions of every man was not sufficient to hold her. the men were compelled to let go the rope and both the canoe and rope went with the stream. the loss of this canoe will I fear compell us to purchase another at an extravigent price. after brackfast all hands . . . were employed in carrying the baggage over the portage 1½ miles which they performed by 4 P.M. . . . in the evening . . . I set out myself accompanied by the Chief of the Chal-clal-lars to the head of the portage, as we passed the remains of an old village about half way the portage, this chief informed me that this old village had been the residence of his Tribe dureing the last Salmon Season. this village I mentioned in decending this river, but did not know the Tribe that had inhabited it that time. . . . Those tribes [Wy-ach-hich, Chalclallah, Wah-clellah] I believe to be all the same Nation their Language habits manner dress &c. are presisely alike and differ but little from those below the Great Narrows of this river."

[LEWIS]

"We purchased one sheepskin for which we gave the skin of an Elk and one of a deer. . . . the big

"the fringe tree has cast the corolla"
Osoberry, flower and fruit.

horned animal is also an inhabitant of these mountains. I saw several robes of their skin among the natives. . . . for the three days last we have made only 7 miles."

•

The "big horned animal" was the bighorn sheep, *Ovis canadensis.* It was first seen on the expedition by Joseph Fields on the Yellowstone. One was killed on the Jefferson River, but none was seen west of Lolo Pass. The bighorn frequents the remotest and most inaccessible reaches of the mountains; its agility in traversing the rocky bluffs is amazing and its enemies must be crafty and lucky to capture one. It was a favored food of

the Indians. Because great numbers of sheep petroglyphs and effigies have been found throughout the West, it is believed that there was a sheep cult, employing magic to attain power for a successful hunt. Campbell Grant explains this theory in detail in *Rock Drawings of the Coso Range.*

13 April 1806.
[L E W I S]

"we loaded and set out [at] 8 A.M. . . . we found the additional laiding which we had been compelled to put on board rendered our vessels extreemly inconvenient to mannage and in short reather unsafe in the event of high winds; I therefore left Capt. C. with the two perogues to proceede up the river on the N. side, and . . . passed over the river above the rapids to the Y-eh-huh village in order to purchase one or more canoes. I found the village consisting of 11 houses crouded with inhabitants. . . . they appeared very friendly disposed, and I soon obtained two small canoes from them for which I gave two robes and four elkskins. I also purchased four paddles and three dogs from them with deerskins. . . . After remaining about two hours at this Village I departed and continued my rout . . . along the s. side . . . the wind being too high to pass over to the entrance of Cruzatts [Wind] river when I expected to have overtaken Capt. C."

•

The Yeh-huh village had moved to its summer site in the center of today's Cascade Locks. The midden of this large town may still be seen in nearby lots. Alexander Henry stopped there on 16 January 1814, and recorded: "We pushed over to the Cathlayackty village on the s., which is situated in the woods, at some distance from the river. The chief, whose house we entered, was a portly old man, who looked more respectable than any other I had seen on the Columbia. He was very civil to us, and spread down near the fire a clean biche-skin [elk skin] for us to sit upon. . . . These houses are sunk about three feet under ground; the entrance is at one end by a narrow oval door, with a knotty log on the inside for a

ladder. Next the door facing it is a plank partition, behind which is the fireplace, about 10 feet square, sunk two feet below the ground floor of the house. At the other end is another partition of planks, behind which a range of beds, raised three feet from the ground, occupies the furthermost end of the house and runs around on both sides to opposite the partition near the door. The front planks of the beds are carved and painted in various styles. At the end of each range are some broad upright planks, on which figures are rudely carved, somewhat resembling fluted pillars. At the foot of the Chief's bed are planted in the ground at equal distances four figures of human heads, about two feet high, adorned with a kind of crown, and rudely carved and painted. Beside these figures are erected in the ground two large, flat, painted stones. On the side of each partition, facing the fireplace, are carved and painted on planks uncouth figures of eagles, tortoises, and other animals, some of them four feet long. The colors used are white, red, black, and green; the sculpture, in some instances, is not bad" (*Journals*, 2:804–5).

14 April 1806.
[LEWIS]

"we took breakfast and departed. at 9 A.M. the wind arrose and continued hard all day but not so violent as to prevent our proceeding. we kept close along the N. shore all day. the river from the rapids as high as the commencement of the narrows is from 1/2 to 3/4 of a mile in width, and possesses scarcely any current. the bed is princi-pally rock except at the entrance of Labuish's [Hood] river which heads in Mount hood and like the quicksand [Sandy] river brings down from thence vast bodies of sand. the mountains through which the river passes nearly to the sepulchre rock, are high broken, rocky, partially covered with fir white cedar, and in many places exhibit very romantic seenes. some handsome cascades are seen on either hand tumbling from the stupendious rocks of the mountains into the river. . . . throughout the whole course of this river from the rapids as high as the Chilluckkit-tequaws, we find the trunks of many large pine trees s[t]anding erect as they grew at present in 30 feet [of] water; they are much doated [de-cayed?] and none of them vegetating; at the low-est tide of the river many of these trees are in ten feet [of] water. certain it is that those large pine trees never grew in that position, nor can I ac-count for this phenomenon except it be that the passage of the river through the narrow pass at the rapids has been obstructed by the rocks which have fallen from the hills into the channel within the last 20 years; the appearance of the hills at that place justify this opinion, they appear constantly to be falling in, and the apparent state of the decayed trees would seem to fix the era of their decline about the time mentioned [*see* 31 October 1805]. at 1 P.M. we arrived at a large vil-lage [Bingen] situated in a narrow bottom on the N. side a little above the entrance of canoe creek [White Salmon River]. their houses are reather

detached and extent [extend] for several miles. They are about 20 in number. These people call themselves We-ock-sock, Wil-la-cum. they dif-fer but litt[l]e . . . from those at the rapids. . . . they have some good horses of which we saw ten or a dousen. These are the fi[r]st horses we have met since last fall, in short the country below this place will not permit the uce of this valuable an-imal. . . . we halted at this village and dined. pur-chased five dogs, some roots, shappalell, filberds and dryed burries of the inhabitants grownd; they were sunk about 8 feet deep and covered with strong timber and several feet of earth in a conic form. these habitations were evacuated at present. they are about 16 feet in diameter, nearly circular, and are entered through a hole at the top which appears to answer the double purpose of a chimney and a door. . . . after dinner we pursued our voyage; Capt. Clark walked on shore with Charbono. I ascended the river about six miles at which place the river washed the base of high clifts on the Lard. side."

[C L A R K]

"met several parties of women and boys in serch of herbs & roots to subsist on[.] maney of them had parcels of the stems of the sun flower. . . . Several canoes over take us with families move-ing up. we passed 3 encampments and came too in the mouth of a small creek [Major] on the N. Side imediately below a village and opposite the Sepulchar rock. this village consists of about 100 fighting men of several tribes from the plains to the north collected here waiting for the

"pine trees s[t]anding erect . . . in 30 feet [of] water"
The drowned forest upriver of the Cascades.

"the river washed the base of high clifts"
Pompeys Pillars on the Columbia. Memaloose
(Sepulchar) Island, now called Rocky Island, right
center.

*"maney . . . had parcels of the stems of the sun
flower"*

(left and above) *"a village . . . opposite the Sepulcher rock"*

Most of the site has been flooded by Bonneville Dam. The banded sinker was found on the water's edge when the photo of the site was taken in 1969.

Salmon. they do not differ in any respect form those above. Many of them visited our camp this evening."

•

The "stems of the sun flower" were from the balsam root, *Balsamorrhiza*, a flowering plant that gilds the dry prairies and hillsides in early spring. The stems were peeled and eaten like celery, and the seeds were gathered and ground into flour. Apparently balsam-root seeds were the only ones gathered by the Indians of the Columbia. The "filberds" were the common hazelnut, *Corylus cornuta californica.*

15 April 1806.

[LEWIS]

"We delayed untill after breakfast in order to purchase some horses of the Indians; accordingly we exposed some articles [but] the natives were unwilling to barter, we therefore put up our merchandize and at 8 A.M. we set out. we halted a few minutes at the sepulchre rock [Memaloose Island], and examined the deposits of the ded at that place. these were constructed in the same manner of those already discribed below the rapids. some of them were more than half filled with dead bodies. there were thirteen sepulchres on this rock which stands near the center of the river and has a surface of about 2 acres above high water mark."

[CLARK]

"from here we returned to the Northern Shore

and continued up it about 4 miles to a village . . . at the enterance of Cateract [Klickitat] river, here we halted and informed the natives of our wish to purchase horses; the[y] produced several for sale but would not take the articles we had in exchange for them. they wanted an instriment which the North W[est] Traders call an eye dag which we had not. . . . we also halted at the two villages of the Chilluckkitequaws a fiew ms. above with no better Sucksess. at 3 in the evening we arrived at the enterance of Quinnett [Mill] Creek which we assended a short distance and Encamped at the place we had called rock fort camp. here we were visited by some of the people at the long narrows & Falls. we informed them of our wish to purchase horses, and agreed to meet them on the opposit or north side on to-morrow for the purpose of bartering with them. . . . those people are much better clad than the nativs below. their men have generaly Legins Mockersons & large robes. maney of them [wear] shirts of the same form of those of the Chopunnish & Shoshonees highly ornamented with the quils of the purcupine, as are also their mockersons & Legins. they conseal the parts of generation with the skins of the Fox or some other small animal drawn under neath a girdle and hanging loosely in front of them like a narrow apron. The dress of their women differ verry little from those about the rapids. both men & women cut their hair in the forehead which comes down as low as the eyebrows, they have long ear locks cut square at the end."

•

The Coues edition of the journals (26 July 1806) makes reference to "eye-dogs [eye-daggs . . . —a sort of war-hatchet]" (*History of the Expedition*, 3:1100). The word "dagg" (or "dag") is from the French dague, meaning dagger. It was probably a tomahawk with a blade like the one illustrated here. Noting this weapon while wintering with the Mandans, Lewis described it as having a blade like an "espontoon" (a sort of halberd or pike) and drew a sketch of it (Thwaites, *Journals*, 1:255; *see* 6 May 1806).

An eye-dag would then be an espontoon-shaped blade with an eye in which to fit a handle. Tomahawks of this type were popular. They are often seen in museums and occasionally found in old village sites.

16 April 1806.
[LEWIS]

"I was visited today by several of the natives, and amused myself in making a collection of the esculent plants . . . such as the Indians use, a specemine of which I preserved. I also met with sundry other plants which were strangers to me which I also preserved, among others there is a currant which is now in blume and has [a] yellow blossom. . . . Reubin Feilds returned in the evening and brought with him a large grey squ[i]rrel and two others of a kind I had never before seen. they are a size less than the grey squirrel common to the middle atlantic states and of a pided

"Encamped at the place we had called rock fort camp"
The camp for 25-27 October and 15-17 April was on top of these rocks, now within the city limits of The Dalles.

grey and yellowish brown colour. . . . we were informed by the Indians that the [Deschutes] river
which falls in on the s. side of the Columbia just
above the Eneshur village heads in Mount hood
and does not water the extensive country which
we have heretofore calculated on."

[CLARK]

"I passed the river with the two interpreters, and
nine men in order to trade with the nativs for
their horses, for which purpose I took with me a
good part of our stock of merchindize. . . . I
formed a Camp on the N. Side and sent [men] to
the Skillute Village and . . . to the Chilluckkite-

"they wanted . . . an eye-dag which we had not"
Espontoon-type blade found on the Snake River near Asotin, Washington.

quaw Village with derections to inform the nativs that if they had horses to sell us to bring them
to my camp. Great numbers of Indians came
from both villages and delayed the greater part of
the day without tradeing a single horse. Drewyer
returned witt the principal Chief of the Skillutes
who was lame and could not walk. after his arival
some horses were offered for sale, but they asked
nearly half the merchindize . . . for one horse. this
price I could not think of giving. the Chief informed me if I would go to this town with him,
his people would sell me horses. I therefore concluded to accompany him to his village 7 [4½]
miles distant. we set out and arrived at the village
at Sunset. after some seriminy I entered the
house of the Chief. . . . The Chief set before me
a large platter of onions which had been sweeted.
. . . in this state the root is very sweet and the tops
tender. the nativs requested the party to dance
. . . and Peter Cruzat played on the violin and the

men danced. . . . this village is moved about 300
yards below the spot it stood last fall [24 October
1805]. We observed maney stacks of fish remaining untouched on either side of the river.
. . . This is the great mart of all this country. ten
different tribes who reside on Taptate [Yakima]
and Catteract [Klickitat] River visit those people
for the purpose of purchaseing their fish, and the
Indians on the Columbia and Lewis's [Snake]
river quite to the Chopunnish Nation visit them
for the purpose of radeing horses buffalow robes
for beeds, and such articles as they have not. The
Skillutes precure the most of their cloth knivs
axes & beeds from the North of them who trade
with white people who come into the inlets to the
North at no great distance from the Tapteet. . . .
I smoked with all the principal men of this nation in the house of their great Chief and lay my
self down on a mat to sleep but was prevented by
the mice and vermin with which this house

"Feilds . . . brought . . . a large grey squ[i]rrel and . . . a kind I had never before seen" Western gray and Beechey ground squirrels.

abounded and which was very troublesome to me."

•

Clark crossed the river to Dallesport, about midway between the Chilluckkilequaw Village and Wishram. After failing in his trading venture, he followed a well-beaten path, parts of which are still visible, across the rocks to the summer village of the Wishram near Wakemap Mound.

The "large gray squirrel" was the Western gray, *Sciurus griseus*, now rare in the oak forests about The Dalles. The other two were California or Beechey ground squirrels, *Sciurus beecheyi*, a destructive creature that is to mammals what the crow is to other birds. They are numerous on the Long Narrows and throughout the cultivated valleys.

The "yellow currant" was the golden variety, *Ribes aureum*, introduced to science by Lewis. The first of these attractive flowering plants we found was on the 23 April campsite of Lewis and Clark; the next was two years later on that of 14 April. Though eaten by the Indians, the berries were not an important food source. Other plants Lewis collected included the serviceberry, popcorn flower, uroppus, and miners lettuce, and type specimens of pestle parsnip, blue-eyed Mary, and large-headed clover. All are in the Lewis and Clark herbarium of the Academy of Natural Sciences in Philadelphia.

17 April 1806.

[LEWIS]

"the inhabitants of the rapids at this time take a few of the white salmon trout and considerable quantities of a small indifferent mullet on which they principally subsist. . . . at this place which is merely on the border of the plains of Columbia the climate seems to have changed[.] the air feels dryer and more pure. . . . the plain is covered with a rich virdure of grass and herbs . . . and exhibits a beautiful seen. . . . there is a species of hiasinth in these plains the bulb of which the natives eat either boiled baked or dryed in the sun. this bulb is white, not entirely solid, and of a flat form. . . . this hiasinth is of a pale blue colour and is a very pretty flower. I preserved a specemine of it."

[CLARK]

"I rose early after [a] bad nights rest, and took my merchindize to a rock . . . at a short distance from the houses, and divided the articles . . . into parsels of such articles as I thought best calculated to pleas the Indians. . . . each parsel was intended for a horse. they tanterlised me the greater part of the day, saying that they had sent out for their horses and would trade as soon as they came. . . . I then packed up the articles and was about setting out for the village above [Celilo Falls] when a man came and sold me two horses, and another man sold me one horse, and several others informed me that they would trade with me if I would continue untill their horses could be drove up. this induced me to continue at this village another day. . . . I purchased 3 dogs for

"There is a species of hiasinth in these plains the bulb of which the natives eat"

the party with me to eate and some chap-pa-lell for myself. . . . the Chief of the Enesher's and 15 or 20 of his people visited me . . . several of them agreed to let me have horses if I would add sundery articles to those I offered which I agreed to do. . . . the chief informed me that their horses were all in the plains with their womin gathering roots. . . . Shabono purchased a verry fine mare for which he gave Hurmin [ermine], Elks Teeth, a belt and some other articles of no great value. . . . I observe at every house scooping nets with which they take the Salmon. I was envited into the house of the 2nd. Chief where concluded to

sleep. this man was pore [with] nothing to eat but dried fish, and no wood to burn. altho' the night was cold they could not rase as much wood as would make a fire."

•

The "hiasinth" was the wild hyacinth, *Brodiaea coronaria*; the type specimen collected by Lewis is in the Lewis and Clark herbarium. This close relative of the onion has a sweet, nut-like corm that can be eaten raw, cooked or dried. Like the *Allium*, there are several species; on some the flower rises on a stem that seems far too long for its burden, like a streamer on a slender mast-head. The bulb of this member of the lily family may be a foot or two beneath the surface—a fortunate circumstance, for it can seek water to survive in a rigorous habitat, and its depth discourages digging, otherwise this savory morsel might have been harvested to extinction.

The permanent Wishram village above Wakemap Mound (not the modern Wishram opposite Celilo) was called Nixluidix; the site is now under water. The Wishram called themselves Ila'xluit, and the word for "I am a Wishram" is "itcxlu'it" from which is derived Lewis and Clark's "Echeloot." The Yakima and Klickitat called these people Wu'cxam, from whence the English pronunciation Wishram, a name indelibly imprinted in literature by the pen of Washington Irving. Wakemap is considered by ethnologists as a separate village, and should have been called Wócem-up, closer to the native pronunciation.

18 April 1806.
[L E W I S]

"Late last evening we were visited by the principal chief of the Chilluckkittaquaws and 12 of his nation they remained with us untill 9 OC. when they all departed except the Cheif and two others who slept at my feet. we loaded our vessels and set out after an early breakfast. . . . we gave the indians a passage to the N. shore . . . and pursued our rout to the foot of the first rapid [Three Mile]. . . . here we found it necessary to unload the perogues and canoes and make a portage of

70 paces over a rock; we then drew our vessels up by a cord and the assistance of seting poles. from thence we proceeded to the bason [Big Eddy] below the long narrows 5 ms. further and landed on the Lard. side. . . . the Cheif when he left me this morning promised to bring some horses to barter with me at the bason. . . . I walked up to the Skillute Village and jouined Capt. [C.]. . . . I shot my airgun in the presents of the natives at the village which excited great astonishment."

[C L A R K]

"Early this morning I was awoke by an Indian . . . who informed me that he lived in the neighbourhood of our horses [Clearwater River]. this man delivered me a bag of powder and ball which he had picked up this morning at the place the goods were exposed yesterday. . . . about 10 A.M. the Indians came down from the Eneesher Villages and I expected would take the articles which they had laid by yesterday. but to my astonishment not one would make the exchange today. . . . I dressed the sores of the principal Chief gave some small things to his children and promised the chief some Medicine for to cure his sores. his wife who I found to be a sulky Bitch and was somewhat afflicted with pains in her back. this I thought a good oppertunity to get her on my side giveing her something for her back. I rubed a little camphere on her temples and back, and applyed worm flannel to her back which she thought had nearly restored her to her former feelings. this I thought a favourable time to trade

Site of Wishram, ancient Indian settlement at the head of the Long Narrows. Wakemap Mound, left center; "Rugid black rock," right center, behind large house. Captain Clark displayed his merchandise on the rocks, center, across railroad tracks. Celilo Falls are at the base of the hill, far right. Photo taken during spring flood, when the river was about 40 feet higher than normal.

Tsagagalal "She Who Watches" overlooking the ancient village of Wishram on the Long Narrows.

with the chief who had more horses than al the nation besides. I accordingly made him an offer which he excepted and sold me two horses. . . . among other nations who visit this place for the purpose of trade is the Skad-datt's [Klickitats]. those people bartered the Skillutes to play at a singular kind of game. in the course of the day the Skillutes won all their beeds skins arrows &c.

This game was composed of 9 men on a side. they set down opposit to each other at the distance of about 10 feet. in front of each party a long pole was placed on which they struck with a small stick to the time of their songs. after the bets were made up which was nearly half an hour after they set down, two round bones was produced about the size of a mans little finger or something smaller and 2¼ inches in length. which they held in their hands changeing it from one hand to the other with great dexterity. 2 men on the same side perforemed this part, and when they had the bone in the hand they wished, they looked at their advorsarys swinging arms around their sholders for their advorsary [to] Guess which they performed by the motion of the hand either to the right or left. . . . in this game each party has 5 sticks. and one side wins all the sticks, once twice or thrice as the game may be set. I observed another game which those people also play . . . 2 persons with 4 sticks. . . . two . . . are black and . . . 2 white. . . . those sticks they placed in different positions . . . under a kind of trencher made of bark round and about 14 inches in diameter. this is a very intricate game and I cannot understand sufficiently to discribe it."

19 April 1806.
[LEWIS]

"This morning early we . . . employed all hands in transporting our baggage on their backs and by means of the four pack-horses, over the portage. . . . there was great joy with the natives last night in consequence of the arrival of the Salmon. . . . They informed us that these fish would arrive in great quantities in the course of about 5 days. this fish was dressed and being divided into small peices was given to each child in the village. this custom is founded on a supersticious opinion that it will hasten the arrival of the salmon. with much difficulty we obtained four other horses . . .

Gambling bones, excavated from sites on the Long Narrows.

303

we wer[e] obliged to dispence with two of our kettles. . . . we have now only one small kettle to a mess of 8 men. . . . I directed the horses to be hubbled & suffered to graize. . . . one of the men Willard was negligent in his attention to his horse and suffered it to ramble off. . . . this in addition to the other difficulties under which I laboured was truly provoking. I repremanded him more severely for this piece of negligence than had been usual with me. . . . [The horses] were extreemly wrestless. . . . all except one were stone horses for the people do not understand the art of gelding them, and this is the season at which they are most vicious."

[CLARK]

"we agreed that I should proceed on to the Enesher Villages at the great falls of the Columbia and if possible purchase as maney horses as would transport the baggage. . . . I set out . . . at half past 5 P.M. for the Enesher Village at which place I arrived at 8 P.M. . . . The long narrows are much more formidable than they were when we decended them last fall, there would be no possibility of passing either up or down them in any vessle at this time. I entered the largest house of the Eneeshers Village in which I found all the enhabitants in bead. they rose and made a light of straw, they haveing no wood to burn. Many men collected we smoked and I informed them that I had come to purchase a fiew horses of them. they promused to sell me some in the morning."

20 April 1806.

[LEWIS]

[at the Long Narrows] "[The Enesher] houses like those of the Skillutes have their floors on the surface of the ground, but are formed of sticks and covered with mats and straw. they are large and contain usually several families each. for fuel they use straw, small willows and the southern wood.° they use the silk grass in manufacturing their fishing nets and bags, the bear grass and cedar bark are employed in forming a variety of articles. . . . in the course of the day I obtained two indifferent horses for which I paid an extravigant price. I found that I should get no more horses and therefore resolved to proceed tomorrow morning with those which I had hand. . . . I bart[er]ed my Elkskin old irons and 2 canoes for beads."

[CLARK, FIRST DRAFT]

[at Celilo Falls] "This morning very cold hills covered with snow. . . . I showed the nativs what I had to give for their horses and attempted to purchase them. they informed me that they would not Sell any horses to me. . . . my offer was a blue robe, callico shirt, a handkerchef, 5 parcels of paint a knife, a Wampom moon 4 braces of ribin, a pice of Brass and about 6 braces of yellow beeds. . . . not a single horse could be precured of those people in the course of the day. . . . I am half frozen at this inhospitable village which is

---

°Probably the big, or common, sagebrush, *Artemisia tridentata Nutt.; see* Moulton, *Journals,* 7:151 n.4, and Cartright, *Lewis and Clark,* 403.

"The long narrows are much more formidable than . . . last fall"

moved from its position above the falls to one below and contains 19 large houses, a village is also established on the other side imedeately above the falls."

[C L A R K]

"and one other a few miles above on the North Side. Those people are great jokers and decitfull in trade. . . . I . . . returned to the lodge which I had slept in last night. great number gathered around me to smoke, I gave them two pipes, and then lay my self down with the men to sleep, haveing our merchandize under our heads and guns &c. in our arms, as we always have in similar situations."

•

The main Eneshur village was on the site of the present railroad town of Wishram, Washington, at Celilo Falls; the original name, Fallbridge, was changed to Wishram about 1920 for more tourist appeal. There were twenty-three lodges in the main village when the party passed down the river. The lodge where Clark stayed was on the point projecting into the river just below the railroad bridge, and remains of the old camp fires may still be seen there in the eroded banks. The village "a few miles above" was near the west entrance of the present railroad tunnel opposite the lower end of Miller Island (*see* 22 October 1805).

The "old irons" must have included Lewis's branding iron (*see* 23 November 1805), found during the early 1890s near this village. Other than medals, this is the only artifact of the expedition to be found along the entire route. A "Wampom moon" is a pendant made from shell. A "brace" is the same as a fathom, or six feet.

The "silk grass" is fiber from the bark of Indian hemp, of the species *Apocynum*. It grows in rich, damp soil in the fields and meadows, often along the river's edge. It is neither plentiful nor particularly attractive. A member of the dogbane family, this plant was extremely important to the natives throughout the Great Basin and Columbian Plateau, for it produced the silkiest fibers of all. David Douglas wrote: "The seine is resorted to as a means of taking salmon in the still parts of the stream with great success. . . . The rope of the net is made from the bark of a species of *Salix* [willow], some of *Thuya* [cedar]; the cord of *Apocynum piscatorium* a gigantic species peculiar to that country, which affords a great quantity of flax" (*Journal*, 57).

The women spun the hemp fibers into threads by rolling them on their thigh with the palm of the hand. The fibers were then twisted into two- or three-ply cord to make dip nets, seines, fish lines, bags, and many other useful objects. A gauge was used to measure the mesh when spinning nets, about two inches for eels and up to five inches for salmon. Gauges were usually made from antler, but sometimes from stone. They are occasionally found in the middens of the old fishing villages.

21 April 1806.
[LEWIS]

"Notwithstanding all the precautions I had taken with rispect to the horses one of them had broken his cord of 5 strands of Elkskin and had gone off spanseled [hobbled]. I sent several men in surch of the horse with orders to return at 10 A.M. with or without the horse. . . . Windsor returned with the lost horse, the others soon after returned also. the Indian who promised to accompany me as far as the Chopunnish country produced me two horses one of which he politely gave me the liberty of packing. We took breakfast and departed a little after 10 OClock."

[CLARK]

"I found it useless to make any further attempts

to trade horses with those unfriendly people who only crowded about me to view and make their remarks and to smoke, the latter I did not indulge them with to day. . . . They are well supplied with straw & bark bags ready to hold their pounded fish. at 12 oClock Capt. Lewis and party came up from the Skillutes Village with 9 horses packed and one which bratten who was yet too weak to walk, rode, and soon after the two small canoes also loaded with the residue of the baggage which could not be taken on horses. we had everything imediately taken above the falls. . . . whilst I remained at the Eneshur Village I subsisted on 2 platters of roots, some pounded fish and sun flower seed pounded which an old man had the politeness to give me in return for which I gave him several small articles. . . . After dinner we proceeded on about 4 miles to a village of 9 Mat Lodges of the Eneshur, a little below the enterance of the *To war hand hi ooks* river and encamped."

•

Clark purchased dogs for the party but, hungry as he was, still would not eat the meat. The village of nine mat lodges was the village "a few miles above" of 20 April; sixteen lodges were seen there on the down-river trip (*see* 22 October 1805).

The sunflower, of the *Helianthus* species, is a member of perhaps the largest of all plant families, *Compositae*; among its more than fifteen thousand species are the thistles and asters. Several different *Helianthus* grow in the West, all of which are easily confused with the balsam root (*see* 14 April 1806). Sunflower seeds, so rich in oil, were eaten by all tribes whose territory included this widespread plant.

22 April 1806.
[CLARK]

"at 7 oClock we loaded and set out, haveing previously sent off the canoe with Colter and Potts[.] we had not arived at the top of the hill which is 200 feet [high] before Shabanos horse threw off his load and with with great speed down the hill to the Village where he disengaged himself of his Saddle & the robe that was under it. . . . Capt. Lewis and the rear party [were delayed] some time before they found the robe which was in a lodge hid. . . . dureing the time the front of the party was waiting for Cap Lewis, I assended a high hill from which I could plainly see the range of mountains which runs south from Mt. Hood as far as I could see. I also discovered the top of Mt. Jefferson. . . . Clarks [Deschutes] river which mouthes imediately opposit to me forks at about 18 or 20 miles, the West fork [White River] runs to the Mt. Hood. . . . after Capt. Lewis came up we proceeded on through an open ruged plain about 8 miles to a Village of 6 Houses on the river. . . . I halted at the mouth of a run above the village . . . to let the horses graze and . . . the party . . . dine. Sent to the huts and purchased a dog & some wood. . . . after we proceeded on up the river about 4 miles to a village of 7 Mat Lodges[.]

"I assended a high hill"
Looking across Miller Island to Clark's hill. The trail followed the level bench.

here our Chopunnish Guide informed me that the next villg was at some distance and that we could not get to it to night. . . . a man offered to sell us a horse for a canoe. . . . we concluded to camp here all night. . . . Serjt. Gass & R. Fields joined us with one canoe this evening. the other canoe with Colter & pots is a head."

•

The party followed the Indian trail up the slope above their camp to the route of today's Highway 14, past the site where the Maryhill Museum now stands, and back down to the river at Maryhill. The noon stop was at what would become the Maryhill ferry landing (now defunct); their evening camp was near that of 21 October 1805.

Colter and Potts were later to share a deadly adventure. They joined the Manuel Lisa expedition of 1808, and, while trapping for beaver in the vicinity of the Three Forks, their canoe was suddenly surrounded by Blackfoot Indians. Ordered to disembark and give up their arms, Potts resisted and met instant death. Colter surrendered and was given the chance to run for his life, stark naked and weaponless, pursued by the swiftest of the war party. He outran them all to the river, where he hid beneath floating driftwood until the Blackfoot gave up the search. One of the earliest of the Mountain Men, Colter is credited with the discovery of Yellowstone Park. He later married a young woman named Sally and became a farmer. He died in 1813. Another member of the Corps of Discovery, Peter Wiser (or Weiser), also joined Manuel Lisa in the Rocky Mountains. He hunted on the upper Missouri and Snake rivers until 1810, then vanished. The Weiser River and an Idaho town commemorate his name.

23 April 1806.
[LEWIS]

"this morning . . . two horses of our Interpreter Charbono were absent; on enquiry it appeared that he had neglected to confine them to picqu[i]ts as had been directed. . . . we immediately dispatched Reubin Feilds and Labuish to assist Charbono in recovering his horses. one of them was found at no great distance and other given over as lost. . . . we therefore determined to proceed immediately to the next village which from the information of our guide will occupy the greater part of the day to reach. . . . we continued our march along a narrow rocky bottom on the N. side of the river about 12 miles to the Wah-how-pum Village of 12 temporary mat lodges near the Rock rapid. these people appeared much pleased to see us, sold us 4 dogs and some wood for our small articles which we had previously prepared as our only resource to obtain fuel and food through those plains. these articles con[s]isted of pewter buttons, strips of tin iron and brass, twisted wire &c. . . . at a little distance below this village we passed five lodges of the same people who like those were waiting the arrival of the salmon. after we arranged our camp we caused all the old and brave men to set around and smoke with us. we had the violin played and some of the men danced; after which the natives entertained us with a dance after their method. this dance differed from any I have yet seen. they formed a circle and all sung. . . . these placed their sholders together with their robes tightly drawn about them and danced in a line from side to side. . . . the whole concluded with a premiscuous dance in which most of them sung and danced. . . . at this village a large creek [Rock] falls in on the N. side which we did not observe as we decended the river. . . . came 12 miles by land. the sands made the march fatieguing."

•

This village of Walla Walla Indians was on Fountain Bar, about one-half mile above Rock Creek, its site now deep beneath the water behind John

"to the Wah-how-pum Village . . . near the Rock rapid"
Rock Rapids, lower center. Arrow points to the village site and Lewis and Clark camp site of 23 April 1806.

Day Dam. The remains of a large village there included many fine petroglyphs. The entire bar, two miles long, showed evidence of extensive occupancy. Along the cliff below the Lewis and Clark campsite were a number of fish leads, fences built of boulders by the Indians to guide the salmon to the rocks where they could be speared or netted. Whitehouse mentions (11 October 1805) similar leads on the Snake River: "we proceeded on passed a great nomber of fishing camps where the nativs fish in the Spring. the Stone piled up in roes So that in high water the Sammon lay along the Side of the line of rocks while they would gig them" (Thwaites, *Journals*, 7:170).

24 April 1806.
[LEWIS]

"We were up early this morning and dispatched the men in surch of our horses, they were all found in a little time except McNeal's. we hired an indian to surch for this horse. . . . we . . . purchased three horses . . . and hired three others of the Choppunish man who accompanys us with his family. . . . the natives had tantalized us with an exchange of horses for our canoes . . . but when they found that we had made our arrangements to travel by land they would give us nothing for them[.] I determined to cut them in peices sooner than leave them on those terms, Drewyer struck one of the canoes and split of[f] a small peice with his tommahawk, they discovered us determined . . . and offered us several strands of beads for each which were accepted. we proceeded up the river between the hills and it's Northen shore, the road was rocky and sandy alternately, the road difficult and fatieguing. at 12 Ms. we arrived at a village of 5 lodges of the Met-cow-wes, having passed 4 lodges at 4. and 2 at 2 Ms. further. we rem[a]ined all night near the Met-cow-we lodges about 2 miles below our encampment of . . . October last. many of the natives pased and repassed us today on the road and behaved themselves with distant rispect towards us. most of the party complain of the soarness of their feet and legs this evening; it is no doubt caused by walking over the rough stones and deep sands after b[e]ing for some months . . . accustomed to a soft soil. . . . The curloos are abundant in these plains and are now laying their eggs. saw the kildee[r], the brown lizzard, and a Moonax which the natives had petted."

•

The moonax was the yellow-bellied marmot, *Marmota flaviventris*, a richly colored, harmless resident of rock slides and crevices in the Transition and Canadian vegetation zones, which lives only in the safety of jumbled rock. The marmot will eat almost any green plant or grass, and in the fall seeks oil-rich seeds to add to the fat needed for a long winter hibernation. The sight of one at attention on a rock, the sound of its sharp warning cry, or the pattern of its trails radiating out through the dry grass add to the pleasure of a hike along the river. Marmots will sun

Ruth Strong exploring the 23 April campsite.

"Stone piled up in roes" Photo taken during low water. In the spring, the river covered this fish lead.

themselves on a stone for hours, presenting a perfect target for a sharpshooter eager for the kill.

The Methow were a Salishan tribe whose territory centered on the Methow River but included the plateau from the Okanogan to the mid-Columbia. Alexander Ross (*Adventures of the First Settlers*, 312) said they were one of twelve tribes constituting the Okanogan Nation, numbering six hundred warriors.

Camp was made this day three miles below what is now Roosevelt, on a barren gravel bar.

25 April 1806.
[L E W I S]

"This morning we collected our horses and set out at 9 A.M. and proceeded on 11 ms. to the Village of the *Pish-quit-pahs* of 51 mat lodges where we arrived at 2 P.M. purchased five dogs and some wood from them and took dinner. this village contains about 7 hundred souls. . . . while here they flocked around us in great numbers tho' treated us with much rispect. we gave two medals of the small size to their two principal Cheifs who were pointed out to us by our Chopunnish fellow traveller. . . . the *Pish-quit-pahs*, may be considered hunters as well as fishermen as they spend the fall and winter months in that occuaption. they are generally pleasently featured of good statu[r]e and well proportioned. both women and men ride extreemly well. their bridle is usually a hair rope tyed with both ends to the under jaw of the horse, and their saddle consists of a paid of dressed skin stuffed with goats hair with wooden stirups. . . . at 4 P.M. we set out accompanyed by eighteen or twenty of their young men on horseback. we continued our route about nine miles where finding as many willows as would answer our purposes for fuel we encamped for the evening. the country we passed through was much as that of yesterday. the river hills are about 250 feet high and generally abrupt and craggy in many places faced with perpendicular and solid rock. this rock is black and hard. leve[l] plains extend themselves from the tops of the river hills to a great distance on either side of the river. the soil is not as fertile as about the falls, tho' it produces a low grass on which the horses feed very conveniently. it astonished me to see the order of their horses at this season of the year when I knew that they had wintered on the drygrass of the plains. . . . I did not see a single horse which could be deemed poor and many of them were as fat as seals. . . . we killed six ducks in the course of the day; one of them was of a speceis which I had never before seen I therefore had the most material parts of it reserved as a specimine. . . . had the fiddle played at the request of the natives and some of the men danced."

•

The large village of the Pisquows was at the outlet of Pine Creek; Gass called the inhabitants Wal-a-waltz. They occupied an extensive area occupied along the riverbank at Pine Creek. A number of petroglyphs were nearby at McCre-

"saw . . . a Moonax"
Yellow-bellied marmot.

die. It is notable that of all the early explorers only Lieutenant Charles Wilkes, who commanded an expedition off the Oregon Coast in 1841, mentions seeing any of the thousands of rock carvings and paintings along the Columbia River. There were great numbers of them in the vicinity of the Long Narrows, and examples were passed almost hourly along the upstream trail.

One reason these petroglyphs and pictographs were unnoticed may have been that they were generally on cliffs and rocks close to the water, where the party would be least likely to pass. Another is that they blend into the background so subtly that they can easily be missed, even by such keen observers as Lewis and Clark. Still, there were so many along the river that it is strange they did not attract the attention of at least one member of the party.

The grass on which the horses fed so conveniently was the bunchgrass, *Agropyron spicatum*, which once covered the plains of the West. Overgrazing has now nearly eliminated it, to be replaced by the unpleasant cheat grass. Occasionally, in places inaccessible to livestock, its evenly spaced hummocks still festoon the hillsides like drum majors' caps. Bunchgrass is a valuable food for horses because it cures into hay while standing, and remains nutritious all winter. Horses paw through the snow to graze on it. The species of duck preserved as a specimen was the shoveller, *Spatula clypeata*.

The party camped for the night at the foot of Crow Butte.

Lewis and Clark's campsite for 24 April 1806, foreground.

26 April 1806.

[LEWIS]

"This morning we set forward and at the distance of three miles entered a low level plain. . . . here the river hills are low and receede a great distance from the river[.] this low country commenced on the s. side of the river about 10 miles below our encampment of last evening. these plains are covered with a variety of herbatious plants, grass, and three speceis of shrubs spec-

Mat lodge outline near 24 April campsite.

Petroglyph at a fishing site on the Columbia.

Campsite on 25 April 1806, at the base of Crow Butte.

imines of which I have preserved. at the distance of twelve miles we halted near a few willows which afforded us a sufficient quantity of fuel to cook our dinner which consisted of the ballance of the dogs . . . and some jirked Elk. we were overtaken today by several families of the natives who were traveling up the river with a number of horses; they continued with us much to our annoyance as the day was worm the roads dusty and we could not prevent their horses from crouding in and breaking our order of ma[r]ch without using some acts of severity which we did not wish to commit."

[CLARK]

"after dinner we continued our march through a leavel plain near the river 16 miles and encamped about a mile below 3 Lodges of the fritened band of the Wallahwallah nation, and

"the river hills are low and receede a great distance"

about 7 miles below our encampment of the 19th. of Octr. last. after we encamped a little Indian boy cought several chubbs with a bone . . . which he substituted for a hook. those fish were of about 9 inches long. . . . Saw a Goat and a small wolf at a distance to day. made 28 miles."

•

The stop for dinner was made about two miles below Paterson, the evening camp one mile below Plymouth. By "fritened band" Captain Clark is referring to the incident of 19 October 1805. The Indian boy was catching the Columbia chub, *Mylocheilus lateralis*, using a straight piece of sharpened bone with a line tied in the center. When swallowed, the bone would swing and catch in the throat.

The goat was an antelope; the small wolf a coyote.

27 April 1806.
[C L A R K]

"This morning we were detained untill 9 AM in consequence of the absence of one of Shabono's horses. the horse being at length recovered we set out and to the distance of 15 [10] miles passed through a country similar to that of yesterday passed Muscle Shell [Umatilla] rapid and at the expiration of this distance [the cliffs] again approached the river, and are rocky abrupt and 300 feet high. we assended the hill and marched through a high plain 10 [8] miles where we again returned to the river. we halted."

Fortified island near Paterson. The top of this island had been fortified by ramparts against all access routes except one. On 26 April 1806, Lewis and Clark stopped for dinner on the far shore. A beaver lodge is in the foreground.

[LEWIS]
"we collected some dry stalks of weeds and the stems of a shrub. . . . made a small fire and boiled a small quantity of our jerked meat on which we dined; while here the principal Cheif of the Wallahwallahs joined us with six men. . . . this Cheif by name Yel-lept! had visited us on the morning of the 19 of October at our encampment a little below this place; we gave him at that time a small medal, and promised a larger one

"passed through a country similar to that of yesterday"
The Lewis and Clark party passed by this house pit in the gravel plain beside Umatilla Rapids. In this village site there were 182 of these "cellers" over which mat lodges were built.

on our return. he appeared much gratifyed at seeing us return. [He] envited us to remain at his village three or four days and assured us that we should be furnished with a plenty of such food as they had themselves, and some horses. . . . after our scanty repast we continued our march . . . to the village which we found at the distance of six miles situated on the N. Side of the river about 12 [10] mi. below the entrance of Lewis's river.

This Cheif is a man of much influence not only in his own nation but also among the neighbouring tribes and nations. This Village consists of 15 large mat lodges. at present they seam to subsist principally on a speceis of mullet . . . which these plains furnish them in great abundance. Yellept haranged his village in our favour . . . to furnish us with fuel and provision and set the example himself by bringing us an armfull of wood and a plat-

"[the cliffs] . . . are rocky abrupt"

ter of 3 roasted mullets. the others soon followed his example. . . . the indians informed us that there was a good road . . . to the entrance of the Kooskooske . . . [and] that the country was level."

•

Although the journals do not record it, the promise to give Chief Yellepit a large medal was apparently kept, for David Thompson saw and described it in 1811 (*see* Glover, *David Thompson's Narrative*, 350). Reference in the journals to a small medal means one of the "Washington Seasons" types, while a large one indicates the "Jefferson Peace and Friendship" type. About 1891 a Jefferson medal was found on an island near the mouth of the Walla Walla River; it must be the one presented to Yellepit. It is now in the Oregon Historical Society's collections.

"promised a larger one on our return"
Jefferson medal found near Wallula; believed to be the one given to Chief Yellepit.

28 April 1806.
[CLARK]

"This morning early the Great Chief Yelleppet brought a very eligant white horse to our camp and presented him to me, signifying his wish to get a kittle but being informed that we had already disposed of every kittle we could possibly spare he said he was content with whatever I thought proper to give him. I gave him my Swoard, 100 balls & powder and some small articles of which he appeared perfectly satisfied. . . . we requested the Chief to furnish us with canoes to pass the river, but he insisted on our remaining . . . [as] he had sent for the *Chim-na-pums*

"signifying his wish to get a kittle"
Copper trade kettle.

[Yakima] his neighbours to come down and join his people this evening and dance for us. We urged the necessity of our proceeding on imediately . . . [but] he said that the time he asked could not make any considerable difference. I at length urged that there was no wind blowing and that the river was consequently in good order to pass our horses and if he would furnish us with canoes for that purpose we would remain all night in our present encampment, to this proposition he assented. . . . we passed our horses over the river safely [by swimming] and hobbled them as usial. We found a *Sho-sho-ne* woman, prisoner among those people by means of whome and *Sah-cah-gah-weah*, Shabono's wife we found means of converceing with the *Wallahwállars*. we conversed with them for several hours and

fully satisfy all their enquiries with respect to our Selves and the Objects of our pursute. they were much pleased. they brought several disordered persons to us for whome they requested some medical aid. . . . [A] man who had his arm broken had it loosely bound in a piece of leather without any thing to surport it. I dressed the arm which was broken short above the wrist & supported it with broad sticks to keep it in place, put [it] in a sling and furnished him with some lint bandages &c. to Dress it in future. a little before sun set the Chimnahpoms arrived; they were about 100 men and a fiew women; they joined the Wallahwallahs . . . and formed a half circle around our camp where they waited very patiently to see our party dance. the fiddle was played and the men amused themselves with danceing about an hour.

we then requested the Indians to dance which they very chearfully complyed with; they continued their dance untill 10 at night. the whole assemblage of Indians about 350 men women and children sung and danced at the same time. Most of them danced in the same place they stood and mearly jumped up to the time of their musick. Some of the men who were esteemed most brave entered the space around which the main body were formed in solid column and danced in a circular manner side wise. . . . they were much gratified in seeing some of our party join them in their dance. one of their party who made himself the most consipicious charecter in the dance and songs, we were told was a medesene man & could foretell things. that he had told of our comeing and was about to consult his God the Moon if what we said was the truth &c. &c."

•

Sergeant Ordway was favorably impressed with the Indians at this village, and his description of the dance is quite dramatic: "the Indians Sent their women to gether wood or Sticks [for a fire] to See us dance this evening. about 300 of the natives assembled at our Camp[.] we played the fiddle and danced a while the head chief told our officers that they Should be lonesom when we left them and they wished to hear once of our meddicine Songs and try to learn it and wished us to learn one of theirs and it would make them glad. So our men Sang 2 Songs which appeared to take great affect on them. They tryed to learn

Singing with us with a low voice. the head chief then made a speech & it was repeated by a warrier that all might hear. then all the Savages men women and children of any size danced forming a circle round a fire & jumping up nearly as other Indians, & keep time verry well they wished our men to dance with them So we danced among them and they were much pleased, and Said that they would dance day and night untill we return. everry fiew minutes one of their warries made a Speech pointing towards the enimy and towards the moon &C. &C. which was all repeated by another meddison man with a louder voice [so] as all might hear the dance continued untill about midnight then the most of them went away peaceable & have behaved verry clever and honest with us as yet, and appear to have a Sincere wish to be at peace and to git acquaintance with us &C. &C." (Quaife, *Journals*, 348–49).

29 April 1806.
[CLARK]

"This morning Yelleppit furnished us with 2 canoes, and We began to transport our baggage over the river; we also sent a party of the men over to collect our horses. we purchased some deer [dogs] and chappallell this morning. we had now a store of 12 dogs for our voyage through the plains. by 11 A.M. we had passed the river with our party and baggage but were detained several hours in consequence of not being able to collect our horses. our guide now informed us that it was too late in the evening to reach an eligible place to camp; that we could not reach any water before night. we therefore thought it best to remain on the Wallahwallah river about a mile from the Columbia untill the morning, accordingly encamped on the river near a fish wear. this weare consists of two curtains of small willows wattled together with four line of withes of the same materials extending quite across the river, parralal with each other and about 6 feet asunder. those are supported by several parrelals of poles. . . . those curtains of willows is either rolled at one end for a fiew feet to permit the fish to pass or are let down at pleasure. they take their fish which at present are a mullet only of from one to 5 pounds wt. with small seines of 15 to 18 feet long drawn by two persons; these they drag down to the wear and rase the bottom of the seine against the willow curtain. they have also a small seine managed by one person, it bags in the manner of the scooping nets. . . . The Wallahwallah River discharges it's self into the Columbia on it's South Side 15 miles below the entrance of Lewis's River . . . this is a handsome Stream about 4½ feet deep and 50 yards wide; its bead is composed of gravel principally with some sand and mud. . . . The Snake indian prisoner informed us that at some distance in the large plains to the South . . . there was a large river running to the N.W. which was as wide as the Columbia at this place, which is nearly 1 mile. this account is no doubt somewhat exagurated but it serves to evince the certainty of the Multnomah being a very large river . . . and that it must water that vast tract of country extending from those mountains to the Waters of the Gulf of California. . . . We gave small Medals to two inferior Chiefs of this nation, and they each furnished us with a fine horse. . . . there are 12 other Lodges of the Wallahwallah Nation on this river a short distance below our Camp. . . . in the evening a man brought his wife and a horse both up to me. the horse he gave me as a present and his wife who was verry unwell the effects of violent coalds was placed before me. I did not think her case a bad one and gave such medesene as would keep her body open and raped [wrapped] her in flannel. . . . Great No. of the nativs about us all night."

•

Gass writes: "Here are a great many of the natives encamped on a large creek which comes from the south [Walla Walla River] and those on the north side are moving over as fast as they can" (*Journal*, 248). He also comments on the number of horses, as does Ordway: "the most of the Savages moved across the river also, & they have a vast Site of horses" (Quaife, *Journals*, 349).

This was indeed horse country, with its mild climate, water, and indispensable winter pasturage of cured bunchgrass; the rolling plains and low mountains between Umatilla and Pasco are aptly named Horse Heaven Hills. Alexander Ross, at the confluence of the Walla Walla only five years after Lewis and Clark, wrote: "The men were generally tall, raw-boned, and well-dressed, having all buffalo robes, deerskin leg-

"this is a handsome Stream"
The Walla Walla River a short distance above its outlet.

gings, very white, and most of them garnished with porcupine quills. Their shoes were also trimmed and painted red; altogether their appearance indicated wealth. . . . The women wore garments of well-dressed deerskin down to their heels, many of them richly garnished with beads, *higuas* [dentalium], and other trinkets. . . . The tribes assembled on the present occasion were the Walla Wallas, the Shaw Haptens [Yakima], and the Cajouses [Cayuse], forming altogether about fifteen hundred souls. . . . The plains were literally covered with horses, of which there could not have been less than four thousand in sight of the camp" (*Adventures of the First Settlers*, 137–38).

Fort Nez Perces, later renamed Fort Walla Walla, was built in 1818 by the North West Company near Lewis and Clark's landing place. Irrigation has reduced the summer flow of the Walla Walla River to a mere trickle of unclean water, discharging into a mud flat bordering the still water behind McNary Dam.

*"we continued . . . through
an open . . . Plain to a bold
creek 10 yards wide"*
Snake River Plains and the
Touchet River where Lewis
and Clark camped.

XI

HOMEWARD BOUND
BY LAND TO CAMP CHOPUNNISH

30 APRIL TO 14 MAY 1806

30 April 1806.
[CLARK]

"We took leave of those honest friendly people the Wallahwallahs and departed at 11 A.M. accompanied by our guide and the Choppunnish man and family. we continued our rout N. 30°. E. 14 Ms [Touchet River] through an open leavel sandy Plain to a bold creek 10 yards wide. . . . This plain as usial is covered with arromatic shrubs, hurbatious plants and tufts of short grass. maney of those plants produce those esculent roots which forms a principal part of the subsistance of the natives. . . . We encamped at the . . . creek where we had the pleasure once more to find a sufficiency of wood for the purpose of makeing ourselves comfortable fires, which has not been the case since we left rock fort camp below the falls. . . . our stock of horses have now increased to 23 and most of them excellent young horses."

[LEWIS]

"I observed the corngrass and rushes in some parts of the bottom."

•

The route they were using, as well as the one they had been following since leaving Celilo, was a well-traveled, ancient Indian trail. Later the same path was used by the Hudson's Bay Company employees, early miners, and army expeditions; it appears on several early maps. County, state, and federal roads now traverse much the same trace over which such colorful brigades plodded through the stifling dust. From the mouth of the Walla Walla, the Indian road struck a little north of east directly across the plains to intersect the Touchet about seven air miles above its outlet into the Walla Walla. Here the present county road from Touchet to State

329

Highway 124 leaves the Touchet River Valley, and the river bends to the northeast.

1 May 1806.

[CLARK]

"This morning we collected our horses and made an early start. . . . We proceeded up the Creek . . . through a countery of less sand and some rich bottoms. . . . at the distance of nine miles we over took our hunters, they had killed one beaver only[.] at this place the road forked, one leaveing the creek and the corse of it nearly North. . . . we deturmined to unlode and wate for our guide, or the Chopunnish man who had accompanied us from the long Narrows. . . . on his arrival . . . he informed us that the road . . . was through a open hilly and sandy countery to the river Lewis's River, and was a long way around. . . . the other roade up the creek was a more direct course, plenty of water wood and only one hill in the whole distance. . . . We traveled 17 miles this evening making a total of 26 mls. and encamped. . . . I see very little difference between . . . the country here and that of the plains of the Missouri, only that those are not enlivened by the vast herds of Buffalow, Elk &c. which animated those of the Missouri. . . . three young men arrived from the Wallahwallah Village bringing with them a steel trap . . . which had been left negligently behind. . . . I think we can justly affirm to the honor of those people that they are the most hospitable, honist and sincere people that we have met with on our Voyage."

•

The trail forked near Lamar, where State Highway 124 meets the Touchet. The northerly fork followed up Winnett Canyon a short distance above, then headed directly for the junction of the Snake and Palouse rivers, continuing up the Palouse into the Spokane country. Lewis and Clark followed the easterly fork along the Touchet and camped near Bolles, about halfway between Prescott and Waitsburg.

2 May 1806.

[LEWIS]

"loaded up and set forward. steered East 3 M. over a hilly road along the N. side of the Creek [Touchet], wide bottom on the s. side. a branch [Coppei Creek] falls in on the s. side which runs towards the s.w. [Blue] mountains which appear to be about 25 Ms. distant[,] low yet covered with snow. . . . more timber than usual on the creek, some . . . hills, also about 50 acres of well timbered pine land. . . . continued up a N.E. branch [Patit Creek]. the bottoms th[r]ough which we passed were wide. . . . encamped on the N. side in a little bottom, having traveled 19 miles today. at this place the road leaves the creek and takes the open high plain. . . . there is much appearance of beaver and otter along these creeks. . . . the three young men of the Wallahwallah nation continued with us. . . . I observed them eat the inner part of the young and succulent stem of a large coarse plant with a ternate leaf. . . . I tasted of this

"about 50 acres of well timbered pine land"
Lewis and Clark Trail State Park between Waitsburg and Dayton near where they "passed the creek."

"continued up a N.E. branch"
The trail led up Patit Creek.

"encamped . . . in a little bottom"
Here the trail left Patit Creek and turned north,
crossing the high plains toward the Tucannon River.

plant found it agreeable and eat heartily of it without feeling any inconvenience."

•

The route this day was up the Touchet to Dayton; here the river turns southeast from its junction with Patit Creek. The party continued up the Patit about eight miles and camped. The trail here, as well as along all streams, frequently left the creek bed and passed over the hills on one side or the other to avoid the brush and timber along the bottom.

The "large coarse plant with a ternate leaf" was the cow parsnip, *Heracleum lanatum*. Only the stems were eaten; the roots and leaves are not edible.

3 May 1806.
[L E W I S]

"set out at 7 A.M. steered N. 25. E. 12 Ms. to Kimooenem [Tucannon] Creek through a high level plain. . . . the bottoms of this creek are narrow with some timber. . . . the hills are high and abrupt. the land of the plains is much more fertile than below, less sand and covered with taller grass; very little of the aromatic shrubs appear in this part of the plain. we proceeded . . . through the high plain to a small creek [Pataha]. . . . the hills of this creek like those of the Kimooenem are high it's bottoms narrow and possess but little timber. lands of good quality, a dark rich loam. we continued our rout up this creek. . . . here we met with We-ark-koomt whom we have usually distinguished by the name of the bighorn Cheif from the circumstance of his always wearing a horn of that animal suspended to the left arm. he is the 1st. Cheif of a large band of the Chopunnish nation. he had 10 of his young men with him. this man went down Lewis's river by land as we decended it by water last fall quite to the Columbia and I beleive was very instrumental in procuring us a hospitable and friendly reception among the natives. he had now come a considerable distance to meet us. after meeting this cheif we continued still up the creek bottoms . . . to the place at which the road leaves the creek and ascends the hills to the plain[.] here we encamped in [a] small grove of cottonwood trees which in some measure broke the violence of the wind. we came 28 *Ms. today.* it rained hailed snowed and blowed with great violence the greater portion of the day. it was fortunate for us that this storm was from the s.w. and of course on our backs. . . . we made but a scant supper and had nothing for tomorrow; however We-ark-koomt consoled us with the information that there was an indian lodge on the river at no great distance where we might supply ourselves with provision tomorrow."

•

Ordway writes: "having nothing to eat bought the only dog the Indians had with them" (Quaife, *Journals*, 352).

The route lay a little east of north eight miles to a crossing on the Tucannon River a mile below

"a large coarse plant with a ternate leaf"
Cow parsnip.

Marengo, then three miles over a steep divide to Pataha Creek below Zumwalt. Following its wide, rich valley east through what is now Pomeroy, the Corps met We-ark-koomt a short distance east of Pataha City.

We-ark-koomt was Apash Wyakaikt or Flint Necklace, whose home village was near Asotin, Washington. He was an influential chief, and historians believe that he was the father of Looking Glass, Sr., whose son, Looking Glass, was the principal war chief during the 1877 Nez Perce war.

4 May 1806.
[CLARK]

"Collected our horses and set out early; the morning was cold and disagreeable. we ascended the Larboard Hill . . . and Steared . . . through a high leavel plain to a ravine which forms the source of a small creek [Alpowa], thence down the Creek . . . to it's enterance into Lewis's river $7\frac{1}{2}$ Ms. below the enterance of the Kooskooske. on the river a little above this Creek we arived at a lodge of 6 families of which *We-ark-koomt* had spoken. We halted here for brackfast and with much difficulty purchased 2 lean dogs. the inhabitants were miserably pore. we obtained a fiew large cakes of half cured bread made of a root which resembles the sweet potatoe, with these we made some soope and took brackfast. . . . the hills of the river are high and abrupt approaching it nearly on both sides. . . . a high leavil plain between the Kooskooske & Lewis' river. . . .

"steered N. 25. E. 12 Ms. to Kimooenem Creek"

it produces great quantities of the quawmash a root of which the nativs are extreemly fond. a Great portion of the Chopunnish . . . are now distributed in small Villages through this plain Collecting the *Cowse* a white meley root . . . the

salmon not yet haveing arived to call them to the river. . . . we continued our rout up the West Side of the river 3 ms opposit 2 Lodges. . . . here we met with *Te-toh-ar-sky* the oldest of the two Chiefs who accompanied us last fall to the Great

"through the high plain to a small creek"
Pataha Creek near where Lewis and Clark crossed.

"here we met with We-ark-koomt"
Looking down Pataha Creek one mile east
of Pataha City.

"to the place at which the road leaves the creek"
Camp was made on Pataha Creek by the trees, left.

Falls of the Columbia. here we also met with our old pilot who decended the river with us as low as the Columbia. . . . we determined to . . . pass the river which with the assistance of three indian canoes we effected in the coarse of the evening. purchased a little wood, some *Cows* bread and encamped, haveing traveled 15 miles today only. . . . the nativs crouded about our fire in great numbers in so much that we could scercely cook or keep ourselves worm."

•

From the camp in the cottonwoods, the Corps passed up the present McKeirnan Grade Road for about half a mile, then directly across country a little south of east to meet today's U.S. 410 near

"down the creek . . . to it's enterance into Lewis's river"
The expedition came down the canyon, far left center, and across the Snake River, in the foreground.

Legge Road. Following the rugged Alpowa Creek Canyon and along the left bank of the Snake River, they crossed to the north side near the mouth of Dry Creek, not far from Clarkston.

5 May 1806.
[LEWIS]
"Collected our horses and set out at 7 A.M. at 4½ miles we arrived at the entrance of the Kooskooske, up the N. Eastern side of which we continued our march 12 Ms. to a large lodge of 10

families . . . & with much difficulty obtained 2 dogs and a small quan[ti]ty of root bread and dryed roots. . . . an indian man gave Capt. C. a very eligant grey mare for which he requested a phial of eye water which was accordingly given him. . . . last fall at the entrance of the Chopunnish river Capt. C. . . . gave an indian man some volitile linniment to rub on his k[n]ee and thye for a pain of which he complained . . . the fellow soon after recovered and has never ceased to extol the virtues of our medicines and the skill of my friend Capt. C. as a phisician. . . . my friend Capt. C. is their favorite phisician and has already received many applications. in our present situation I think it pardonable to continue this deseption for they will not give us any provision without compensation in merchandize and our stock is now reduced to a mere handful. We take care to give them no article which can possible injure them. . . . after dinner we continued our rout 4 miles to the entrance of Colter's Creek. . . . we encamped on the lower side of this creek at a little distance from two lodges of the Chopunnish nation having traveled 20½ Ms. today. one of these lodges contained eight families the other was much the largest we have ever seen. it is 156 feet long and about 15 wide built of mats and straw, in the form of the roof of a house having a number of small doors on each side, is closed at the ends and without divisons in the intermediate space[.] this lodge contained at least 30 families. their fires are kindled in a row in the center of the house and about 10 feet assunder. all the lodges of these people are formed in this manner. we arrived here extreemly hungry and much fatiegued, but no articles of merchandize in our possession would induce them to let us have any article of provision except a small quantity of bread of *cows* and some of those roots dyed. we had several applications to assist their sick which we refused unless they would let us have some dogs or horses to eat. a man whose wife had an absess formed on the small of her back promised a horse in the morning provided we would administer to her accordingly Capt. C. opened the absess introduced a tent and dressed it with basilicon; I prepared some dozes of the flour of sulpher and creem of tarter which were given with directions to be taken on each morning. . . . This is the residence of one of 4 principal Cheifs . . . whom they call Neesh-ne-park-ke-ook or *the cut nose* from . . . his nose being cut by the snake indians with a launce in battle. to this man we gave a medal of the small size with the likeness of the president. . . . we met with a snake Indian man at this place through whome we spoke at some length to the natives this evening with rispect to the objects which had induced us to visit their country. . . . We-ark-koomt rejoined us this evening. this man has been of infinite service to us on several former occasions and through him we now offered our address to the natives."

•

A tent is a roll of lint inserted into a wound so that it drains and heals from the inside. Basilicon

"all the lodges of these people are formed in this manner."

is a salve made from wax, grease, or most likely anything that was handy; if it smarted a little or smelled good it was thought to possess more virtue. Colters Creek is now the Potlatch River. During railroad construction across its outlet an Indian grave was uncovered, from which a Jefferson medal was taken that must be the one presented to Neesh-ne-park-ke-ook, or Cut Nose.

John Work, a Hudson's Bay brigade leader, traded for horses with this chief in 1825 on the Clearwater. The early Methodist missionary Jason Lee met a Nez Perce chief with the same name near the Green River in 1834; perhaps it was the very same man.

In order to address this group of Indians, Lewis and Clark had to give their message in

"we gave a medal"
Jefferson medal found at the outlet of Potlatch River, probably the one given to Cut Nose.

English to Labiche, who translated it into French for Charbonneau, from whom it went in Hidatsa to Sacagawea and thence in Shoshone to the Snake prisoner, who put into Nez Perce for the natives. The answer then traveled the same tedious route in reverse.

6 May 1806
[CLARK]

"This morning the husband of the sick woman was as good as his word. he produced us a young horse in tolerable order which we imediately had killed and butchered. the inhabitents seemed more accommodating this morning, they sold us some bread. we received a second horse for medecine & pro[s]criptions to a little girl with the rhumatism whome I had bathed in worm water, and anointed her a little with balsom capivia. . . . I was busily imployed for several hours this morning in administering eye water to a crowd of applicants. we once more obtained a plentiful meal, much to the comfort of all the party. Capt. Lewis exchanged horses with *We ark koomt* and gave him a small flag with which he was much pleased and gratifyed. . . . At this place we met with *three* men of a nation called the *Skeets-so-mish* [Coeur d'Alene] who reside at the falls of a small river [Spokane] dischargeing itself into the Columbia. . . . this river they informed us headed in a large lake [Coeur d'Alene] in the mountains. . . . these people are the same in their dress and appearance with the Chopunnish, tho' their language is entirely different. . . . at 3 P.M. we set out accompanied by the brother of the twisted hair and We-ark-koomt. we derected the horse which I had obtained for the purpose of eateing to be led as it was unbroke, in performing this duty a quarrel ensued between Drewyer and Colter. We continued our march along the river on its North side 9 miles to a lodge of 6 families built of sticks mats and dryed Hay, of the same form of those hertofore discribed. . . . a little after dark our young horse broke the rope by which he was confined and made his escape much to the chagrin of all who recollected the keenness of their appetites last evening. the brother of the twisted hair & *Wearkkoomt* with 10 others encamped with us this evening. The nativs have a considerable Salmon fishery up Colters Creek. . . . The Chopunnish about the mouth of the Kooskooske bury their dead on stoney hill side generally, and as I was informed by an Indian who made signs that they made a hole in the Grown[d] by takeing away the stones and earth where the[y] deposit the dead body after which they laid the body which was previously raped [wrapped] in a robe and secured with cords. over the body they placed Stones so as to secure the body from the wolves and birds &c. they sometimes inclose the grave with a kind of sepulcher like the roof of a house formed of the canoes of the disceased. they also sacrifice the favorite horses of the deceased, the bones of many of which we see on the ground about the graves."

•

Balsam copaiba is a salve made from aromatic plant resins.

Ordway wrote in his journal on 6 May 1806: "Several of the natives gambled in the same way as those below[.] had buffaloe robes war axes &C Staked up[.] the war axes these Indians have they get from the Grouse-vauntares [Gros Ventres] on the Missourie & they got them from us at the Mandans" (Quaife, *Journals*, 353; *see* 24 August 1805).

During the winter of 1804–05 at Fort Mandan, Lewis and Clark found to their considerable benefit how fond the Indians were of a certain type of "battle ax" or hatchet.

These weapons, which were sold for corn, were in such demand that the expedition's blacksmith was constantly kept busy in their fabrication. Captain Lewis said the axes were "formed in a very inconvenient manner in my opinion. . . . of iron only, the blade is extreemly thin, from 7 to nine inches in length and from 4¾, to 6 Inches on it's edge, from where it's width is generally not more than an inch. . . . the great length of the blade of this ax, added to the small size of the handle renders a stroke uncertain and easily avoided" (Thwaites, *Journals*, 1:254–55).

Camp for this day was made on the right bank of the Clearwater about five miles downstream from what is now Lenore, Idaho; Ordway says "near a small village" (Quaife, *Journals*, 355).

7 May 1806.

[CLARK]

"This morning we . . . set out early accompanied by the brother of the twisted hair as a guide; Wearkkoomt and his party left us. we proceeded up the river 4 miles to a lodge of 6 families just below the enterance of a small Creek [Bed Rock Creek], here our guide recommended our passing the river. . . . we . . . accordingly unloaded our horses and prepared to pass the river which we effected by means of one canoe in the course of 4 hours. a man of this lodge produced us two canisters of Powder which he . . . had found by means of his dog where they had been berried in the bottom near the river a fiew miles above. they were the same which we had berried as we decended the river last fall. as he had kept them safe and had honisty enough to return them to us, we gave him a fire Steel by way of compensation. . . . we renewed our march along the S.E. side of the river about 2 miles over a dificuelt stoney road, when we left the river and assended the hills to the right which are here mountains high. the face of the country when you have once assended the river hills, is perfectly level and partially covered with the long leafed pine. the soil is a dark rich loam, thickly covered with grass and herbatious plants which afford a delightful pasture for horses. in short it is a butifull fertile picteresque country. Neeshneparkeeook over-

took us and after rideing with us a fiew miles turned off to the right to visit some lodges of his people who he informed us were gathering roots in the plains at a little distance from the road. our guide conducted us through the plan and down a steep and lengthy hill to a creek [Canyon Creek] which we call Musquetoe Creek in consequences of being infested with sworms of those insects. . . . we proceeded up the Creek one mile and on the S.E. Side we arrived at an old Indian encampment of Six Lodges which appeared to have been recently evacuated. here we remained all night haveing traveled 12 ms. only. . . . we deturmined to remain here untill noon tomorrow in order to obtain some venison, and accordingly gave orders to the hunters to turn out early in the morning. The spurs of the rocky mountains which were in view from the high plain to day were perfectly covered with snow. The Indians inform us that the snow is yet so deep on the mountains that we shall not be able to pass them untill after the next full moon or about the first of June. . . . this [is] unwelcome intiligence to men confined to a diet of horsebeef and roots, and who are as anxious as we are to return to the fat plains of the Missouri, and thence to our native homes. . . . I observed in all the Lodges which we have passed since we crossed Lewis's river decoys . . . for the deer . . . formed of the skin of the head and upper portion of the neck of that animale extended to the nateral shape by means of a fiew little sticks placed within. the hunter when he sees a deer conseals himself and with his hand

"axes formed in a very inconvenient manner"
Blade found in Nez Perce territory similar to those made by the expedition's
blacksmith while wintering with the Mandans.

givs to the decoy the action of a deer at feed, and this induces the deer within arrow shot; in this mode the Indians near the woody country hunt on foot in such places where they cannot pursue the deer with horses which is their favourite method when the grounds will permit. The orniments worn by the Chopunnish are, in their nose a single shell of Wampom [dentalium], the pirl & beeds are suspended from the ears. beads are worn arround their wrists, neck and over their sholders crosswise in the form of a double sash. the hair of the men is cewed in two rolls which hang on each side in front of the body. Collars of bear claws are also common; but the article of dress on which they appear to bestow most pains and orniments is a kind of collar or brestplate; this is most commonly a strip of otter skins of about six inches wide taken out of the center of the skin it's whole length including the head. this is dressed with the hair on. this is tied around the neck & hangs in front of the body the tail frequently reaching below their knees; on this skin in front is attached pieces of pirl, beeds, wampom, pices of red cloth and in short whatever they conceive most valuable or ornamental."

•

The members of the party crossed the Clearwater near Rattlesnake Canyon, following it upstream to a point opposite Lenore, Idaho, whereupon they climbed the steep canyon to the plains above, camping near Peck. The "butifull fertile

"assended the hills which are mountains high"

"his people . . . were gathering roots in the plains"
Mrs. Elizabeth Wilson, a Nez Perce from Kamiah, Idaho,
harvesting camas bulbs with a digging stick.

pictoresque" country is now the rich Camas Prairie farmlands of Idaho. Some of the succulent plants and roots that fed a native empire may still be found there in pasture corners and marshy bottoms.

8 May 1806.

[CLARK]

"This morning our hunters was out by the time it was light. about 8 oClock Shields brought in a small deer, on which we brackfast. . . . Drewyer & P. Crusat brought in a deer each & Collins wounded one which our Dog caught near our camp."

[LEWIS]

"Shields killed a duck of an uncommon kind. the head beak and wing of which I preserved."

[CLARK]

"on the small creek which passes our Camp, the nativs have laterly encamped and as we are informed have been much distressed for provisions, they have fallen a number of small pine in the vicinity of this Encampment for the Seed which is in the bur of which they eate. we are informed that they were compelled to collect the moss off the pine boil & eate it in the latter part of the last winter. on the creek near our camp I observed a kind of trap which was made with great panes to catch the small fish which pass down with the stream. This was a dam formed of stone so as to collect the water in a narrow part not exceeding 3 feet wide from which place the water shot with great force and scattered through

some small willows closely connected and fastened with bark, this mat of willow switches was about 4 feet wide and 6 feet long lying in a horozontal position, fastened at the extremety. the small fish which fell on those willows was washed on the Willows where they [lie] untill taken off &c. I cought or took off those willows 9 small trout from 3 to 7 Inches in length. Son after I returned from the fishery an Indian came from a similar kind a little above with 12 small fish which he offered me which I declined axcepting as I found from his signs that his house was a short distance above, and that those fisheries afforded the principal part of the food for his children. . . . The Snake Indian was much displeased that he was not furnished with as much Deer as he could eate. he refused to speake to the wife of Shabono, through whome we could understand the nativs. we did not indulge him and in the after part of the day he came too and spoke very well. one of the Indians drew me a sketch of the river[,] in this sketch he makes the 1st. large Southerly fork of Lewis's river much the longest and on which great numbers of the Snake Indians reside &c. . . . we loaded up and set [out] . . . on the roade leading . . . to the lodge of the twisted hair, the Chief in whoes care we had left our horses. . . . we assended the hills which was steep and emencely high to a leavel rich country thinly timbered with pine. we had not proceeded more than 4 miles before we met the *twisted hair* and several men. . . . we were verry coolly receved by the twisted hair. he spoke aloud and was answered by the Cut nose. we could not learn what they said, but plainly discovered that a miss-understanding had taken place between them. we made signs to them that we should proceed on to the next water and encamp. accordingly I set out. . . . we had not proceeded far before the road crossed a small handsom stream on which we encamped. The parties of those two Chiefs took different positions at some distance from each other and all appeared sulkey. after we had formed our camp we sent Drewyer with a pipe to smoke with the twisted hair and lern the cause of the dispute between him and the Cut nose, and also to invite him to our fire to smoke with us. The twisted hair came to our fire. . . . we then sent drewyer to the Cut Noses fire with the same directions. . . . it appears that the cause of the quarrel between those two men is about our horses and we cannot lern the particulars of this quarrel which probably originated through jel-ousy on the part of the Cut nose who blames the twisted hair for suffer[ing] our horses to be rode, and want water dureing the winter &c. twisted hair says the horses were taken from him &c. The Cut nose joined us in a short time[.] We smoked with al the party of both Chiefs, and told them that we were sorry to find them at variance with each other[.] the cut nose said that the twisted hair was a bad man and wore two faces, that he had not taken care of our horses as was expected, that himself and the broken arm had caused our horses to be watered in the winter and had them drove together, and that if we would proceed on

to the village of the great chief [for] whome we had left a flag last fall the broken arm he would send for our horses, that he had himself three of them. he also informed us that the great Chief hereing of our distressed situation had sent his son and 4 men to meet us and have us furnished on the way &c. that the young men missed us, that the great Chief expected us to go to his lodge which was near the river and about half a days march above &c. . . . The *twisted hair* told us that he wished to smoke with us at his lodge which was on the road leading to the Great Chiefs lodge, and but a fiew miles ahead. if we would delay at his lodge tomorrow he would go after our saddles and horses which was near the place we made our canoes last fall. we deturmined to set out early in the morning and proceed on to the lodge of the twisted hair and send for our saddles and powder which we had left burried near the forks, and the day after tomorrow to proceed on to the lodge of the Grand Chief. ac-cordingly we informed the Indians of our inten-tions. we all smoked and conversed untill about 10 PM. the Indians retired and we lay down. Derected 5 hunters to turn out early to hunt and meet us at the twisted hair's lodge."

•

The "duck of an uncommon kind" was the shov-eler, *Anas clypeata*. This bird, often mistaken by hunters for the mallard, nests in the Great Basin and northward as far as central Alaska, and mi-grates southward in the late fall. Its long, spatu-

"we sent Drewyer with a pipe"
Prehistoric stone pipes with wooden container, Columbia River.

late bill, edged with a strainer, roots out seeds, bulbs and aquatic worms from the bottoms of shallow ponds, and separates them from the mud.

The "small pine" was the yellow pine, *Pinus ponderosa*. Forests of this most beautiful of the pines, with its rich brown bark and symmetrical bole, look like a well-kept park. In the spring the bark was sometimes stripped from the tree for its nutritious cambium layer. The "moss" is a lichen, *Alectoria jubata*, which hangs from the limbs in a mass of black filaments like a luxuriant beard on a buccaneer. Steamed in pits for a day or so, the mucilaginous mess was pressed into a layer, cut into squares, dried, and stored for winter. The squares, looking like enlarged dominoes, were boiled into a soup that was said to be very good. As a starvation diet, the lichen could be eaten raw, but it was very bitter when uncooked.

The site of this day's camp has not been located, but it was about two miles south of Ah-sahka, Idaho.

9 May 1806.
[CLARK]

"The hunters set out very early agreeable to their derections. we were detained untill 9 A.M. for our horses which were much scattered. . . . set out and proceeded on through a butifull open rich country for 6 miles to the camp of the twisted hair. this Campment is formed of two Lodges built in the usial form of mats and straw. the largest and principal Lodge is calculated for 2 fires only and contains about [12] persons."

[LEWIS]

"even at this small habitation there was an appendage of the soletary lodge, the retreat of the tawney damsels when nature causes them to be driven into coventry [refers to the menstrual cycle]."

[CLARK]

"this custom is common to all the nations on this river as well as among all other Indian nations with whom I am acquainted. at the distance of 2 miles we passd. a lodge of 2 fires on a fork of the road. . . . before 2 P M all our hunters joined us haveing killed only one deer which was lost in the river and a pheasent. Soon after we halted at the lodge of the twisted hair he set out with two boys and Willard with a pack horse down to the river near the place we made the canoes for our saddles and a cannister of powder and some lead buried there, also a part of our horses which re-sorted near that place. late in the evening they returned with 21 of our horse[s] and about half of our saddles with the powder and ball. The greater part of the horses were in fine order. . . . we precured some pounded roots of which a supe was made thick on which we suped. the wind blew hard from the s.w. accompanied with rain untill from 7 oClock untill 9 P.M. when it began to snow and continued all night. several Indians came from the village of the Chief with whome we had left a flag and continued with us all night. they slept in the house of the twisted hair and two of them along side of us."

•

Gass writes: "Between the great falls of the Columbia and this place, we saw more horses, than I ever before saw in the same space of country. They are not of the largest size of horses, but very good and active" (*Journal*, 255).

And Ordway: "these plains are Smooth Soil rich & filled with commass wild onions and white roots calld halse & other roots good for food which the natives live on at this Season of the year" (Quaife, *Journals*, 355).

10 May 1806.
[CLARK]

"This morning the snow continued falling untill 1/2 past 6 A M when it seased. the air keen and cold the snow 8 inches deep on the plain. . . . we set out . . . and proceeded on through an open plain. the road was slipry and the snow cloged and caused the horses to trip very frequently. . . . at 4 P M we arrived at the village of *Tin nach e moo toolt* the Chief whome We had left a flag. this flag was hoisted on a pole[.] unde[r] the flag the Chief met me and conducted me to a spot near a small run about 80 paces from his Lodges where he requested me to halt which I did. Soon after Cap Lewis who was in the rear came up and we smoked with and told this Chief our situation in respect to provisions. they brought forward about 2 bushel of quawmash 4 cakes of bread made of roots and a dried fish. we informed the Chief that our party was not accustomed to eate roots without flesh & proposed to exchange some of our oald horses for young ones to eate. they said they would not exchange horses, but would furnish us with such as we wished, and produced 2[,] one of which we killed and informd. them that we did not wish to kill the other at this time. We gave medals to the broken arm or *Tin-nach-e-moo-tolt* and *Hoh-hást-ill-pilp* two Chiefs of the Chopunnish Nation and was informed that there was one other Great Chief . . . who had but one eye. he would be here tomorrow. a large Lodge of Leather was pitched and Capt. Lewis and my self was envited into it. . . . the Chief requested that we might make the Lodge our homes while we remained with him. here after we had taken a repast on roots & horse beef we resumed our council with the indians which together with smoking took up the ballance of the evening. I was surprised to find decending the hill to *Commearp* [Lawyers] Creek that there

had been no snow in the bottoms of that stream. . . . as those people had been liberal I directed the men not to crowd their Lodges in serch of food [in] the manner hunger has compelled them to do at most lodges we have passed, and which the *Twisted Hair* had informed us was disagreeable to the nativs. . . . The Village of the *broken Arm* consists of one house or Lodge only which is 150 feet in length built in the usial form of sticks, Mats and dry grass. it contains 24 fires and about double that number of families. from appearance I prosume they could raise 100 fighting men. the noise of their women pounding the cows roots remind me of a nail factory. The Indians appear well pleased, and I am confident that they are not more so than our men who have their stomach once more filled with horse beef and the bread of cows. Those people has shewn much greater acts of hospitallity than we have witnessed from any nation or tribe since we have passed the rocky Mountains. in short be it spoken to their immortal honor it is the only act which diserves the appelation of hospitallity which we have witnessed in this quarter."

•

"Hoh-hást-ill-pilp" was Hohots Illppilp or Red Grizzly Bear, one of the greatest Nez Perce leaders; he was sometimes called Bloody Chief because of his many battle wounds. His primary village was on the Salmon River near White Bird, Idaho. He was at Spalding's mission in 1842, at the age of about ninety years.

"the Chief . . . conducted me to . . . a small run"
The village and spring were on Lawyer Creek near the
building, right center, top photo. The spring appears in
the bottom photo.

11 May 1806.

[CLARK]

"Some little rain last night. we were crouded in the Lodge with Indians who continued all night and this morning Great numbers were around us. The One Eyed Chief Yoom-park-kar-tim arived and we gave him a medal of the small size and spoke to the Indians through a Snake boy[,] Shabono and his wife. we informed them [of] . . . our intentions towards them, which pleased them very much. a young man[,] son to the great Chief who was killed not long sence by the Indians from the N.E., brought an elegant mare and coalt and Gave us, and said he had opened his ears to what we had said and his heart was glad: and requested us to take this mare and coalt as a token of his deturmination to pursue our Councels &c. The twisted hair brough[t] six of our horses all in fine order. Great numbers of Indians apply to us for medical aid which we gave them cherfully so far as our skill and store of Medicine would enable us. schrofla, ulsers, rhumitism, sore eyes, and the loss of the use of their Limbs are the most common cases among them. the latter case is not very common but We have seen 3 instances of it among the Chopunnish. a very extroadinery compl[ai]nt. . . . We are now pretty well informed that Tunnachemootoolt, Hohastillpilp, Neshneparkkeeook, and Yoomparkkartim were the principal Chiefs of the Chopunnish Nation and ranked in the order mentioned; as all those chiefs were present in our lodge we thought it a favourable time to repeat what had been said and to enter more minutely into the views of our government with respect to the inhabitants of this Western part of the Continent, their intentions of establishing tradeing houses for their relief, their wish to restore peace and harmony among the nativs, the strength welth and powers of our nation &c. to this end we drew a map of the country with a coal on a mat in their way, and by the assistance of the Snake boy and our interpreters were enabled to make ourselves understood. after this council was over we amused ourselves with shewing them the power of magnetism, the spye glass, compass, watch, *air gun and* sundery other articles equally novel and incomprehensible to them. . . . In the evening a man was brought in a robe by four Indians and laid down near me. they informed me that this man was a Chief of considerable note who has been in the situation I see him for 5 years. this man is incapable of moveing a single limb but lies like a corps in whatever position he is placed, yet he eats hartily, dejests his food perfectly, enjoys his understanding. . . . were it not that he appears a little pale . . . he might well be taken for a man in good health. . . . The Chopunnish notwithstanding they live in the crouded manner before mentioned are much more clenly in their persons and habitations than any nation we have seen sence we left the Illinois."

Dried roots were pounded with a stone pestle in a bottomless basket cemented to a stone. Sometimes a rawhide sack with a stone enclosed in the bottom was used. Both of these objects are from Nez Perce territory.

12 May 1806.

[CLARK]

"a fine morning[.] great numbers of Indians flock about us as usial. after brackfast I began to administer eye water and in a fiew minits had near 40 applicants with sore eyes, and maney others with other complaints. . . . the Indians had a grand Council this morning after which we were presented each with a horse by two young men at the instance of the nation. we caused the chiefs to be seated and gave them each a flag a pint of Powder and 50 balls. . . . the broken arm or Tunnachemootoolt pulled off his leather shirt and gave me. In return gave him a shirt. We retired into the Lodge and the natives spoke in the following purpote, i.e. they had listened to our advice and that the whole nation were deturmined to follow it, that they had only one heart and one tongue on this subject. . . . they wished to be at peace with all nations &c. as a great number of men women & children were wateing and requesting medical assistance. . . . we agreed That I should administer and Capt L to here [hear] and answer the Indians. I was closely employed untill 2 P.M. administering eye water to about 40 grown persons. . . . Those people are much affraid of the blackfoot indians. . . . those indians kill great numbers of this nation whenever they pass over to hunt on the Missouri. . . . we gave the twisted hair a gun, powder and 100 ball in part for takeing care of our horses. . . . early last Summer 3 of their brave men were sent with a pipe to the Shoshones. . . . their pipe was disregarded and their 3 men murdered, which gave rise to the War expedition against that nation last fall."

13 May 1806.

[CLARK]

"a fine morning[.] I administered to the sick and gave directions. we collected all our horses and set out at 1 P.M. and proceeded down the Creek [Lawyers] to the *Flat head* [Clearwater] River a short distance below the enterance of the Creek. . . . we halted . . . unloaded our horses and turned them out to feed. . . . in the evening we tried the speed of several of our horses. these horses are strong active and well formed. Those people have emence numbers of them 50 or 60 or a Hundred head is not unusial for an individual to possess. The Chopunnish are in general stout well formed active men. they have high noses and maney of them on the acqueline order with chearfull and agreeable continances. . . . in common with other Indian Nations of America they extract their beard, but the men do not uniformly extract the hair below, this is more particularly confined to the females. they appear to be cheerful but not gay, they are fond of gambling and of their amusements which consists principally in shooting their arrows at a targit made of willow bark, and in rideing and exersiseing themselves on horseback, raceing &c. they are expirt marks men & good riders. they do not appear to be so much devoted to baubles as most of the nations we have met with, but seem anxious always to

"we . . . formed a Camp around a very convenient Spot"
Site of Camp Choppunish on the far shore of the Clearwater River near Kamiah.

riceve articles of utility, such as knives, axes, Kittles, blankets & mockerson awls. blue beeds however may form an exception to this remark; This article among all the nations of this country may be justly compared to gold and silver among civilized nations. They are generally well clothed in their stile. their dress consists of a long shirt which reaches to the middle of the leg, long legins which reach as high as the waist, mockersons & robe. those are formed of various skins and are in all respects like those of the Shoshone. Their ornamints consists of beeds, shells and pieces of brass variously attached to their dress, to their ears around theire necks wrists arms &. a band of some kind usially serounds the head, this is most frequently the skin of some fir animal as the fox otter &c."

•

The resistance of the Nez Perce to "baubles" occasioned some concern on the part of the Hudson's Bay Company. A number of years later, in 1824, the company's governor, George Simpson, would write: "returns this season are estimated at 2000 Beaver got principally from a branch of the Nez Perces tribe called the Caiuses [Cayuses] and it does not appear to me that there is a prospect of any considerable increase unless trappers are introduced as the Indians cannot be prevailed on to exert themselves in hunting; they are very independent of us requiring but few of our sup-

plies and it is not until absolutely in need of an essential article or an article of finery such as Guns and Beads that they will take the trouble of hunting" (Simpson, *Fur Trade and Empire*, 54).

14 May 1806
[CLARK]

"a fine day. we had all our horses collected by 10 AM dureing the time we had all our baggage Crossed over the Flat head [Clearwater] River. . . . after the baggage was over to the North Side we crossed our horss without much trouble and hobbled them in the bottom after which we moved a Short distance below to a convenient Situation and formed a Camp around a very convenient Spot."

•

The place has come to be called Camp Chopunnish. There they remained until 10 June, awaiting the snow melt in the Bitterroot Mountains so that they could recross Lolo Pass.

After some nine months of trekking mountains, plains, valleys, rivers, and streams, punctuated by a rain-soaked winter at Fort Clatsop, the Corps of Discovery was concluding its activities west of the Great Divide. And so, to the people they called "Chopunnish," and for whom Lewis and Clark had nurtured a genuine admiration, the expedition offered medical assistance, in a fitting gesture of peace and friendship.

EPILOGUE

Many difficult and dangerous miles lay ahead of the expedition before it would reach St. Louis, that outpost of civilization from which the Corps of Discovery had departed some two years earlier. In describing their return, Sergeant Ordway says that when they stepped ashore at St. Louis—around noon, on 23 September 1806, near the center of town—"people gathered on the Shore and Hizzared three cheers. . . . the party . . . much rejoiced that we have the Expedition Completed and now we look for boarding in Town and wait for our Settlement and then we entend to return to our native homes to See our parents once more as we have been so long from them" (Quaife, *Journals*, 402).

The three huzzahs were well earned, and the expedition's members had every right to rejoice over their survival and achievement. Only one of the original party, Sergeant Charles Floyd, had perished. The subsequent fates of the expedi-

tion's other members, however, would sometimes prove little happier than his.

Consider, for example, Meriwether Lewis. Within three years of his triumphal return to St. Louis, he was dead of gunshot wounds suffered at an obscure roadside inn called Grinder's Stand, some seventy miles southwest of Nashville, Tennessee. As the newly appointed governor of the Louisiana Territory, Lewis was having difficulties getting officials in the new federal capital at Washington City to honor vouchers he had issued in the course of his duties. Thus, in October of 1809, he set out to confront his bureaucratic antagonists, traveling along an ancient thoroughfare in the wilderness of northern Mississippi and western Tennessee known as the Natchez Trace. To this day the circumstances of his death are debated. Some believe (as did Thomas Jefferson) that Lewis committed suicide in a fit of despondency; others (among them

Lewis's mother) have contended that he was murdered in the course of being robbed. Considering that Lewis had made two previous, unsuccessful attempts to end his own life, current opinion seems inclined to favor suicide (*see* Fisher, *Suicide or Murder?*, Cutright, "Rest, Perturbed Spirit," and Moulton, "On Reading Lewis and Clark," 32).

Then there is the case of Sacagawea. What appears to be her epitaph was entered by the fur trader John Luttig in his journal, as alluded to earlier in this work (17 August 1805). His entry for 20 December 1812 at Fort Manuel (in what is now South Dakota) reads, "this Evening the wife of Charbonneau a Snake Squaw, died of a putrid fever she was a good and the best Woman in the fort, aged abt 25 years she left a fine infant girl" (*Journal of a Fur Trading Expedition*, 106). In apparent confirmation of Sacagawea's youthful demise, an account book discovered in 1955, originally belonging to William Clark and dated to 1825–28, lists "Se car ja we au" with the stark notation "Dead" (Jackson, *Letters*, 2:638–40).

Belief to the contrary—that the Shoshone woman who accompanied Lewis and Clark lived to be over ninety years old—has been advanced most notably by Grace Raymond Hebard, late professor of political economy at the University of Wyoming, and Charles A. Eastman, who held various posts with the Bureau of Indian Affairs. They theorized that the "wife of Charbonneau" who died at Fort Manuel was not Sacagawea, but a different wife, another Shoshone woman

known as Otter Woman (*see* Hebard, *Sacajawea*, 90, 111).

This contention has not been easy to dispute conclusively. Luttig failed to specify the name of the woman whose death he witnessed, and the credibility of Clark's knowledge about the subsequent fates of expedition members has been questioned because he mistakenly and prematurely included Patrick Gass among the departed. Nevertheless, the preponderance of evidence favors the view that Sacagawea did not live much beyond her twenty-fifth year, and that her remains lie buried in an unmarked grave somewhere at or near the site of Fort Manuel (*see* Howard, *Sacajawea*, 175–92; and Anderson, "Probing the Riddle," 12–17).

As for York, Clark's African-American servant, he seems to have lived longer than Lewis and Sacagawea, but not particularly happily. In 1832 Washington Irving recorded a conversation he had with Clark, in which he learned of York's fate. After granting him his freedom, his erstwhile master gave him, in Irving's words, "a large waggon & team of 6 horses to ply between Nashville and Richmond." But York's career as a wagoner would prove neither lengthy nor successful, and eventually he sought to return to Clark's service." "He . . . set off for St. Louis," Irving relates, "but was taken with cholera in Tennessee & died" (*Journals*, 82).

Reminiscent of the legends of Sacagawea's supposed survival to old age, word sometimes filtered out of the upper Louisiana wilderness of a black man living among the Indians who claimed to be York. The fur trader Zenas Leonard, for example, reported that he saw and talked with such a man on Wyoming's Shoshone River during the winter of 1832. John C. Ewers, the editor of Leonard's narrative, however, asserts that this man was in fact "the mulatto, Edward Rose, who went up the Missouri with Manuel Lisa in 1807 and remained among the Crows to become a leader of influence among the tribes" (*Adventures of Zenas Leonard*, 51–52 n.31).

Within two decades of the expedition's return, if we may rely on Clark's long-lost account book, close to half of the original party that crossed the Continental Divide to explore western waters had subsequently died or been killed. No doubt this is a grim reflection of the rigors of the frontier life so many of them chose to pursue after the expedition's return. Yet it may also be seen as testimony to how remarkable their achievement was in surviving that epic journey west of the Rocky Mountains. It is fair to say that their respective lives culminated in those ten months between August 1805 and May 1806, whatever else befell them later.

Sacagawea's son, Jean Baptiste Charbonneau, would prove more fortunate in later life than his mother. In some measure this was because Clark took "Pomp"—as he often called the lad—under his protection, seeing that he received a formal education at St. Louis. Baptiste was befriended in 1824 by a member of the German nobility, Prince Paul Wilhelm of Württemberg, who had come to the Louisiana Territory in quest of scientific knowledge. With Clark's consent the prince took the twenty-one-year-old Baptiste to Germany, where his education was further enhanced. His fluency in French, German, and Spanish, added to his prior knowledge of English and several Indian languages, made him a linguist whose services as an interpreter were in considerable demand on his return to America in 1829 (*see* Anderson, "J.B. Charbonneau," 248–49).

With his formative years behind him, Baptiste adopted the life of the Mountain Men, ending his days as a frontier guide and interpreter. He was associated with such important figures in the history of the American West as Joe Meek, Jim Bridger, Nathanial Wyeth, T.J. Farnham, John C. Frémont, Jim Beckwourth, and the commander of the Mormon Brigade, Philip St. George Cooke. After a brief retirement in California from his career as frontiersman, Baptiste returned to the rigorous life he seems to have loved, seeking Montana gold, only to fall victim to pneumonia en route. He died at the age of sixty-three, on 16 May 1866, near the southeastern Oregon locality of Danner, where he lies buried today (*see* Anderson, "J.B. Charbonneau," 250–55).

William Clark's life after the expedition was to prove lengthier than most, and more notable than any, of the lives of his companions in the venture. Commissioned by President Jefferson to the rank of brigadier general of the militia of the Louisiana Territory, he was simultaneously appointed to the office of territorial Indian agent. Subsequently, among other positions that he filled with distinction, he served as governor of Missouri Territory and surveyor general of the States of Illinois and Missouri. In 1822 Congress created the office of superintendent of Indian Affairs, to which President Monroe appointed Clark, who remained in the post until his death in 1838 at age sixty-eight. Twice married, Clark had five children, only three of whom survived him (*see* Coues, *History*, 1:xxxiii–xlv; and Steffen, *William Clark*, 53, 129).

No member of the expedition, however, would surpass Patrick Gass for longevity. After military service in the War of 1812, he left the frontier to settle in Wellsberg, West Virginia, where he eventually married, and fathered seven children. Contrary to what Clark believed in the late 1820s, Gass remained very much alive, and lived on at Wellsberg until 1870. On 2 April of that year, he finally expired at the remarkable age of ninety-nine, the last surviving member of Lewis and Clark's Corps of Discovery (Gass, *Journal*, xvi).

Regardless of their eventual fates, all the expedition's members had shared an experience that was unlikely to be eclipsed later in their lives. Even now, nearly two centuries later, things are being learned about their westward venture that continue to enhance its prestige and importance. The modern sciences of archaeology, botany, ethnology, geology, and zoology owe the Lewis and Clark expedition a particularly large debt insofar as they concern the geographic province surveyed in this volume. Current studies in these fields involving the Columbia River Basin routinely review the Lewis and Clark records as an embarcation point for their own efforts. In this, probably nothing better attests to the lasting value of those nine months the expedition spent seeking western waters.

SOURCES

Allen, John Eliot, Marjorie Burns, and Sam C. Sargent. *Cataclysms on the Columbia*. Portland, Oreg.: Timber Press, 1986.

Allen, John Logan. *Passage Through the Garden: Lewis and Clark and the Image of the American Northwest*. Urbana, Chicago, and London: Univ. of Illinois Press, 1975.

Allen, Paul [and Nicholas Biddle]. *History of the Expedition . . . under the Command of Captains Lewis and Clark*. 2 vols. Philadelphia and New York: Bradford and Inskeep, H. Inskeep, 1814.

Anderson, Irving W. "J.B. Charbonneau, Son of Sacajawea." *Oregon Historical Quarterly*, 71 (September 1970): 246–64.

———. "Probing the Riddle of the Bird Woman," *Montana: The Magazine of Western History*, 23 (October 1973):2–17.

Andrist, Ralph. *The Long Death, The Last Days of the Plains Indians*. New York: Macmillan, 1969.

Bakeless, John. *Lewis and Clark: Partners in Discovery*. New York: William Morrow, 1947.

Balch, Frederick Home. *The Bridge of the Gods*. Portland, Oreg.: Binford and Mort, 1965.

Bolton, Herbert E., trans. and ed. *Pageant in the Wilderness*. Salt Lake City: Utah Historical Society, 1950.

Boyd, Robert T. "Demographic History, 1774–1874." *Handbook of North American Indians*. Vol. 7. Washington: Smithsonian Institution, 1990.

Brown, Dee. *Bury My Heart at Wounded Knee: An Indian History of the American West*. New York: Holt, Rinehart and Winston, 1970.

Cook, S.F. *The Epidemic of 1830–1833 in California and Oregon*. Berkeley and Los Angeles: Univ. of California Press, 1955.

Cook, Warren L. *Flood Tide of Empire: Spain and the Pacific Northwest, 1543–1819*. New Haven: Yale Univ. Press, 1973.

Corning, Howard McKinley. *Dictionary of Ore-*

gon History. Portland: Binford and Mort, 1956.

Coues, Elliott, ed. *History of the Expedition under the Command of Lewis and Clark*. 3 vols. Reprint. New York: Dover, 1965.

Cox, Ross. *The Columbia River; or, Scenes and Adventures During a Residence of Six Years on the Western Side of the Rocky Mountains*. 2 vols. London: Henry Colburn and Richard Bentley, 1832.

Cressman, Luther. "Cultural Sequences at The Dalles, Oregon: A Contribution to Pacific Northwest Prehistory." *Trans. of the American Philosophical Society* 50, pt. 10 (1960).

Cutright, Paul Russell. *Lewis and Clark: Pioneering Naturalists*. Urbana, Chicago, and London: Univ. of Illinois Press, 1969.

———. "Rest, Rest, Perturbed Spirit." *We Proceeded On* 12 (March 1986): 7–16.

Deacon, Richard. *Madoc and the Discovery of America*. London: Frederick Muller, 1967.

Dobbs, Caroline C. *Men of Champoeg*. Portland: Metropolitan Press, 1932.

Douglas, David. *Journal Kept . . . During his Travels in North America, 1823–1827*. New York: Antiquarian Press, 1959.

Ewers, John C. *Adventures of Zenas Leonard, Fur Trader in North America*. Norman: Univ. of Oklahoma Press, 1959.

Fisher, Vardis. *Suicide or Murder? The Strange Death of Governor Meriwether Lewis*. Denver: Alan Swallow, 1962.

Franchère, Gabriel. *Adventures at Astoria,*

1810–1814. Translated and edited by Hoyt C. Franchère. Norman: Univ. of Oklahoma Press, 1967.

Gass, Patrick. *A Journal of the Voyages and Travels of a Corps of Discovery*. Edited by Earle R. Forrest. Minneapolis: Ross and Haines, 1958.

Gibbs, George. *Indian Tribes of Washington Territory*. Fairfield, Wash.: Galleon Press, 1967.

Glover, Richard, ed. *David Thompson's Narrative, 1784–1812*. Toronto: Champlain Society, 1962.

Grant, Campbell, James W. Baird, and J. Kenneth Pringle. *Rock Drawings of the Coso Range*. China Lake, Calif.: Maturango Museum, 1968.

Gunther, Erna. *Ethnobotany of Western Washington*. Seattle: Univ. of Washington Press, 1970.

Hebard, Grace Raymond. *Sacajawea*. Glendale, Calif.: Arthur H. Clark, 1933.

Henry, Alexander, and David Thompson. *The Manuscript Journals of Alexander Henry*. Edited by Elliott Coues. 2 Vols. 1897. Reprint. Minneapolis: Ross and Haines, 1965.

Hezeta, Bruno de. *For Honor and Country, the Diary of Bruno de Hezeta*. Translated and edited by Herbert K. Beals. Portland: OHS Press, 1985.

Howard, Harold P. *Sacajawea*. Norman: Univ. of Oklahoma Press, 1973.

Howay, Frederic W. "A Yankee Trader on the Northwest Coast, 1791–1795." *Washington Historical Quarterly* 21 (April 1930): 83–94.

————, ed. *Voyages of the "Columbia" to the Northwest Coast, 1787–1790 and 1790–1793.* Boston: Massachusetts Historical Society, 1941.

Ingraham, Joseph. [letter] "to Don Estephan Joseph Martínez, Commander of His most Catholic Majesties Ship Princesa." English-language text and Spanish translation, n.d. Mexico City. Archivo General de la Nación. Ramo: Historia 65, fojas 52–65. Microfilm copy in the manuscript collection of OHS, Portland.

————. *Voyage to the Northwest Coast of America.* Edited by Mark D. Kaplanoff. Barre, Mass.: Imprint Society, 1971.

Irving, Washington. *The Western Journals of Washington Irving.* Edited by John Francis McDermott. Norman: Univ. of Oklahoma Press, 1944.

Jackson, Donald. "Call Him a Good Dog, But Don't Call Him Scannon." *We Proceeded On* 11 (August 1985): 5–8.

————, ed. *Letters of the Lewis and Clark Expedition with Related Documents, 1783–1854.* 2 vols. 2d ed. Urbana, Chicago, and London: Univ. of Illinois Press, 1978.

————, and Mary Lee Spence, eds. *The Expeditions of John Charles Frémont.* 3 vols. Urbana, Chicago, and London: Univ. of Illinois Press, 1970.

Jewitt, John R. *A Journal Kept at Nootka Sound.* Fairfield, Wash.: Galleon Press, 1988.

————. *A Narrative of the Adventures and Sufferings of John R. Jewitt; Only Survivor of the Crew of the Ship* Boston. . . . Middletown, Conn.: Lewis and Richards, 1815.

Journal of Geology 32 (1922): 139. Univ. of Chicago Press.

Kane, Paul. *Wanderings of an Artist Among the Indians of North America.* 1859. Revised reprint. Rutland, Vt., and Tokyo: Charles E. Tuttle, 1968.

Large, Arlen J. "The Empty Anchorage, Why No Ship Came for Lewis and Clark." *We Proceeded On* 15 (February 1989): 4–11.

Luttig, John. *Journal of a Fur Trading Expedition on the Upper Missouri, 1812–1813.* Edited by Stella M. Drumm. St. Louis: Missouri Historical Society, 1920.

Lyman, Horace S. *History of Oregon, the Growth of an American State.* 4 vols. New York: North Pacific Publishing Society, 1903.

McArthur, Lewis A. *Oregon Geographic Names.* 5th ed. Portland: OHS Press, 1982.

McKelvey, Susan Delano. *Botanical Exploration of the Trans-Mississippi West, 1790–1850.* Jamaica Plains, Mass.: Arnold Arboretum of Harvard University, 1955.

Meares, John. *Voyages Made in the Years 1788 and 1789, from China to the North West Coast of America.* London: Logographic Press, 1790.

Moulton, Gary E., ed. *The Journals of the Lewis and Clark Expedition*, vols. 5, 6, and 7. Lincoln: Univ. of Nebraska Press, 1988–91.

————. "On Reading Lewis and Clark: The Last

Twenty Years." *Montana: The Magazine of Western History* 38 (Summer 1988): 28–39.

Parker, Rev. Samuel. *Journal of an Exploring Tour Beyond the Rocky Mountains*. 4th ed. Ithaca, N.Y.: Andrus, Woodruff and Gauntlett, 1844.

Peattie, Donald Culross. *A Natural History of Western Trees*. Boston: Houghton Mifflin, 1953.

Pursh, Frederick. *Flora Americae Septentrionalis*. 2 vols. London: White, Cochrane, 1814.

Quaife, Milo M., ed. *The Journal of Captain Meriwether Lewis and Sergeant John Ordway*. Madison: Historical Society of Wisconsin, 1916.

Ray, Verne F. "Lower Chinook Ethnographic Notes." *University of Washington Publications in Anthropology* 7 (May 1938): 29–165.

Ross, Alexander. *Adventures of the First Settlers on the Oregon or Columbia River*. Edited by Milo M. Quaife. New York: Citadel Press, 1969.

———. *The Fur Hunters of the Far West*. Edited by Kenneth A. Spaulding. Norman: Univ. of Oklahoma Press, 1956.

Silverstein, Michael. "Chinookans of the Lower Columbia." *Handbook of North American Indians*. Vol. 7. Washington: Smithsonian Institution, 1990.

Simpson, George. *Fur Trade and Empire: George Simpson's Journal*. Edited by Frederick Merk. Cambridge: Harvard Univ. Press, 1931.

Skarsten, M.O. *George Drouillard, Hunter and Interpreter for Lewis and Clark and Fur Trader, 1807–1810*. Glendale, Calif.: Arthur H. Clark, 1964.

Steffen, Jerome O. *William Clark: Jeffersonian Man on the Frontier*. Norman: Univ. of Oklahoma, 1978.

Stejneger, Leonhard. *Georg Wilhelm Steller, the Pioneer of Alaskan Natural History*. Cambridge: Harvard Univ. Press, 1936.

Stuart, Robert. *On the Oregon Trail: Robert Stuart's Journey of Discovery*. Edited by Kenneth A. Spaulding. Norman: Univ. of Oklahoma Press, 1953.

Swan, James G. *The Northwest Coast, or Three Years' Residence in Washington Territory*. 1857. Reprint. Seattle: Univ. of Washington Press, 1977.

Thwaites, Reuben Gold, ed. *Brackenridge's Journal up the Missouri, 1811, Early Western Travels, 1748–1846*. Vol. 6. Cleveland, Ohio: Arthur H. Clark, 1904.

———. *Original Journals of the Lewis and Clark Expedition, 1804–1806*. 8 vols. New York: Dodd, Mead, 1905.

Townsend, John Kirk. *Narrative of a Journey Across the Rocky Mountains to the Columbia River, and a Visit to the Sandwich Islands, Chili etc*. Philadelphia and Boston: Henry Perkins and Perkins and Marvin, 1839.

Vancouver, George. *A Voyage of Discovery to the North Pacific Ocean and Round 1791–1795*. 4 vols. Edited by W. Kaye Lamb. London: Hakluyt Society, 1984.

ILLUSTRATION LIST

Unless otherwise attributed, all photographs are from the Oregon Historical Society Photographic Archive.

INDEX

THE AUTHORS

The co-authors of this book were a rare combination. A native of Mosier, Oregon, Ruth Beacon Strong was a graduate of Mills College, with an MA from the University of Oregon. For most of her working life she taught school, but she was also an avocational botanist specializing in the native plants of the Pacific Northwest. Her husband, Emory Strong, was born in the small community of Burton, northeast of Vancouver, Washington, and grew up on a farm near Sandy, Oregon. In 1933 he graduated in engineering from what was then called the Oregon Agricultural College (now Oregon State University). Employed for a time with the Forest Service in the Mount Hood National Forest, Emory Strong joined the Bonneville Power Administration in 1938 as a mechanical engineer, a position he held—except for wartime service in the shipbuilding industry—until his retirement in 1967.

An interest in the archaeology and prehistory of the Columbia River region led him to help found the Oregon Archaeological Society in 1951. Serving twice as its president, he wrote its first publication, *Wakemap Mound, A Stratified Site on the Columbia River* (1959). That same year he wrote *Stone Age on the Columbia*, which helped him achieve prominence as an amateur archaeologist and prehistorian. In collaboration with Ruth Beacon Strong, who contributed an ethno-botanical dimension to the book, he wrote a sequel, *Stone Age in the Great Basin*, which was published in 1969.

However, it was the Lewis and Clark saga, in which human prehistory and history meet and blend with natural history, that most engaged the couple's interest. *Seeking Western Waters*, a work of true collaboration, is the final product of their partnership in the pursuit of knowledge.

In their last years, the Strongs came to reside at Skamania, Washington, amidst the scenic splendors of the Columbia River Gorge that were so much an inspiration in their lives. Emory passed away in 1980 and Ruth followed in 1985. Emory Strong's artifact collection as well as his library of over seven hundred texts is now installed at the Columbia Gorge Interpretive Center in Stevenson, Washington. Permission for restricted use of the collection can be obtained from the Interpretive Center. They can be reached at (509) 427-8211.

COLOPHON

The typeface used for text in this volume is New Caledonia and the display face is Bodoni Poster. The script on the cover is Carpenter.

Seeking Western Waters is printed on 70lb. Pacesetter Matte.

Production of this volume was accomplished through the skill and cooperation of the following:

Design: Caroline Hagen
Editing: Philippa Brunsman
Maps: Connie Bartos
Typesetting: Irish Setter
Printing and Binding: Paramount Graphics Inc.